Eating Tomorrow

Eating Tomorrow

AGRIBUSINESS, FAMILY
FARMERS, AND THE BATTLE
FOR THE FUTURE OF FOOD

Timothy A. Wise

NEW YORK
LONDON

Requests for permission to reproduce selections from this book
should be mailed to: Permissions Department, The New Press,
120 Wall Street, 31st floor, New York, NY 10005.

Published in the United States by The New Press, New York, 2019
Distributed by Two Rivers Distribution

ISBN 978-1-62097-423-0 (ebook)

Names: Wise, Timothy A., 1955– author.
Title: Eating tomorrow : agribusiness, family farmers, and the battle for the
future of food / Timothy A. Wise.
Description: New York, NY : New Press, [2019] | Includes bibliographical
references and index.
Identifiers: LCCN 2018036746 | ISBN 9781620974223 (hc : alk. paper)
Subjects: LCSH: Food supply. | Agricultural industries. | Family farms.
Classification: LCC HD9000.5 .W489 2019 | DDC 338.1—dc23
LC record available at https://lccn.loc.gov/2018036746

The New Press publishes books that promote and enrich public discussion and
understanding of the issues vital to our democracy and to a more equitable world.
These books are made possible by the enthusiasm of our readers; the support
of a committed group of donors, large and small; the collaboration of our many
partners in the independent media and the not-for-profit sector; booksellers, who
often hand-sell New Press books; librarians; and above all by our authors.

www.thenewpress.com

Composition by dix!
This book was set in Fairfield LH

Printed in the United States of America

2   4   6   8   10   9   7   5   3   1

R07100 41940

Contents

Foreword

Raj Patel

More people are hungry today than yesterday. For the first time in a generation, global hunger is increasing. It's not just the absolute number of malnourished people on the rise. The percentage of humans facing food shortages is climbing too.

Not everyone will eat tomorrow *because* of how we eat today. Every study that troubles itself with the question finds that climate change trends and industrial agricultural practices will cause staple foods to become more expensive in the future. Either that or there just won't be any food at all: fish could be commercially extinct by 2050.

Industrial agriculture is an engine for the exploitation of humans and the web of life. If you want to invent pandemic disease, you couldn't imagine a better laboratory than the hells of concentrated animal feeding operations, in which the constant drip of antibiotics creates a perfect breeding ground for the next deadly swine or bird flu. Along the food production line, workers in the food chain are treated as brutally as the product they butcher. And a complex web of social and ecological subsidies allows the system to produce food that appears as a bargain but is increasingly likely to contribute to chronic disease and ecological destruction.

Ask not, then, how the existing food system is going to kill us. Ask why it is allowed.

At every turn, the architects of the industrial food system ap-
pear to have created a world without alternative. Economic bumper
stickers are presented as imperatives never to be questioned. You'll
hear slogans from the thought leaders like: "developing countries
can export their way to success" or "without cheap food, the world
will starve" or "industrial agriculture is the only way we can feed
the world" or "technology can feed the 9 billion" or "organic food
just yields less." You may have uttered one or two of these slogans
yourself.

When you begin with the conviction that you're going to feed the
world, there's nothing that can prick your conscience. That's what
hubris feels like. If peasants need to be displaced in order to increase efficiency, their lives don't even rise to the level of collateral
damage. They're being liberated from work they didn't particularly
want to do, emancipated to find higher-paying jobs and a better
future in the cities, where they can eat tomorrow. The GDP data
prove it. Except with safety nets shredded and food prices higher,
that's not true at all. In India, the epicenter of this magical thinking, the poor are consuming fewer calories than they once did. Despite the fact that GDP is soaring. *Because* GDP is soaring, and the
only way to count development that matters is money. The urban
poor earn more money than their rural brethren and have higher
costs for food, so they eat less, spend more on cell phone airtime
and water, and live in sprawling slums. Progress.

The turn toward sustainability in the food industry is similarly
bitter. If you're growing crops to feed the world, are environmentalists just getting it wrong when they point out the absurdity of
biofuel industries that grow corn not to eat but to set on fire? No.
There is a difference between renewable resources and sustainable
ones. Sure, the corn will come out of the ground this year, and then
come out of it next year. It is renewed. But the system into which
corn-based ethanol plays, mortgaged to the internal combustion
engine and the fossil fuel industry, is bringing the planet to new
kinds of state-shift. Unsustainable.

This is the world that conventional agriculture has made. Yet it's unclear how most people have agreed to it. Where was the convention at which conventional agriculture was established? When? If you want dates, they're long gone, yet not even past. They're dates like 1492, the moment that some still refer to as the inauguration of the Columbian Exchange, when Christopher Columbus saw the New World and wrote to his patrons, "I can never tire my eyes in looking at such lovely vegetation, so different from ours. I believe there are many herbs and many trees that are worth much in Europe for dyes and for medicines but I do not know them, and this causes me great sorrow." Thus, lamenting his ignorance, did one of history's greatest criminals christen the plunder of a continent.

Another date: 1885, the Berlin Conference, in which Africa was divided among Europe's great powers. (The United States was invited to observe proceedings and its plenipotentiaries asked to bless the outcome.)

What's the Berlin Conference's contemporary analogue? Perhaps historians will mark it as 2001, when China joined the World Trade Organization. China's gambits, in its Belt and Road Initiative and global investments, have been played in Africa against increasing U.S. military base presence, which in turn has rubbed up against the alliances forged by Brazilian and Japanese capital. Tim Wise sees as much in his travels in Mozambique.

Whether there's a bipolar world of the West versus the Soviet Union, or the decade of post–Cold War U.S. supremacy, or the multi-polar world of great powers, the follies of the old food system remain. Unless there's a widespread recognition that they are, indeed, madness. Wise in his journeys has come across these absurdities time and again, and his frustrations should be everyone's.

Yet Wise travels to find transformations too. In Malawi, where he and I have both seen corners of the Malawi Farmer-to-Farmer Agroecology Project, women like Esther Lupafya and Rachel Bezner Kerr lead research into what a just transition away from the conventions of agriculture might look like. They're not asking about how to feed the world. They know that peasants are already feeding most of the global south and, with the right kinds of support, can do a better job under climate change than industrial agriculture can. Their visions for eating tomorrow do violence to the economists' slogans, because such a path requires not the great minds of agricultural science and commerce, but the combined entrepreneurship and democracy of social movements.

Wise has done us a great service in showing us the paths to a better food system that we might choose, and he offers us the tools to take the first step. From Mexico to Mozambique, Iowa to India, he takes us behind the lines in the battle for the future of food, to feel the impacts of land grabbing, the latest flashpoints in a Long Green Revolution, and the ravages of "free trade." Through his travels, we come to realize the magnitude of the choices ahead: whether to rid ourselves of the existing food system, or let it get rid of us. If we choose well, we'll need to organize and share successes and failures, analysis and criticism, anger and hope, if we're all to eat tomorrow.

Amritsar, India, August 2018

1

Introduction

In Mozambique's lovely capital city of Maputo, the afternoon temperature had just hit 104 degrees Fahrenheit. Maputo is in the tropics, but this was October 2017, its springtime, and no one could remember a hotter October day. Inside the air-conditioned Radisson Blu Hotel on the city's waterfront, African government representatives and international experts gathered for the African Union's annual agricultural research conference. Organized by the Washington-based International Food Policy Research Institute, these conferences have monitored and supported African governments' ambitious commitments since 2006 to invest in agricultural development. Well-dressed participants sipped bottled water and took on the theme for this year's conference: "Climate-Smart Agriculture."

The day before, I'd been with farmers in Marracuene, just forty-five minutes up the coast from Maputo. They weren't embracing the experts' climate-smart initiatives but rather defending themselves from them. They wanted no part of synthetic fertilizer, which was labeled climate-smart even though it came from fossil fuels. Small-scale family farmers often referred to such practices, and the "technology package" of which they were a part, as "climate-stupid agriculture."

In Southern Africa, there is nothing abstract about climate change. In the unseasonable spring heat, the women of Marracuene told me of the climate roller coaster they had been riding the last few years. They had seen their rainy seasons turn erratic and undependable, shortening the growing season. They'd seen unusually frequent and intense storms bring floods through their well-tended fields, washing away seeds, crops, and topsoil. They had suffered two consecutive years of drought, worsening the cyclical El Niño weather pattern that wreaks havoc with farmers. In those droughts, they had sweltered in heat waves they said were unprecedented, with temperatures climbing out of the nineties to 100 degrees Fahrenheit, then 106. In 2017, the thermometer hit 110 and crops baked to a crisp in the parched fields. Blessed with irrigation that allows them a second crop in the dry season, they had even seen that backfire on them. In the 2015 drought, the Incomati River, which fills their irrigation ditches with water, saw water levels so low that the Indian Ocean, four miles downriver and swollen with rising sea levels, flowed back up the dried riverbed. Irrigation canals in parts of the region filled with salt water, destroying crops and land.

The women who lead Marracuene's 7,000-member farmer associations seemed undaunted. They had their own climate adaptation strategies, and those did not involve using more fossil fuels or growing monocultures of commercial seeds. They had improved their own preferred vitamin-rich, drought-tolerant maize variety. They had created seed banks that saved the day when climate calamities wiped out many farmers' maize and with it the next year's seeds. Their steady intercropping, with diverse food crops growing within the same field, was improving their soils as it fed their families, with drought-tolerant crops—cassava, cowpeas, sweet potatoes, okra—preventing a food crisis when the maize crop failed. Their rich soil now retained moisture when rains were poor and better absorbed the downpours. These farm families were eating today, despite the damaging climate, and they were steadily improving their chances of eating tomorrow by enriching rather than depleting the resource base that gives them their sustenance.

They were getting no significant help from their government or from the international agencies gathered in the Radisson Blu

Marracuene, Mozambique: Climate change has devastated
Southern Africa, leaving farmers desperate for resilient farming
methods. *Timothy A. Wise*

air-conditioning to address global warming. Neither were family
farmers in other parts of Africa. Instead, they were being pressured
to abandon their native seeds in favor of commercial varieties or,
worse still, genetically modified seeds; to give up the crop diversity
that provides them diet diversity in favor of intensified monocultures of maize or other cereal crops; and to shortcut their patient soil-building practices, substituting expensive, fossil-fuel-based
fertilizer for their own homemade compost. Family farmers in the
developing world know they will never grow crops like farmers do
in Iowa, and mostly they don't want to. But that is the path that

their governments and the Western donors and philanthropists who back them are insisting poor farmers follow.

Going from Marracuene's farmers to the policy-maker conference in the Radisson Blu, I saw the kind of disconnect I'd seen repeatedly in the ten years since food prices spiked, food riots broke out in many developing countries, and African leaders decided they needed to grow more of their own food.

Most of the climate-smart initiatives being hailed at the conference as "win-win" solutions, I realized, had only one consistent winner: agribusiness, the conglomerates that dominate the production of seeds, fertilizers, and other farm inputs. There, as elsewhere in the various halls of power, farmer initiatives that grew more food while reducing dependence on multinational agribusiness were marginalized in favor of business-friendly programs that boosted corporations' profits, increased corporate control of our food systems, and deepened farmers' dependence while undermining the very resource base on which they—and the hungry world—depend for food.

That is why I decided to write this book. I needed to understand why our leaders, after the wake-up call of a global food crisis, remained so blindly committed to business-as-usual policies that ignored the affordable solutions all around them. These solutions could help hungry farmers eat today while giving them the natural and financial resources that could allow them—and all of us—to eat tomorrow.

Business, as Usual

As I saw in four years of research, governments kept following business-as-usual policies because they were designed to support agribusiness, as usual. Agribusiness ran the show. Agribusinesses mostly don't farm, but they make a great deal of money off of agriculture. They produce inputs like fertilizer, seeds, pesticides, and tractors. On the output side, you have traders that store grain and ship it and other farm products within and between countries, and processing companies that take what comes out of the ground and turn it into food and other products—the slaughterhouses, yogurt companies, sugar and corn sweetener factories, breakfast cereal companies, ethanol refineries, cotton ginners. At a global scale, and in many African countries, the dominant agribusiness players are household names: Monsanto, DuPont, Syngenta, John Deere, Yara (fertilizers), Cargill, Archer Daniels Midland, Tyson, Smithfield, Nestlé, Kellogg's. In many cases, these companies' revenues exceed the gross domestic products of the countries in which they operate.

Farmers, meanwhile, assume all the risks that go with growing food and other agricultural products, but they receive a declining share of the rewards. They are squeezed between input-suppliers who sell them ever-more-costly goods and traders and processors who use their market power to bid down the prices farmers can get for their crops. The share of consumers' food dollar going to farmers has been steadily declining for decades. In the United States, the farmer share fell 25 percent between 1993 and 2016, leaving farmers with just 15 percent of the consumer food dollar.[1] Who is getting the rest of that food dollar? Retailers like Walmart, food processors like Archer Daniels Midland, meat companies like Tyson, grain traders like Cargill, seed companies like Monsanto.

Agribusiness companies have such a powerful hold in the United States that they have convinced policy-makers and the general public—and even many farmers—that their interests are completely aligned with those of farmers. Nothing could be further from the truth, despite claims to the contrary by the self-proclaimed "farm lobby." Farmers want low costs and high prices. Agribusinesses want maximum production to maximize input sales and low farm prices to reduce the costs of processors' raw materials. Conveniently enough for agribusiness, maximum production tends to result in low farm prices. Ever-concentrating monopoly power up and down the food chain gives global agribusinesses inordinate power to dictate the terms of trade, the high prices farmers must pay for their inputs and the low prices they can get for their crops.

Their economic power translates into political power, where they dictate national and global policies. That did not change when food prices spiked in 2008, though many of us hoped it would. The so-called food crisis was sparked not by scarcity but largely by the massive diversion of food and land into biofuel production and the sudden surge of speculative capital into a destabilizing new array of commodity-based investment vehicles. The ensuing food riots delivered a wake-up call to international leaders. The number of chronically malnourished surged past 1 billion. With climate change looming and a population of 9.7 billion projected by 2050, leaders called for massive investments to increase food production.[2] For the first time in years, government officials in developing countries realized the perils of relying on cheap imported food. They asked the question many of their own farmers had been asking for years: How can we grow more of our own food?

Soon an expert consensus emerged within international agencies like the UN Food and Agriculture Organization (FAO). Developing countries should grow more of their own food, and to do so they should turn to the farmers who already grew most of the food—small-scale producers. Suddenly, those farmers were not the problem, the "backward" peasants dragging down national development, they were a key part of the solution. And not just to hunger but to climate change. Their low-input methods contributed little in the way of greenhouse gases to the atmosphere compared to industrial agriculture and allowed them to adapt more effectively to the rapidly changing climate.

Plenty of research backed the new consensus. It largely demonstrated the obvious. The largest productivity improvements could be made among small-scale farmers, precisely because they had received very little investment or technical support in the preceding decades. With so many farmers producing at levels so far below their potential, relatively small investments could produce large gains. Because most farmers produced basic food crops, those productivity improvements would first address hunger in the farming families themselves. Once farmers began producing more than their families needed, they would enter the market and a virtuous cycle of economic development would emerge, with the most successful farmers becoming commercial growers as rising incomes generated demand for new goods.[3]

This felt like a revelation to many, but it was, in fact, nothing more than the rediscovery of traditional agricultural development theory. That theory was needed now more than ever, given the urgency of reducing the environmental costs of industrial farming. The world loses 25 million acres of cropland each year as some 80 percent of agricultural land suffers from moderate-to-severe erosion. Overuse of synthetic fertilizer on monocropped agricultural lands is causing acidification, reducing organic matter and soil microbial diversity. Half or more is not taken up by crops, with much of it ending up in waterways or groundwater. Much of the excess is emitted as nitrous oxide, one of the most damaging of greenhouse gases. Overuse of insecticides and herbicides is leaving the soil lifeless; broadcast spraying of herbicides on herbicide-tolerant genetically modified crops is undermining the diversity of surrounding ecosystems and breeding "superweeds" resistant to treatment. Nearly 70 percent of the fresh water humans use is for irrigation, with intensive meat and commodity crop production draining aquifers at unsustainable rates.[4] While many warn that the spread of meat-based diets in developing countries will prove unsustainable, the truth is that overproduction and overconsumption of meat and dairy products in more developed countries is the real environmental threat. According to one recent report, the top twenty global livestock conglomerates together emit more greenhouse gases than Germany, Canada, Australia, the United Kingdom, or France.[5] Any future-oriented response to the food crisis would need to reverse these resource-consuming trends.

Agribusiness pretty quickly hijacked the food crisis response. To do so, they called on an old friend, eighteenth-century philosopher Thomas Malthus, who had warned that soaring populations, which grow exponentially, would overrun the resources needed to put food in all those hungry mouths. Monsanto's Robert Fraley fed the fears of scarcity, warning that food production must double by 2050, and that only technology such as his company's seeds and chemicals can feed the hordes. Leaders at the FAO amplified the neo-Malthusian alarms, echoing the agribusiness claim that we needed to double food production.

Never mind that the FAO's own researchers had shown no such cause for concern.[6] The data showed clearly that global population had not been growing at an exponential rate for decades.[7] Frances Moore Lappé's wise words, that hunger is not caused by a lack of food, were as true in 2008 as they were when she published *Diet for a Small Planet* nearly fifty years ago. Estimates show that today's production could feed 10 billion.[8] Scarcity was still a myth, but a convenient one for agribusiness. In the panic, they could open more markets for their seeds, chemicals, and machinery. After all, how else will we feed a hungry world?

The myth that "we" feed "the world" is the ultimate first-world conceit.[9] The world is mainly fed by hundreds of millions of small-scale farmers who grow 70 percent of developing countries' food. The crops grown in the United States, by farmers like the ones I met in Iowa, feed pigs, chickens, and our cars (with corn ethanol), with some left over to feed China's and Mexico's pigs and, indirectly, their middle classes. Moreover, there is no abstract "world" out there needing to be fed. There are about 1 billion hungry people, nearly all in developing countries. Paradoxically, and unconscionably, the majority of the hungry are some of those same small-scale farmers.[10] The others are underemployed workers, including many farmworkers, who need decent jobs to earn enough to feed their families.[11]

Increasing the industrial production of agricultural commodities does almost nothing for the hungry. It may lower urban food prices slightly, if agribusiness monopolies actually pass the savings on to consumers. But within developing countries capital-intensive farming reduces employment in rural areas, which increases migration to urban centers and reduces wages for low-skill workers. For hungry farmers, those commodities that "we" export to "feed the world" can even make them hungrier, as cheap imports undercut local food producers.[12]

Eating Tomorrow

Everywhere I traveled in researching this book, agribusiness interests were being aggressively promoted, to the detriment of family farmers, the environment, and the food and nutritional security of the world's poor. I went to Mexico, where I'd done research for years. There, the North American Free Trade Agreement had been the vehicle to expose small-scale farmers to a flood of low-priced imports that had devastated rural communities and left Mexico heavily dependent on food imports, even for its staple crop, maize. Now, Monsanto and other biotechnology companies were trying to open the country to genetically modified maize seeds despite the risks of cross-pollination with the country's rich diversity of native maize varieties.

Meanwhile, the U.S. government was using outdated World Trade Organization rules to challenge India's ambitious National Food Security Act, an unprecedented effort to provide basic food rations to some 800 million poor Indians in the world's hungriest country. The claim, from a U.S. government known for subsidizing its farmers, was that India was procuring those food rations from farmers at an above-market price, which constituted an unfair agricultural subsidy. Galled by the hypocrisy, I traveled to India to better understand the controversial program, which seemed to be working effectively, much like the early U.S. agricultural policies from the Great Depression on which India's policies were modeled.

To understand the roots of this maladaptive model I went to Iowa, blanketed in genetically modified corn and soybeans, dotted with industrial hog factories and ethanol refineries. In 2013, the Des Moines–based World Food Prize was awarded to three biotechnology scientists, one from Monsanto. Coincidentally, the company had just donated a sizeable sum to help refurbish the grand World Food Prize Hall of Laureates on the banks of the Des Moines River, a conflict of interest so commonplace in the agribusiness-dominated U.S. heartland that it barely stirred a complaint. Meanwhile, the Des Moines water supply had nearly been shut down when nitrate levels in the river from fertilizer runoff upstream hit unsafe levels. Why was this the model for global agriculture in the wake of the food crisis?

And why was it being exported to Africa? The continent is certainly the area in greatest need of agricultural development; most national economies are heavily dependent on farming, and productivity remains low. The global food crisis focused welcome attention on Africa, supporting national governments in efforts already under way to raise crop yields and promote rural development. But agribusiness had largely hijacked those reform efforts as well via the Gates Foundation–inspired Alliance for a Green Revolution in Africa, with its narrow but well-financed marketing of commercial seeds and chemical fertilizers. I traveled extensively in Southern Africa, an area heavily dependent on corn production for livelihoods and nutrition, documenting the consistent failures of this agribusiness-driven approach.

How had we gone so terribly wrong? Why were leaders so blind to the limitations of this model? How could policy-makers at the Maputo conference on climate change and agriculture focus so narrowly on industrial-scale practices? How could they not see the real solutions that were all around them?

Farmers mostly weren't granted entrance to the air-conditioned gathering in the Radisson Blu. I didn't have to go far to find them. I walked ten minutes up the globally warmed street to the modest Kaya Kwanga conference center. There, over the din of giant fans blowing hot air, peasant farmers lectured a representative from the Mozambican government about why they did not want foreign-financed industrial agriculture, which they denounced as "land-grabbing." They wanted secure land rights and government support to help them grow more food in the country's relentlessly changing climate. They didn't want climate-smart agriculture, they wanted more sustainable and resilient farms, the kinds of low-input practices that could restore rather than deplete the fertility of their land. In a country with more than half of rural residents in poverty, they wanted to eat today. And they wanted to restore their soil so they could eat tomorrow.

Part I

Into Africa: The New Colonialism

IN THE WAKE OF the food crisis, the issue that grabbed the headlines was land-grabbing, a wave of foreign investment in industrial-scale farming in the developing world explained as a way to secure land and food production for resource-poor countries like China. Africa was a particular target. With thousands of farmers and their communities displaced in the land rush, the sudden surge in capital was widely denounced as the "new colonialism," even as cash-starved African governments brokered the deals as a fast track to modern agriculture.[1]

A more patient response came from international donors and agencies, which took seriously the goal of increasing the productivity of Africa's family farmers. Public investment poured into agricultural research while governments increased support to their own farmers.[2]

Unfortunately, much of that support favored agribusiness, which found its champion in the Bill and Melinda Gates Foundation. The world's largest private foundation, endowed by the fortune of technology monopolist Bill Gates, of Microsoft, got lucky. Barely one year before the first food price spikes in 2007, the foundation launched a new agricultural development initiative to supplement its global health and education programs. Much of the initial funding came from investor Warren Buffett, awash in cash from the speculative bubble that would burst the following year. In 2006, the Gates Foundation tapped that new cash and joined the Rockefeller Foundation to launch the Alliance for a Green Revolution in Africa (AGRA), which would prove to be the ready-made answer to the coming question: How can Africa grow more food?

The diagnostic was as compelling as it was false: Africa was behind because it was left out of the first green revolution, the technology-led effort credited with bringing Asia and Latin America into high-yield agriculture in the 1960s and 1970s through the incorporation of high-yield seeds, the application of inorganic fertilizers and other chemical inputs, and investments in irrigation. Production increased, feeding growing populations and dissuading restive farmers from joining radical movements for land reform or wholesale revolution. The designation "green revolution" came from its offer of an economic antidote to "red revolutions," not from being environmentally friendly.[3] Environmentally friendly it was not, causing long-term damage to land and water resources.[4]

In 2006, with more-advanced seeds and agro-chemicals at the rich world's disposal, the new Masters of the Agricultural Universe could make a green revolution designed just for Africa, tailored to its specific needs and conditions. Coming from a high-tech giant like Bill Gates, the answer to Africa's agricultural underdevelopment was, not surprisingly, technology. Having the Rockefeller Foundation, the lead promoter of the first green revolution, on board gave AGRA the air of invincibility.

With the onset of the food crisis, donor governments from industrialized countries joined AGRA. As if agribusiness needed further help, U.S. president Barack Obama in 2012 launched the New Alliance for Food Security and Nutrition, a multiyear, multi-donor effort focused on agribusiness-led "public-private partnerships" (PPPs) as the vehicle for African agricultural development. Donors would provide aid, private companies like Cargill, Yara, Monsanto, and DuPont would make a nonbinding promise to invest, and participating African governments would commit to reforming their national laws and regulatory systems to "enable the business of agriculture," in the words of a new World Bank index that measures such reforms.[5] Reforms included new seed laws to protect commercial plant breeders, land laws to give investors easier access, and a host of other pro-agribusiness policies. The New Alliance was immediately denounced with the same term used to describe land-grabbing: "the new colonialism." The New Alliance was seen as taking over where the World Bank and the International Monetary Fund had left off with their "structural adjustment" conditionalities in the 1990s.[6] Its business-friendly policy prescriptions complemented AGRA's technology-based approach perfectly.

From its founding in 2006, AGRA was the Gates Foundation's second-largest grantee, receiving more than $400 million.[7] For cash-starved African governments fearing food riots in 2008, AGRA and its $100 million per year in funding was an offer they could scarcely refuse.[8] African governments had in 2006 launched their ambitious Comprehensive African Agricultural Development Program, which committed governments to spend at least 10 percent of their budgets on agriculture. Here was Bill Gates & Co. ready to tell them what to spend it on.

AGRA preached improved seeds (mainly commercial hybrid and genetically modified varieties), soils (mainly through increased use of synthetic fertilizer), and markets (for the distribution of such inputs and the infrastructure to bring products to market). And it offered cash payments for those who converted to its particular version of African agricultural development, dispensed as grants to governments, nongovernmental groups, and even for-profit initiatives. The approach was buttressed by expensive farm input subsidy programs (FISPs), which subsidized farmers to use those green-revolution seeds and fertilizers.

The biggest difference between Africa's green revolution and the first one wasn't the new technology, it was the failure to include the old technology. GR 2.0 didn't have more features, it had fewer. Specifically, Gates & Co. left irrigation out of the technology package, and they left out other key features like infrastructure, credit, and marketing support. A reliable supply of water had been critical to the success of the new seed and fertilizer package in Asia. India became the world leader in local tube-well irrigation, with generous support from international donors. By recent accounts, irrigation (not seeds or fertilizer) was the input most responsible for the yield increases in wheat and rice.[9] Sure, the improved seeds responded to fertilizer—they were bred to do just that—but they needed water to thrive.

It is well established that irrigation is one of the most effective inputs in any agricultural system. In Southern Africa, with climate change making rainy seasons erratic, it can save the year's harvest and give farmers a second cropping season. Irrigation makes a huge difference no matter the other inputs, no matter what seeds or fertilizer a farmer is using. Commercial seeds and fertilizers are expensive, making them an inappropriate technology for many poor farmers. Without irrigation, how could Africa's own green revolution expect to increase agricultural productivity?

I started my research in the home of the "Malawi Miracle," a widely acclaimed green-revolution success story.

2

The Malawi Miracle and the Limits of Africa's Green Revolution

I first visited the small, landlocked country of Malawi in southeastern Africa in late January 2014, and it was hard to believe its people often go hungry. The rainy season was well under way, and in the central region around the capital city—and even within the city limits—the landscape was lush and green. Look closely, and you'd notice it was green with food crops. Nearly every inch of unpaved space seemed to be planted in maize (corn). Along roadsides in the capital city of Lilongwe, the green stalks rose five feet above moist, dark soil.

This scarcely seemed like a land that could not feed itself. But that is what Malawi had been, at least until 2006. National food production, particularly for the national staple, maize, regularly fell short of demand from a rapidly growing population, leaving the country perennially on the international dole for food aid. The World Food Program had permanent offices in Malawi, and for good reason.

After yet another crop shortfall in 2005, the government took a stand, rejecting World Bank and International Monetary Fund advice by launching broad-based government subsidies for the country's small-scale farmers to buy seeds and fertilizers. It worked. Maize production doubled, and the "Malawi Miracle" was proclaimed. Most donors had to concede success. Even the World Bank grudgingly accepted that subsidies could work.[1] "The impact [of Malawi's

subsidy programme] has stunned the sceptics and the doomsayers,"
gushed Glenn Denning and Jeffrey Sachs in the *Financial Times*; "it
seems that an African green revolution is possible after all."[2]

It certainly had gotten my attention. Here was a poor government doing just what the experts now said they should do in the
wake of the food crisis—support small-scale farmers to grow more
food. And it worked. I wanted to know more.

Even in early 2014, I could see that Malawi's green revolution
was losing momentum. The rains had come late but strong, and
harvests the previous year had been decent. Yet some 1.8 million
of the country's 16 million people faced severe food insecurity. According to news reports, some had starved. Maize production was
strong, but hunger persisted. Productivity was no longer climbing
so rapidly, subsidy costs were devouring the government's budget,
and fertilizer imports were draining scarce dollars.

As it turned out, I would be witness over the coming three years
to the unraveling of the Malawi Miracle. Flooding and drought,
the evil twins of climate change, devastated farmland and reduced
harvests in 2015 and 2016. According to the World Food Program,
more than 8 million people—almost half of Malawi's population—
faced hunger after the 2016 crop failures. Malawi was very much
back on the international dole.[3]

There was a lot to learn from Malawi's successes and its failures
in its quest to ensure everyone could eat today and tomorrow. I
would be surprised by how many of those lessons involved agribusiness influence over government policies, and how much of that
influence was exerted by Monsanto.

The Malawi Miracle

The countryside looked pretty miraculous in January 2014. Outside the capital city, on the road south toward the former colonial
capital of Zomba, the hills rolled with maize, not in vast tracts rem-
iniscent of Iowa but in small, neatly bordered plots. It is paradoxical
only to outsiders that this greenest of seasons is also the hungriest.

By planting time, many peasant farmers have consumed the last of their saved grain, even following a decent harvest like they'd had the previous year. Until the new crop comes in late March or April they have to rely on meager cash income to feed themselves and their families. For two-thirds of Malawi's farm families, the harvest doesn't last the year; on average, maize stores have run out within six months of bringing in the grain.[4]

Malawi's victories over the hungry season were impressive and hard-fought. Between 1998 and 2001, Malawi's government had acceded to World Bank and IMF recommendations that it cut spending. Neoliberalism was at its zenith, and governments were simply advised to get out of the way so markets could work their magic. Among its cost-cutting reforms, Malawi's government eliminated a small but effective program of seed and fertilizer distribution. The program had been partly credited with raising Malawi's maize production to record levels.[5]

The Southern African country of Malawi depends heavily on corn for its people's livelihoods and diets. *Timothy A. Wise*

The twin towers of economic orthodoxy then added insult to injury by persuading the government to sell off most of its food reserves, which were deemed "market distorting" and too expensive to maintain. Even with a food crisis looming in 2001 after heavy flooding damaged fields, the government declined to restock its silos, citing IMF advice. That decision proved deadly by early 2002. As many as 1,000 people died in the ensuing famine, the worst ever recorded in the country. National maize production had fallen 40 percent by 2002, in part because of the floods but also because of the elimination of seed and fertilizer handouts.[6]

Drought in 2005 caused yet another food crisis. In this landlocked country, the hungry can wait months for food aid, and many grow desperate. "I have nothing, no food or crops," villager Maria Binda told a British newspaper. "Two of my children are dead from disease and my remaining child is very hungry."[7] Food aid prevented as high a death toll as in 2002, but it was the sixth consecutive year of production shortfalls and hunger.

Officials had had enough. The government rebuilt its food reserves, critical in a country where emergency food donations can take 3–5 months to reach the hungry. Malawi's leaders then had the audacity to ignore World Bank and IMF advice by establishing its broad farm input subsidy program (FISP) intended to put high-yield seeds and fertilizer into the hands of poor farmers.

When international donors refused to support the initiative, calling it inimical to free market principles, Malawi's cash-strapped government launched the program with its own funds. The program was a success. With the help of steadier rains, maize production jumped to record levels in 2006. The first five years of Malawi's FISP showed average maize production 91 percent higher than the previous five-year average. Malawi was even growing enough maize in some years to export to neighboring countries.[8]

Soon, other African countries followed Malawi's lead, and now such farm input subsidy programs are common across Sub-Saharan Africa.[9]

It would be comforting to believe that the replication of Malawi's input subsidy program, in the face of World Bank and IMF opposition, is a shining example of the new politics of food in the wake of the food crisis. But the deeper I got into Malawi's agricultural policies, the more it seemed like the real beneficiaries of the new subsidy programs weren't small-scale farmers or the rural poor. Hunger indicators showed little improvement, if any.[10] But the subsidies were undeniably a boon to multinational seed and fertilizer companies and the donors who saw them as the true engines of modernization in Africa. The closer I looked, the more I saw Malawi's FISP creating a market for seeds and fertilizers where one barely existed. In the process, they were promoting a long-term transition away from sustainable practices of seed-saving, intercropping, and using compost for fertilizer.

Subsidizing the Multinational Seed Giant

"We are very much in favor of the input subsidy program," said Alick Maulawo, technology development manager at Monsanto Malawi. Maulawo, young and outgoing, was a plant breeder by training. He received me warmly in the company's small Lilongwe offices, which serve mainly for distribution and marketing in the country. Like most of Africa, Malawi still does not allow genetically modified maize to be grown in the country, so Monsanto's market is overwhelmingly hybrid maize, patented but developed through conventional breeding methods. In 2014, when I met Maulawo, that market was strong and growing.

Maulawo said Monsanto had about 50 percent of the Malawian market for hybrid maize seeds. Seed Co, a Zimbabwe-based regional seed company, had a good share of the rest of the market. He didn't know—or wouldn't say—how much of Monsanto's sales came from FISP coupons. But he knew full well that the program was significantly responsible for the company's success.

"The perception of hybrids has changed a lot because of the government programs," Maulawo said, betraying a slight smile.

By "perception," of course, he meant sales. Estimates vary, but the share of hybrid maize in Malawian fields has grown steadily since the introduction of the FISP. Maulawo expressed confidence that the company would continue to gain converts among the maize farmers who still keep a majority of their land planted in so-called local seeds they can plant year after year.[11]

The subsidies overcome two major obstacles to the widespread adoption of the green-revolution technology package. First, they primarily support hybrid maize seed, not the so-called open-pollinated varieties (OPVs) or local varieties that can be saved from one harvest and planted the next. Hybrid maize can be replanted, but yields decline significantly after the first year. Poor farmers are unaccustomed to buying seed every year; they've been saving seeds, and exchanging them with neighbors, for generations. And in Malawi, most farmers are too poor to risk such an outlay of scarce cash.

Private seed companies have little incentive to develop or sell OPVs; they want annual customers for their products. Most improved OPVs have come from public-sector plant breeding. The government subsidy, which covers three-quarters or more of the seed cost, puts hybrid seeds within reach. And it encourages farmers to abandon their often lower-yielding varieties, which leaves them dependent on the commercial seed market, without saved seeds, in subsequent years.

Second, and more important, the subsidies provide fertilizer, which produces undeniable results in Malawi's depleted soils, no matter what kind of maize seed a farmer is using. The modern hybrids, however, respond particularly well to synthetic fertilizer; they were bred to do just that. By covering 90 percent of the cost of a 50-kilo bag of fertilizer (about 100 pounds), the government is enticing farmers who otherwise could not find the cash to buy what for most would be prohibitively expensive fertilizer.

The first drugs are often free, I thought. In this case they were just heavily subsidized.

Still, the technology package has to produce. I asked Maulawo what kind of yields small-scale farmers in Malawi were getting with Monsanto's hybrids. He hesitated, but he answered.

"Between 800 kilos and 1 ton per hectare," he said (about 14 bushels per acre). I didn't think I'd heard him right; 1 ton or less? Those are very low yields by almost any standard, and even below average for Malawi as a whole. Depending on the measure one uses, Malawi's average maize yields are around 2 tons per hectare, about 30 bushels per acre, far below the U.S. average of 12 tons per hectare (177 bushels per acre). Maulawo said that the Monsanto seeds' potential is up to 10 tons per hectare, under optimal management and growing conditions. Those include tractors and irrigation, key planks in the first green revolution, which are rarely discussed in Africa's current version. But he confirmed that Malawi's smallholders, who don't farm under anything resembling optimal conditions, are getting 1-ton yields with Monsanto's seeds.

Still, he argued, the yields from Monsanto's maize are better than the alternatives, and certainly superior to the half ton per hectare that farmers get from their saved local maize seeds.[12] Not much better. I asked him if he thought the company would still be able to sell its seeds if there were no government subsidies.

"We could still sell seeds without the input subsidy program," he answered, "but not as much."

Edson Musopole, former agricultural ministry employee and a self-proclaimed "seed elder" in Malawi due to his long tenure in the sector, was dubious. "If the input subsidy program ended, it is not clear that the multinational seed companies would be sustainable here."

The math is pretty simple. If Maulawo's yield estimates were accurate—and why would he, of all people, underestimate the yield of his company's seeds?—the per-hectare yield gain of using hybrid maize and fertilizer may be higher, but it is just half a ton. That extra maize, if sold on the Malawian market, earns only about $70. A hectare's worth of the seed costs about $14, unsubsidized, and the fertilizer costs $193. That adds up to a $137 per hectare *loss* from the technology—$207 in added costs and just $70 in added income. Even with the subsidies, farmers may be getting such low yields that they don't justify the added out-of-pocket costs. Stephen Greenberg, of the Johannesburg-based African Centre for Biodiversity, estimated that at prevailing prices farmers would need to get at least 1.5 tons more maize per hectare from the investment in green-revolution technologies to recoup their costs. "Our findings show net transfers away from farming households to agribusinesses," said Greenberg.[13]

Why would a poor farmer sink cash she doesn't have into inputs that produce such marginal—or negative—returns? She wouldn't, and Monsanto knows it.

Farmers Make Their Own Calculations

Near Dedza in the area of Lobi, off the road south from Lilongwe toward Zomba, I saw farmers making that cost-benefit calculation for themselves. And they were slowly moving away from hybrid maize and synthetic fertilizer.

Edwin Kasamba, a muscled middle-aged farmer, posed proudly in front of maize plants that looked particularly robust. The stalks were tall, the leaves luminescent, the ears just beginning to develop. I'd been told that farmers here were working to improve their soils and harvests by intercropping maize with leguminous crops—beans, pigeon peas, groundnuts, soybeans. The goal was to diversify diets too dependent on maize and offer crops that ripen at different times of the year. The legumes also replenish the soil by replacing nitrogen heavily drained by maize monocultures while adding organic matter to Malawi's depleted land.

Kasamba was enthusiastic about this experiment in agro-ecology. He said that this was only his second season intercropping, but already he'd seen his soil improve so much that he'd skipped the usual post-planting application of synthetic fertilizer on his one acre of maize. He thought he wouldn't need the usual midseason application either to get good yields.

The Lobi project is associated with a long-running effort in Ekwendeni, in Northern Malawi, the "Soil, Food, and Healthy Communities" project.[14] The original goal was to improve nutrition

Farmer in Lobi in Central Malawi shows off his orange maize crop. *Timothy A. Wise*

and food security by encouraging on-farm crop diversity, an anti-dote to the "cornification" of Malawi.

I asked if his high-yield maize didn't need those fertilizers to thrive. He smiled. This was a local variety, he told me, so it didn't depend on synthetic fertilizer, just composted manure farmers were producing in the community. He told me proudly that he was growing "orange maize." Orange? The ears weren't in yet, so I couldn't tell. He said it was a local variety, which had been grown widely in the region before hybrids took over the landscape. In the interests of dietary diversity, farmers were trying it because the grain is high in vitamin A, which is chronically in deficit in developing countries. Vitamin A deficiencies can lead to blindness and a range of other ailments, all common in Malawi. Apart from the nutritional advantages, Edwin said it was much better than hybrid white maize for the local porridge staple, *nsima*; it produced more grain and was easier to mill at home.

I was encouraged to see intercropping taking hold, in part because the government had, to its credit, added coupons for legume seeds to its input subsidy program to encourage the practice. The big seed and fertilizer companies had opposed the move. They didn't market legume seeds in Malawi, and the last thing they wanted to see was a drop in fertilizer demand. But land planted to legumes had more than doubled since the introduction of the legume seed subsidy in 2009.[15]

And in Lobi, at least, the seeds being sown in farmers' fields were coming mainly from those same fields, saved from last year's crops.

Why in the face of such positive examples was the Malawian government so fixated on maize, and hybrid maize at that, which had to be purchased every year? More perplexing still, the green-revolution package did not seem to be working as well as it had when the input subsidy program first started.

Getting Through the Maize Maze

David Mkwambisi, a professor of environmental sustainability at Malawi's Bunda College of Agriculture and Natural Resources, used to work in the seed industry. He scoffed at Monsanto's claim of superiority. He said that Malawi's former seed breeding program, and the now-defunct National Seed Company of Malawi, had gained renown for producing maize seeds especially suited to Malawian conditions and preferences.

Small-scale African farmers are often loath to adopt the high-yield varieties, mostly developed by Northern scientists for industrialized agricultural markets. Malawian breeders realized that yield was only one of a range of characteristics farmers were seeking. For Malawi's farmers, additional priority traits included drought tolerance, storability, and poundability.

The first relates to Malawi's erratic rainy season. Maize is a remarkable plant. Not only does it produce among the largest amount of energy (calories) per unit of land, it can adapt to a wide range of agro-ecological conditions. But it requires a lot of moisture. Most varieties suffer from even relatively short periods without water, particularly if they occur during one of the crucial times in the

plant's development. Some varieties, so-called short-season varieties, grow more quickly. Farmers tended to favor those varieties,
particularly with climate change shortening the rainy season in
some years and making it more erratic in others.

Storability relates to the grain's capacity to resist diseases and
pests for the relatively long periods it may need to be stored after
the harvest. In rain-fed agriculture in Malawi, there is one harvest, which means that the grain must last the family for the entire
year, into the next rainy season until the next crop comes in. Some
varieties store better than others; many hybrids have proven to be
prone to infestation with weevils and other pests.[16]

Poundability refers to the utility of the grain for farmers' food
needs. Mostly they use maize for *nsima*, a grits-like cornmeal mixture that is the staple food of the poor in the country. To make cornmeal, farmers pound the grain into meal, often by hand, and some
maize varieties pound better than others. It's hard work, mostly done
by women, so poundability matters a lot. Malawians tend to prefer
so-called flint and semi-flint varieties of maize, as opposed to the
dent varieties more commonly marketed by multinational seed companies. The grain-to-husk ratio is better, giving them more edible
food from each kernel. The taste is also widely preferred.[17]

So preferred, in local lore, that Malawian women have called too
much hybrid maize "a marriage breaker" because the *nsima* made
from it won't satisfy their husbands. Local varieties, with their filling grain content, are known as "marriage builders."[18]

Mkwambisi told me that Malawi's plant breeders had teamed up
with international experts in the 1980s to produce a set of national
OPVs and hybrids that had a reputation for being relatively tolerant
of erratic rains, storing for long periods without spoilage, and being
easily pounded for *nsima*. A particularly popular national hybrid
was MH18 (Malawi Hybrid 18).

"They got 6 to 7 tons per hectare on medium-sized farms, 2 to 3
on small farms," he said.

Those yields dwarfed those of Monsanto's current maize varieties. Where are those seeds now? Mkwambisi wasn't sure; he'd

since left the seed business to focus on environmental matters. He explained that an economic crisis forced major cutbacks in government funding. They reduced the research station budget, preventing the breeders from reproducing the most popular seeds for distribution. With the public sector no longer providing inexpensive, productive, and desirable seeds, the terrain—literally—was opened for the multinational firms' seeds.

"The private sector has benefited more than small farmers have from the subsidy program," Mkwambisi said, shaking his head.

Blessings Chinsinga, a professor of political economy at Malawi's Chancellor College in Zomba, didn't mince his words when I met him at the Centre for Social Science Research. He is known for his candor. Chinsinga ran me through the twists and turns in the input subsidy program, a very helpful lesson in politics. Not only does the program benefit multinational seed and fertilizer companies, it provides a steady source of patronage for national politicians, who now see those coupons as indispensable for winning rural votes. Lucrative contracts, for transportation or seed production, can feather the nests of cronies.

He confirmed that Malawi's national maize breeding had basically collapsed, but he said the input subsidy program had not always had its myopic focus on hybrid maize, which now accounts for 70 percent or more of subsidized maize. In its first year, the government actually subsidized only open-pollinated maize varieties, precisely because of their affordability for farmers. Why the change?

Chinsinga smiled. He said, carefully, that the "donor community" wanted the government to let "the private sector" play more of a role, for reasons of "efficiency." Those were a whole lot of euphemisms to pack into one sentence. Chinsinga unpacked them. Before the 2006–2007 growing season, the U.S. Agency for International Development, a major program donor, was particularly insistent that Malawi open up its seed program to Monsanto and other transnational seed companies, ostensibly to take advantage of their high-yield seeds. The government added hybrid maize seeds to the subsidy program.

"That's when the hybrid share jumped to 70 percent," Chinsinga went on. "The program is a cash cow for the seed companies. They don't need to tender competitive bids for their seeds, and they don't need to advertise. They have a guaranteed market."

I walked a short way down the hill to the economics department, a small, plain building on the main road through Chancellor College's tidy campus. With Michigan State professor Andrew Dorward, economist Ephraim Chirwa had just published a book on the recent history of the input subsidy program.[19] He'd been inside the government and out, and I found him to be warm and friendly, like so many in Malawi, and a straight talker. Short and stocky, perhaps in his late forties, he smiled easily, but he was plenty serious about the FISP.

Amid a chorus of current critics, Chirwa still defended the program. His research showed that maize production roughly doubled (depending on the estimates you use), a result of a rising share of hybrid maize, rising fertilizer use, and increased area planted to maize. He and his colleagues regularly evaluate the FISP, and they generally find benefits exceeding costs by 60 to 80 percent, the main economic benefit being the reduction in maize imports when there are shortages.[20] Impacts on food security are less impressive.[21]

Chirwa disputed some of the charges leveled at the FISP, but he was no cheerleader. He, too, saw the need for deep reform. Seeds were one of those areas. Chirwa's best estimate was that nationally on-farm yields from modern hybrid maize were 1.2 to 1.5 tons per hectare. "They are not good," he said, and only marginally better than the best-yielding local varieties.

Chirwa said that Monsanto and Seed Co's joint share of the government seed subsidy program was 70 percent, up from 35 percent previously. These are oligopolistic markets, with those two players controlling such a large share of the market that they can collude to set prices, including in negotiations with the Malawian government on the value of seed vouchers.[22]

"I call it forced adoption," said Chirwa firmly. "The test will come when the subsidy is finished. If adoption continues, the seed companies can thank the government subsidy program."

A Piece of the Yield Puzzle

I was given a missing piece in the yield puzzle at the Millennium Villages Project off the Chancellor campus in Zomba. I was curious to meet their director, Andrew Daudi. He had been the principal secretary in the agriculture ministry until 2010 and was an architect of the input subsidy program. The Millennium Villages were part of economist Jeffrey Sachs's grand and well-funded project to implement the UN's Millennium Development Goals in a set of model villages. The projects were widely criticized for not being cost-effective or easily replicable.[23] Their lessons for cash-strapped Malawi seemed limited. But they had the resources and the independence to try things, and I'd been told Daudi was now thinking well outside the box.

Daudi looked like a former bureaucrat, in his fifties and slightly round. He told me he was very busy, but he had a lot to say; I had to work to squeeze in my questions. He was far more interested in talking about seeds than about his project.

An economist by training, he pulled out a pen and drew a simple graph of yield growth over time for different maize varieties—hybrids, OPVs, local seeds. He pointed out two things. First, the yield rises fairly quickly if synthetic fertilizer is applied, for most any variety but especially for hybrids. Hybrid yields were marginally higher on his graph. But then yields tend to plateau, sometimes requiring more fertilizer as time goes on just to maintain productivity. He implied that this was a part of Malawi's current problem.

Second, though, and more revealing, he included on his graph a line for hybrids without optimal fertilizer application. It was well below his line for OPVs without optimal fertilizer. He said I was right that the yield differences were not great between hybrids and Malawian OPVs, and when you factor in tolerance for inconsistent fertilizer applications the OPVs were less risky for poor farmers.

Monsanto's modern hybrids, he said, do very poorly if they don't get the right amount of fertilizer at the right time. In the demonstration plots on company land, with optimal management, their seeds get great yields, 5 to 7 tons per hectare or more. In the real world of Malawi's smallholders, nothing is optimal, least of all fertilizer applications. The subsidies give farmers only two 50-kilo bags of fertilizer, enough for about a quarter-hectare of intensive cultivation.[24] Farmers not only aren't shown when and how much to apply, they don't have enough to sustain the hybrid seeds. They usually can't afford the recommended amount, and they often share their rations with other family members who may not have gotten a subsidy that year. They will sometimes spread it more thinly to cover more land, arguably a rational choice to give a smaller boost to more maize. Or they just apply the top dressing at the beginning of the growing season but skip the crucial mid-season application.

The results are decidedly suboptimal, but entirely predictable.

Anticipating eventual subsidy cutbacks, Daudi explained that in their Millennium Villages Project they were experimenting with OPVs. Those seeds had the advantage that they only needed to be "renewed" (purchased) by the farmer every three years, that they would hold their yield for that long. And they were storable, pound-able, and drought-tolerant. But most important to Daudi, they were also tolerant of inconsistent applications of fertilizer.

This last characteristic seemed like a missing piece of the yield puzzle, and a crucial limitation of the new green revolution. Not only was the revolution failing to mobilize irrigation and credit in its march through Africa, its well-heeled revolutionaries weren't even equipped with enough fertilizer to make its hybrid maize transform the landscape, like modern artillery without the gun-powder to launch its shells.

Daudi was dealing with that in his Millennium Villages by mix-ing a bag of subsidized fertilizer with two parts chicken manure and two parts corn husks, from local sources. Daudi said they were getting very good results from this mix, which stretched fer-tilizer purchases, cut costs by 80 percent, and improved the soil with needed organic matter. Many recommend just this sort of "in-tegrated soil fertility management"—ISFM, as it's known in the field—with its less exclusive reliance on synthetic fertilizers. In fact, AGRA itself endorses such an approach, even if it mostly just ends up promoting fertilizer use.

Daudi said the public sector already has the kinds of high-yield OPVs farmers need, the government just needs a private company to grow them out and distribute them.

"Sounds like a perfect opportunity for a public-private partnership," I said, partly joking. He laughed, a common response to the new fetish for PPPs.

"They don't see a market," Daudi said.

Plenty of demand, but no market. Not as long as farmers are cash-poor and subsidies go mainly for hybrid maize and synthetic fertilizer.

Falling off the Yield Plateau

Most experts I spoke with decried the nearly exclusive focus on maize, for both ecological and dietary reasons. Maize monocultures, grown on the same land year after year, deplete soils, and Malawi's are generally poor. Some studies suggest many are "technically infertile," producing only when the land is stocked with synthetic fertilizer.[25]

Monoculture cropping produces a monoculture diet deficient in many basic nutrients. Malawians get a higher share of their calories from maize than even Mexicans, who domesticated the plant. Production gains aside, the country's food security indicators remain terrible. Over 20 percent of Malawians are undernourished, according to the FAO.[26] Malawi's proportion of children underweight was 17 percent in 2014, one percentage point higher than in 2006 before the FISP began (but better than the 26 percent recorded in 1998). In 2014, 42 percent of children under five were stunted, the height-to-age measure that is widely used to estimate chronic child malnourishment.[27] More than half of rural Malawians are in poverty, according to a range of official sources.[28]

What I really wanted to know was why a government so strongly committed to increasing maize production in the country would overlook its own history of innovation, relying on expensive and apparently low-yielding multinational hybrid seeds that require expensive fertilizers, when its own scientists had produced comparable—or perhaps much better—varieties.

In several meetings with officials in the agriculture ministry, I'd gotten the party line: Yes, the input subsidy program needed some changes, but its emphasis on hybrid maize had paid off. I'd been told that Alex Namaona, the respected head of planning in the agriculture ministry, might be more forthcoming. He received me like the busy man that he was, gracious but apologizing for having only limited time. He touted the government's irrigation programs. He bemoaned the sorry state of the extension services. He expressed support for new efforts to bring foreign capital into the country. It seemed I would get the party line once again.

The conversation turned easily to hybrid seeds, but only with the obligatory detour through fertilizers. (Like the seeds themselves, my conversations about them only seemed to work with fertilizers.) Namaona was visibly proud of what the FISP had accomplished, but he grew refreshingly candid about its limitations.

"Fertilizer is only a temporary measure," he said without hesitation. "It is poisonous to the health of the soil." He agreed that being dependent on fertilizer imports was not much better than being dependent on food imports. "We are still agro-dependent." I was surprised to hear him call for intercropping with legumes in order to reduce the use of inorganic fertilizer. Namaona said synthetic fertilizers were too expensive, they didn't build soil fertility, and Malawi couldn't afford the import bills.

There on the front lines of the green revolution, Namaona sounded downright counterrevolutionary.

Namaona acknowledged that yields had plateaued, just as Andrew Daudi had alleged. He worried that they would continue to stagnate or, worse, decline as the soils deteriorated and the plants' response to nitrogen fertilizer slipped. He talked of green manure, intercropping, rotations, and the desperate need for extension workers to support the effort. But he said nothing about seeds.

I popped my question. "If you want to wean the country from its dependence on imported fertilizer, don't you also need to wean it from its dependence on modern hybrids?" He nodded. "Why not distribute some of those national seeds developed by Malawian breeders? Why not revive the national seed company?"

He smiled and shook his head, clearly pained to deliver bad news to a naïve U.S. researcher. "Don't you know?" he asked. I shook my head. "Monsanto bought the national seed company fifteen years ago."

I imagined he could hear the gentle click as that key piece of the seed puzzle fell into place for me. Of course: Who else would buy the national seed company but a multinational firm? It could then take what it wanted, shelve varieties it didn't want on the market anymore, and open new markets for its own patented seeds. Indeed, after Monsanto took over the National Seed Company of Malawi (NSCM) in 1998, it discontinued the distribution of the popular hybrid, MH18. The stated reason was a leaf blight that harmed many hybrid maize varieties, but the real reason was that Monsanto didn't own the patent and profits were therefore lower than for its less popular patented varieties.[29]

Monsanto hadn't discontinued production of MH18 because it was unproductive. It had done so because it *was* productive.

I got the full story when I came back to Malawi two years later, and it was worse, with an added multinational villain: Cargill, the grain-trading behemoth.

Elizabeth Sibale, a regal, understated crop breeder, met me for tea. Trained first in Malawi, then at the University of Missouri, and with a PhD from Cornell, she had helped lead the effort in the 1980s within the national research department to develop some of those popular seeds I had heard so much about, including MH18. She told me that the research was not limited to maize hybrids but also included open-pollinated maize varieties and improved legume seeds that could appeal to cash-poor smallholder farmers while diversifying their diets. The NSCM would grow them out and market them, and they were popular.

What happened when NSCM was privatized? Cargill, one of the world's largest grain traders, bought a controlling interest in the national company in 1988. "Cargill had no interest in legumes or OPVs, and they stopped producing the seeds," said Sibale. It was all maize hybrids all the time. They kept producing MH18 and other national hybrids until Monsanto bought the controlling interest in NSCM from Cargill in 1998.

Sibale said her commitment had always been to creating affordable improved seeds, so she resigned in 1996 after Cargill shelved its OPV and legume distribution. For a decade, after Monsanto took over what remained of NSCM, Sibale led a European Commission effort to fill the gap, continuing her work to breed improved maize OPVs, legumes, and other traditional crops such as millets and sorghum. She helped found the Association of Smallholder Seed Multiplication Action Group (ASSMAG) to promote smallholder seed production and Malawian commercial seed companies. Eventually, she moved away from her breeding roots, first to the FAO and then to the NGO sector to work on crop diversity and nutrition. But it was easy to see that her heart was still with smallholder food producers. And she decried the loss of seed development to the private sector.

"I don't like where we are heading," she told me. "Our mistake was to adopt the monoculture system. My mother grew other crops with her maize—pigeon peas, cowpeas, yams." Like many in Malawi, she thinks the goal should be crop diversification, for nutritional reasons and for soil health. The answer, she says, is in improving soils, not seeds. "The rain just runs off the fields when we get it now."

I had the answer now to my question about what seemed to be Malawi's irrational commitment to green-revolution solutions delivered by multinational seed and fertilizer companies. What happened in Malawi has happened in many other countries. Economic crisis forces cutbacks. International debt or shortages of foreign exchange prompt the World Bank and IMF to step in with a structural adjustment program, a set of market-oriented reforms designed to reduce the government role in the economy. Under those programs—and Malawi has seen its fair share, including one in late 2012—a lot gets privatized.[30] And where there is privatization there are multinational firms ready to move in.

In Malawi's seed sector, Monsanto seemed not only to have moved in, it got the government to furnish its house and, with the input subsidy program, provide it with a steady source of income.

It seemed Malawi was on a classic high-input treadmill that keeps the people and their government running, but getting nowhere. The farmers are subsidized by the government to use imported inorganic fertilizers and hybrid seeds from outside companies like Monsanto. Sometimes they get higher yields—but not always, not if they can't afford extra fertilizer, which the seeds require. If the subsidies run out, the farmers can't afford the seeds or the fertilizer.

Even though production improves initially with fertilizer-induced yields, it takes more and more fertilizer just to sustain those gains. Farmers run hard mostly just to stay in place. The numbers are clear: Malawi is getting less bang for its fertilizer buck as yields stagnate due to poor soil fertility.[31]

Unfortunately, that treadmill was only picking up speed when I first visited Malawi in 2014. The previous year, the government had committed itself to the G-7 countries' New Alliance for Food Security and Nutrition, a controversial agricultural development scheme designed to entice foreign investors—and their precious hard currencies—to invest in Malawi.[32] In return, the Malawian government was expected to reform its policies, laws, and regulations so they are more conducive to business. Seed policies were at the top of that list of reforms. So were land policies, for which donors and multinational firms were demanding private land they could purchase outright or at least easy access to large tracts of agricultural land. In Malawi, that land mostly stretched through the so-called green belt that runs along the fertile shores of Lake Malawi, which covers much of the country's eastern border with Tanzania. Malawi's Green Belt Initiative was set up to secure

500,000 acres of land to attract foreign investors. They hadn't gotten many takers.

Small Can Still Be Beautiful, with Public Support

The global fetish for foreign investment and PPPs diverts attention from two of the things that have historically been proven to work to increase smallholder food production: farmer cooperatives and small-scale irrigation. Geoffrey Mamba, head of Malawi's irrigation department, suggested I stop in Lifuwu and Ngolowindo to see two such government-funded irrigation projects.

Irrigation department engineers Bennett Siwenbe and Fenwick Simfukwe climbed into our car outside the lakeside town of Salima and took us to Lifuwu Rice Cooperative, several kilometers off the main road. It was midmorning, and members—the majority women—were wading in calf-deep water on their plots, which together covered around 250 acres.[33] Each member farms his or her own plot, but they cooperate in the processing and marketing of the rice and in the maintenance of the irrigation system. The system pumps water from boreholes kept productive by an easily accessible water table fed by the nearby lake.

Co-op president Yusufu Charles received us along the path between the flooded fields. His white beard and whiter smile shone from his dark, sweaty face. He said they'd made good profits in recent years, but this last dry season the electricity bills, inflated by the IMF-mandated price hikes, had consumed those earnings. The great advantage of irrigation in a place like Malawi, which has one rainy season but a year-round tropical climate, is the addition of a second or even third crop each year. Here they got two, but Charles told us that this year many co-op members left their fields fallow in the dry season rather than spend the money to pump the water. "It was going to cost $20,000 a month," he said, and fertilizer prices had also increased. Still, he said co-op members were much more food secure than most Malawian farmers.

Irrigation is not cheap. Once it's up and running, Malawian

farmers are responsible for its upkeep and the engineers are there for technical advice. Fenwick said the farmers at our next stop, the Ngolowindo Horticultural Co-operative Society, had failed to maintain the system so it broke down recently, costing the members a dry-season winter crop. It was working now, after some technical support from the government.

Three co-op members received us at the small hut that serves as the organization's headquarters. Healthy maize plants lined the overgrown muddy road, leaning almost into the open windows of our car. This was a different cooperative model, with 140 members sharing just 42 acres of land.

"How much land does each member get?" I asked Saidi Asiri, an older man who seemed ready to speak for the three of them.

"One-tenth of a hectare," he responded, through the translator. Just one-quarter of an acre. He explained that each co-op member also has their own separate field, generally planted in maize for their own consumption. The co-op is for cash crops, and here the cash crops are mostly vegetables. They get good prices for the year-round supply of vegetables made possible by their small-scale, government-built irrigation system. They even make good money from the limited maize they grow under irrigation, since they can sell it as "green maize," picked early and grilled right on the cob. Green maize generally gets a higher price, particularly in the winter because the hungry season is just starting for many rural Malawians.

Again, no public-private partnership here, just a good old-fashioned farmers' cooperative that relies on a small initial government investment in irrigation. Bennett and Fenwick told us it cost between $9 and $15 per hectare to build irrigation. I did the math in my head. It would have cost around $2,000 to irrigate 42 acres. The result was vegetables for home consumption, cash income from sales, and a better supply of needed vegetables for consumers, particularly in the dry season. From the perspective of food security, that seemed a good return on investment.

I was encouraged to see such positive examples in Malawi, but I was mystified that such projects were not at the center of the country's agricultural development strategy. The government was still deeply committed to its collapsing green-revolution programs alongside desperate pro-business efforts to reform its policies and laws to entice foreign investors onto lands it didn't have.

The Great Unraveling

I was back in Malawi two years later after a drought ravaged much of Southern Africa, leaving Southern Malawi parched and hungry. Floods the previous year had wiped out crops in much of the same region. National maize production had fallen more than 30 percent in 2015, and it was projected to fall another 15 percent in 2016, leaving production barely above pre-subsidy levels.[34]

The government was ill-equipped to respond. A corruption scandal had prompted the suspension of much donor support, on which the government relied for 40 percent of its budget. Imports of synthetic fertilizer, the backbone of the subsidy program, were absorbing 12 percent of Malawi's limited foreign exchange, with rising prices increasing the import tab more than 75 percent from 2012 to 2013.[35] The input subsidy program faced a 50 percent budget cut. Half the country's people needed emergency food aid. Donors were refusing to fund ongoing government programs due to well-documented fears of corruption, leaving Malawi's agricultural development budget crippled at its time of need.

Even Monsanto seemed to be doing poorly, according to Alick Maulawo, who again received me with a smile in Malawi's headquarters in Lilongwe in mid-2016. He confirmed the continued low yields from the company's hybrid maize seeds and admitted that conditions were much worse, in more ways than I realized.

The government's budget crisis had resulted in severe cutbacks in the FISP the previous growing season. Despite the aid cutoff, donors agreed to support some fertilizer subsidies, as a food security measure, but they refused to support seed subsidies. The Malawian government ended up providing limited support for seeds, but not in the manner to which multinational seed companies were accustomed.

Most important, Maulawo said the drought was so severe in Southern Malawi that many farmers just didn't plant at all, or at least they didn't plant the seeds that matter to Monsanto—hybrids. Many farmers opted for lower-cost, lower-risk local seeds, saved by them or their neighbors. So the drought shrank the market for commercial maize seed. One survey indicated that the share of maize land planted in hybrids dropped from 45 percent to 38 percent with the floods of 2014–2015 and then to 33 percent with the 2015–2016 drought.[36]

Not only that, the public sector, through publicly funded international research networks and national breeders, had produced more than 200 new drought-resistant maize varieties under the Drought Tolerant Maize for Africa (DTMA) program. Early results from across Eastern and Southern Africa suggested that drought-tolerant hybrid and OPV maize both were outperforming the most popular commercial hybrid by 35 to 50 percent.[37]

What did all that mean for Monsanto? Nothing good. Drought makes fertilizer and seed investments look particularly foolish—for the government and for farmers. Local seeds and homegrown compost fertilizer often do as well or better in such conditions. The climate makes farmers more risk-averse, and with FISP subsidies in decline, that risk looks even riskier. Meanwhile, a whole new set of inexpensive, publicly funded, drought-tolerant maize seeds have come on the market, out of Monsanto's control. Some are OPVs, but some are hybrids that will compete directly with the company's core business.

Maulawo said the company had no real answer yet to drought-tolerant maize. Monsanto is trying to regain some of that market while opening the door for its genetically modified maize by donating a transgene for splicing into DTMA maize varieties, supposedly to confer additional drought tolerance. The effort is part of the Water Efficient Maize for Africa (WEMA) project. There is little indication that the gene is particularly effective, and Malawi was not close to allowing GM food crops to be grown in the country.[38]

For now, Monsanto was left to license DTMA technology from

the public sector, which is what Malawian seed companies were doing, but that was certainly not Monsanto's business model. That business model, like Monsanto's seeds, was not looking particularly climate-resilient.

Homegrown Solutions

What looked very climate-resilient was that intercropped orange maize I'd seen two years earlier in Lobi. Mangani Katundu, the human ecology professor at Chancellor College, met me for a lunch of goat stew and *nsima* in the faculty cafeteria. He was as refreshing as the meal. Young and eager, he's an agriculture and food scientist by training, and he is not consumed with narrow economic measures such as yield. He was helping run the Malawi Farmer-to-Farmer Agroecology (MAFFA) project in Lobi and another in Thyolo in Southern Malawi. He took me to Lobi, where they had by then had four years of experimenting with orange maize, high in vitamin A.

When I was there before I'd seen only the healthy plants, not the maize itself. This time I arrived right after the harvest. The ear was beautiful, an unusually deep orange, with the kernels somewhat spaced and with shorter cobs. It reminded me of some of the pure landraces I'd seen in Mexico over the years. Like those carefully cultivated varieties, this one displayed great stability over time, resisting the genetic erosion associated with most local Malawian varieties. These have been replanted over generations, and uncontrolled cross-pollination has resulted in poor yields. By all indications, this orange maize is different.

You wouldn't have known from the farmers gathered in Lobi that drought had seriously depressed harvests in the recent growing season. To be sure, they hadn't suffered the worst of the country's devastating heat and dry spell. Farmers to the south saw crops wither in their baked fields.

At a community gathering of some forty farmers from nearby villages, I heard a range of testimonies about their farming

They had with orange maize, known locally as *mthikinya*. Farmers talked about its high yields, comparable to hybrid maize and with mostly compost for fertilizer. It matures early, making it more drought-tolerant as the rainy season grows shorter with climate change. That also gives the household an earlier source of food, bringing the hungry season to an end. When pounded or milled into flour, it yields a lot of grain and less bran, a much-sought attribute for local diets. Women farmers sang its praises as a tasty food, sweeter and more filling than white maize. (I did not ask if it was a good "marriage builder," but the men looked happy too.) And made into *nsima*, farmers said the flour "gelled" quickly, meaning they could produce more *nsima* from the same amount of flour. One farmer said it was the ideal maize to save for the hungry season, when stores from the last harvest are running out.

If orange maize was so great, why were they still growing so much hybrid white maize? For the region as a whole (not just those in the MAFFA program), the data on the blackboard showed hybrid maize production with slightly higher yields than OPV maize but at nearly double the total production levels of OPVs and local varieties combined. (The project organizers did not yet have data on orange maize production.) Didn't they have to buy seeds for hybrids every year and fertilizer, too? The data on the blackboard showed a 30 percent drop in yield for the hybrids after the drought, with much smaller yield reductions for OPVs and local maize. If yields for orange maize were just as good, why grow hybrid white maize at all?

"We grow hybrid white maize to sell in the market," explained Kasamba. "We grow orange maize to eat at home." I asked if there was any market in which they could get cash for their orange maize, and they said no. Katundu told me later that the project was working on developing markets, but for now they just had the occasional purchase from Save the Children and other relief organizations interested in providing high–vitamin A maize in their feeding programs.

This market was heavily biased. In Malawi, perhaps even more than in Mexico, market institutions, heavily influenced by government policies, are set up for white maize. On the input side, subsidies go mainly for hybrids, so of course that is what the agro-dealer shops stock, supplied overwhelmingly by Monsanto and Seed Co of Zimbabwe. What little technical support farmers get comes mainly from those companies, and a few extension agents trained in hybrid maize systems and inorganic fertilizers. ADMARC, the government grain agency, buys only white maize for its stores and for the national grain reserve. So if a farmer needs to sell some of her maize at harvest, to pay for school fees or maybe medical care, she'd better be growing some white maize.

I asked the group what seemed an obvious question: If there were a market to sell orange maize, would you grow less hybrid maize? The response was resounding: "Of course!" came a voice from the crowd of farmers, to unanimous applause.

Katundu asked about other varieties of local maize, and a woman came forward with her own samples to show us. She had purple and red varieties that would have made the Maya proud. They had hard kernels, and she explained that she mainly used them to make a sweet malt beverage for children and, of course, an alcoholic version for the men.

An older man took the recorder and smiled, revealing few remaining teeth. He explained, staring straight into the recorder, that he'd been growing red maize for many years; he even keeps a store of it in his house. He says it keeps particularly well. He protects it from cross-pollination by planting soybean buffers around it. He says people come to him when their maize has run out because they know he will always have some red maize on hand. He says it is good for *nsima*, not just for drinks.

Farmers in Lobi were showing that they were willing to adopt new varieties, just as others in Ekwendeni had shown they would shift their cropping patterns if they saw a better way to farm. The myth of the backward peasant is indeed a myth. Small-scale farmers are certainly risk-averse, and for very good reasons. But if intercropping orange maize with legumes and other nutritious crops could reduce their costs, rebuild their soils, and increase their families' food security, they were clearly willing to change their ways.

What was less clear in Malawi was whether the government, the private sector, and the international donors who call so many of the shots there were willing to change their ways. Dr. Willkson Makumba, head of research for the agriculture ministry, certainly wasn't when I spoke with him in 2017. Decrying farmers' "primitive ways," he said that anyone (like me) who questioned the value of hybrid seeds was "keeping developing countries in poverty." He dismissed native orange maize as inferior to the new biofortified orange hybrid that was just coming on the market.

Native orange maize, intercropped with other healthy food crops, is a Malawian natural resource. It appears to be drought-tolerant in a changing climate, high-yielding even without imported fertilizer, well suited to intercropped systems designed to restore soil fertility, and it offers nutritional qualities desperately needed by the population. Japanese researchers even confirmed these advantages in an academic study in which they compared *mthikinya* with a popular Monsanto hybrid. They found the local maize to be superior in: edible grain yield; storability (with lower losses to pests); performance with low levels of fertilizer; and nutritional value (protein, iron, and zinc, not just vitamin A). "It appears therefore that the orange local variety . . . is beneficial for low-input sustainable agriculture among the smallholder farmers," the Japanese researchers concluded.[41]

In the face of such evidence, and with the unraveling of its own green-revolution strategies, would the government abandon its fixation on hybrid maize fed with unaffordable fertilizer?

Opening Africa to the Seed Giants

Malawi has largely followed the dominant advice on seed policy, delivered with the kind of pressure only donor governments can exert. Seed policy reform is among the thirty-five pro-business changes promised in Malawi's New Alliance agreement. Such policies directly threaten the more widespread adoption of orange maize.

Malawi is not alone in pursuing misguided seed policies that favor commercial plant breeders over local farmers. The so-called Arusha Protocol on "Plant Variety Protection" is now the leading edge of an international effort, supported by Western donor governments, foundations, and of course multinational seed companies, to open Africa to commercial seeds.[42] The initiative comes out of the African Regional Intellectual Property Organization (ARIPO), which promotes laws that protect the intellectual property rights of formal-sector plant breeders, ostensibly to promote the use of certified high-yielding seeds. Farmer groups, such as the African Food Sovereignty Alliance, warn that such policies are designed to undermine farmers' rights to save and exchange seeds and then to open the door, eventually, to genetically modified seeds.[43]

In theory, the goal is to certify the quality of seeds, a real problem in many areas, and also to encourage innovation in seed development for food security. In practice, of course, such laws can impose a regimen of high-cost purchased seeds on poor farmers, the vast majority of whom can't afford them. In its most draconian forms, the Arusha Protocol could advocate policies that make the saving and exchange of seeds, from which most African farmers live, illegal. Civil society representatives have warned of the threats to "farmers' rights," the phrase used to describe the right to free use and exchange of seeds for food and forage crops. Those rights are enshrined in the International Treaty on Plant Genetic Resources for Food and Agriculture.[44] Malawi is a signatory, as are many of the African governments now considering seed laws that violate both the spirit and the letter of the treaty.

Farm leaders in Lobi were certainly worried about their rights. Malawi's initial draft seed policy seemed to outlaw seed exchange and local sales unless seeds were certified by the government. The draft policy would define farmer-saved orange maize seed—the same kernels people make into staple foods—as a "grain" but not a "seed," worthy of eating but not planting.

To Katundu, declaring something that can be planted to grow such nutritious food somehow "not a seed" was beyond cynical. "How can such a valuable native variety of maize not be a seed?"

I posed that question to Tamani Nkhono-Mvula, longtime director of CISANET, the country's umbrella network on agricultural policy. Nkhono-Mvula had recently left CISANET to pursue doctoral studies. He and the organization had supported the government's seed policy, much to the consternation of some of the member groups. I was arguing with him over dinner. Why did the policy need to threaten farmers' rights? I asked. Farmers are not responsible for counterfeit seeds, sold as certified seeds.

"The way the policy reads," I told him in frustration, "it could have been written by Monsanto!"

There was a long pause. "Actually," Nkhono-Mvula told me with a sheepish smile, "a Monsanto official was one of the two authors of the seed policy." I would later learn that this was Paul Chimimba, Monsanto's former country manager in Malawi.

"It is a chilling revelation that the seed policy was authored by an ex-Monsanto employee," said Blessings Chinsinga, Chancellor College professor, when I told him this news. Indeed. It is difficult to imagine a more egregious conflict of interest than allowing a seed company executive to write a government policy that threatens to outlaw farmers' saving and exchanging of seeds, which clearly would open new markets for his company.

Thanks to lobbying by farmer groups and other advocates, some of the more severe provisions were removed from Malawi's seed policy. The final draft seemed to allow seed saving and sharing, but it could prohibit the sale of any seed not certified by the government. Katundu told me the MAFFA project had sold more than 4 tons of orange maize seed this year to NGOs looking to promote healthier and more sustainable food production. Would that now be illegal? As this book goes to press, Katundu and others are lobbying to ensure that the implementing legislation does not restrict farmers' rights, and they plan to take the government up on its stated commitment to pass a separate Farmers' Rights Policy.

Evelyn Njolomole, an experienced farmer from Lobi, certainly did her part to lobby for "seed sovereignty"—the right of farmers and governments to freely choose the seeds they want to use. She joined Katundu and the MAFFA team in the capital of Lilongwe in early June 2016, staffing a Chancellor College booth for the opening of the African Union–sponsored "Ecosystem-Based Adaptation for Food Security" program. The booth featured large professionally produced posters on the orange maize project and offered samples of orange maize flour and other local products.

Njolomole would later see herself on television on the evening news as she eloquently explained the virtues of their crop to Malawi president Peter Mutharika when he stopped by the booth. His first question, according to Katundu, was, "Does it come from Monsanto?" For his government, it seemed, only multinationals could be expected to produce anything of value. He'd allowed Monsanto, after all, to draft the national seed policy.

Njolomole explained that no, it was actually saved seed from Malawi. She handed him a bag of their orange maize flour. President Mutharika promised he would make *nsima* with it that night. One hoped he would taste the national pride in each bite.

Drought-Tolerant Farms

What the president would not have been able to taste is the crop and seed diversity on the farms that grew that maize. Nor would he have sensed the careful alignment of farming practices with nature, from composting to intercropping. The result is the slow and steady rebuilding of degraded soils, with nutrients restored and organic matter nourishing the crops and holding precious moisture. President Mutharika, with half of his citizens facing hunger in 2016 after the drought, probably did not recognize the tremendous opportunity Njolomole was offering him, beyond her orange maize *nsima*.

"What Malawi needs are drought-tolerant farms, not drought-tolerant seeds," said Stacia Nordin when I asked her about the new maize seeds on the market. A U.S.-born nutritionist, she and her husband have their own permaculture farm outside Lilongwe, planted in perennial and seasonal trees and crops designed to maximize year-round food output without external inputs. Nordin's nutritionist training, as much as anything, has her frustrated with Malawi's maize-obsessed agricultural policies. Her own farm demonstrates that the land and climate can grow an abundance of nutritious foods without relying on expensive seeds and fertilizers.

Malawi is not the only African country to see poor results from its input-subsidy program. A recent survey of seven such programs showed that yield gains were often temporary, and they rarely generated the prosperity to sustain commercial fertilizer purchases without subsidies.[45]

No one thinks Malawi could or should stop growing maize; it is now a deep part of the culture, and it can be a critical component of a healthy diet. But monocultures of hybrid white maize, fed by expensive synthetic fertilizer, address none of Malawi's problems. With climate change bringing shorter growing seasons and occasional crippling droughts, the costs of such practices are high.

Vandana Shiva referred to the reductionism of modern agriculture as the "monoculture of the mind"—reducing agriculture to isolated problems of one nutrient such as nitrogen, one seed such as hybrid maize, even one gene within one genetically modified seed.[46] Njolomole, Kasamba, and their fellow farmers were showing Malawi's president how to reduce costs by farming with nature, rather than against it. Hopefully, he and his government were not too bewitched by agribusiness and its green revolution to listen.

3

The Rise and Fall of the Largest Land Grab in Africa

If Malawi's green-revolution dream was slowly dissolving with the fertility of its soils, I still had to give the government credit for investing in small-scale farmers producing food for its own hungry population. The same could not be said in neighboring Mozambique. When I first traveled there in 2014, the country was one of the top targets in Africa for "land-grabbing," the pejorative term coined to describe the great land rush that followed the food crisis. And the tallest lightning rod in the land-grab storm was Pro-SAVANA, the ambitious plan led by Japan and Brazil to turn more than 25 million acres of Mozambique's fertile savannah lands in its northern Nacala Corridor into an export platform for soybeans modeled on Brazil's success in taming its own savannah lands in the *cerrado* region.[1]

For the cash-strapped Mozambican government still licking its wounds from a brutal civil war, the promise was a fast track to modern agriculture for an underdeveloped country struggling to feed itself. Lacking the resources, capacity, and patience for meaningful investments in the country's millions of small farms, the government was betting on foreign capital, with its advanced know-how and technologies, to leapfrog the often slow process of agricultural development, landing with both feet in the brave new world of emerging economies, alongside China, Brazil, and neighboring South Africa. Hoe-wielding peasant farmers would ride the wave of modernization, as laborers, contract farmers, and a new class of entrepreneurial "emerging farmers" ready to act like businessmen (and -women) as they integrated into the "value chains" that the new investments and markets would open for them.

The peril, as I saw in Mozambique and other parts of Southern Africa, was that when foreign capital landed with both feet it was usually on land already occupied and cultivated by farming communities. And the wave of modernization didn't usually carry peasant farmers forward with a rush, it buried them along with their crops and communities. It often didn't even carry the investors very far. And when the wave's waters receded, the landscape left behind often looked more like post-tsunami devastation than modern agriculture.

For investors, of course, the promise of such land deals had nothing to do with agricultural development, it had to do with money. As the global financial crisis engulfed rich countries and investors pulled their money out of subprime real estate and the crashing stock markets, they fled to commodities markets, which were starting to see spectacular price increases. These so-called refuge goods, such as oil, gold, and food grains, are thought to run counter-cyclically to financial markets, in normal times providing a hedge for investors against downturns. Speculative capital flowed into commodities markets, taking advantage of commodity index funds and other creative derivatives designed to "financialize" food markets. The speculation further drove up prices, attracting more speculators, further driving up prices: the bulging end of the investment balloon that expands when its other end is squeezed.[2]

It is no surprise that land speculation soon followed, particularly as food price spikes fed a wave of neo-Malthusian warnings of rising populations causing looming food shortages. Speculators presented land as an appreciable asset with returns, the appreciation coming from scarcity, the returns from what you could grow on that land.

Mark Twain famously quipped, "Buy land, they're not making it any more."[3] That sounded especially prescient to land- and water-poor countries with capital, such as China and some Arab states, which feared a future of declining domestic food production, rising food prices, and restive populations. It was not lost on government leaders that food price increases had been among the main triggers of the Arab Spring and other protest movements. Why not buy or rent land overseas to grow food for your people back home?

By the time I got to Mozambique in 2014, there had been 956 concluded transnational land deals globally, with another 46 under negotiation, according to the Land Matrix Project, which was trying to track the surge. A far larger number showed intended land acquisitions, in which some intention on the part of the investor or the government had been made public. But just the completed agreements covered 150 *million* acres—an area about the size of France—and more than half of that land was under formal contract.[4]

Though China was loudly criticized after a series of highly publicized planned acquisitions, most never materialized. The emerging profile of grabbed land looked markedly different from the simplistic image that dominated the headlines. In fact, the top land-grabber—by far—was the United States, with 6 million acres under contract, more than twice the level of the second-largest investor country, Malaysia. China was eleventh on the list. The investors were not mostly sovereign wealth funds from land-poor countries but investors from rich countries. OECD countries accounted for more than half of the deals. And food crops represented only about one-quarter of all acquired land. Biofuel crops or "flex crops" such as sugar—for either sweetener or ethanol—accounted for nearly as much land, as did forest concessions. In Africa, only 39 percent of agricultural projects were for food. Finally, Land Matrix found that the land was hardly unoccupied. For projects on which there was data on former use, the majority was converted from cropland and much of that was being cultivated by small-scale farmers before the takeover.[5]

Africa, with the world's largest supply of underutilized arable land, topped Land Matrix's list of the regions targeted by investors. That was no surprise. Governments were desperate for investment and yearned for quick fixes to low agricultural productivity, and big money was knocking on their doors ready to invest. What could go wrong?

In 2008, the government of Madagascar found out. It had quietly signed a deal to cede half its arable land—more than 3 million acres—rent-free on a ninety-nine-year lease to South Korean multinational Daewoo for the production of palm oil and corn to ship back home.[6] When the *Financial Times* reported the story, protests erupted in the streets, the government fell, and the land deal was rescinded.[7]

Most land grabs were neither as grandiose nor as well publicized. Many went forward, particularly in authoritarian states where land was relatively plentiful and government dominion over it could be enforced. In Africa, the Democratic Republic of the Congo and South Sudan led the giveaways, with Ethiopia also showing a frighteningly impressive ability to clear land through forced removals and deliver it to foreign investors.

In Mozambique, investors found a willing government and a lot of underutilized land, but also a rural population ready to defend its interests. As investors came shopping, the first way farmers learned of the deals was often when the fences went up across land they had been cultivating for years. There was rarely notification, let alone the kind of consultation expected of such projects. The rural population, not far removed from a liberation struggle whose main rallying cry was "Free the Man, Free the Land," and wary of encroachments after a brutal sixteen-year civil war, fought back. Some 300 local land conflicts had been registered by 2011, some turning violent.[8]

In 2009, the government instated a moratorium on land deals larger than 25,000 acres, partly to allow its own laws and regulations to catch up with the fast-moving realities on the ground.[9] By 2011, with some guidelines in place and with a new mapping and zoning of potentially available land, the moratorium was lifted and the land rush began anew.[10]

The New Face of South-South Investment?

I was interested in ProSAVANA because out of all the large-scale projects I'd studied this one sounded almost feasible. It wasn't some fly-by-night venture capitalist looking to grow a biofuel crop he'd never produced commercially for a market that barely existed. That's what I saw in Tanzania, and such failed land grabs litter the African landscape.[11]

ProSAVANA had a few things going for it. Its architects knew the investors it wanted to attract: Brazil's agribusiness giants. The planners also knew their crop—soybeans—and they knew their technology—soybean varieties Brazilian researchers had adapted to the harsh tropical conditions of Brazil's *cerrado*. They also knew their market: Japan's and China's hog farms with their insatiable appetite for feed, generally made with soybeans. Demand for soybeans within Mozambique was also growing to feed a slowly emerging domestic poultry industry.[12] Maybe Brazil would do things differently, bringing the kind of strong developmental focus that had characterized the country's ascendance under the leadership of the left-leaning Workers' Party.

As it turned out, the project's most basic premise was just wrong. The promoters assumed that the soil and climate in the Nacala Corridor of Mozambique were similar to those found in the *cerrado*, so technology could be easily adapted to tame a region inhospitable to agriculture. After all, PowerPoints proclaimed, they were at the same latitude and had roughly the same geography.

Someone should have gone to the Nacala Corridor before they issued the press releases. It turns out that the two regions differ dramatically. The *cerrado* had poor soils, which technology was able to address. That's also why it had few farmers, and those who were there could be moved by Brazil's then-military dictatorship. The Nacala Corridor, by contrast, has good soils, which is precisely why it is the most densely populated part of rural Mozambique.[13] (If there are good lands, you can pretty well bet civilization has discovered them and is farming them.)

Still, when I set out for the Nacala Corridor in late 2014 in search of ProSAVANA, project promoters were sounding every bit as ambitious as when they first started. At the time, Mozambique ranked fifth among all target countries in the amount of land given away and under contract (behind Papua New Guinea, Indonesia, South Sudan, and the Democratic Republic of the Congo).[14] Land Matrix identified ninety-nine concluded projects covering 5.5 million acres. But three-quarters of that was for forestry projects. Of the agriculture projects, one could find just a few comparatively small soybean projects in the Nacala Corridor, ProSAVANA's target region. One had to move to the large category of "intended but not concluded" projects to find a 1.7-million-acre project that listed Brazilians as the investors and the Brazilian, Japanese, and Mozambican governments as partners.[15] ProSAVANA? What happened to the 25 million acres? I set off to find out.

Into the Nacala Corridor

We set off early from the state capital of Nampula, in the heart of the Nacala Corridor that runs from Tete east across Malawi 560 miles to the port city of Nacala. My Brazilian colleague and reluctant interpreter, Mariana Santarelli, had been there not too long before to research her dissertation on ProSAVANA. We headed to Monapo, about two hours' drive, where we had heard from the Nampula district peasant union about current land conflicts.

Justina Wisiarro, union vice president, said farmers from outside the region were coming in and cutting deals with traditional leaders for land. "They talk to the chief, there is no consultation with his people."

Costa Estevão, the muscular, energetic president of the union, nodded. "The Land Law here is not respected. It is a good law, but it is not followed." He said the union was helping farmers get the formal land titles known as DUATs. "Of course it is important, it gives more security, but even then it is not certain. But even without a DUAT, the government should respect the occupancy rights in the law."

ProSAVANA certainly had farm leaders on edge, desperate to identify any signs of land-grabbing so they could educate peasant farmers about their rights under the Land Law and help them organize to defend their farms.

The mistrust was easy to understand. Controversy had dogged the project since its "Master Plan" had been unceremoniously leaked the year before.[16] No one had been notified about the project nor consulted on it, yet the Master Plan declared ProSAVANA *the* agricultural development plan for the Nacala Corridor, driven by massive land concessions to foreign investors. The ProSAVANA directorate, with representatives from Brazil, Japan, and Mozambique, quickly disavowed the document as just an early draft, unapproved by the government. But the damage was done. It soon came out that Agriculture Minister José Pacheco had been courting the most powerful Brazilian soybean producers as early as 2009,[17] with the support of the Brazilian Getulio Vargas Foundation, which largely drafted the Master Plan, and notably included a large investment fund to provide incentives to Brazilian soybean magnates.[18]

The campaign to stop the project formed quickly, spearheaded by UNAC, Mozambique's national farmers' union, which took farmers to Brazil for a tour of the *cerrado*. They produced a crudely made short video of the tour. The images of unending expanses of soybeans, without a small farmer in sight, spread quickly through Mozambique, as did tales of environmental destruction in the *cerrado*.[19]

Within months of the release of the Master Plan, a tri-national campaign in Japan, Brazil, and Mozambique formed. An open letter to presidents of the three countries caused a stir, particularly in Japan, where the country's international development agency was accused of violating long-standing principles calling for a separation of development assistance from commercial interests.[20] Japan's Mitsui multinational had large energy and infrastructure investments in the corridor. A few months before I'd arrived, the tri-national campaign adopted a militant "No to ProSAVANA" stance vowing no further engagement with the program until farmers and local communities were consulted on development plans for the region.[21] The declaration divided civil society and farmer groups. Some groups in the corridor were desperate for agricultural investment.

It was easy to see why. The landscape along the road to Monapo was dry and unplanted, mostly untended, a stark contrast with Malawi, where every inch seemed planted in maize. But the early rains hadn't come to Mozambique and the crops weren't in the ground yet, so it looked more barren no doubt than it really was. Mozambique does indeed have underutilized land, which is what has allowed rural communities to live from so-called shifting cultivation. Soil fertility is maintained by allowing land to lie fallow after it's been harvested, which farmers can afford to do because they have access to additional land. Of course, government land surveyors often identified fallow land as unused and unoccupied, making it subject to grabbing.

I was surprised at the low level of technological development in the countryside, at least around Monapo. Farmers cultivated only with hoes. There was little sign of powered hand cultivators or tractors of any size. Estimates are that only 12 percent of farmers even use plow animals.[22] This leaves the labor productivity on Mozambique's farms well behind Africa's average. Some estimate that with such limited tools a family can barely manage to farm one hectare of land, hardly more than a subsistence. More striking still, compared to Malawi the government seemed to have very few programs to support small-scale farmers. No input subsidy programs, though I was told there were occasional seed and fertilizer distributions, but only sporadically. According to the World Bank, only 5 percent of the country's small and medium-size farms use pesticides or fertilizers, 3 percent have access to credit, and just 10 percent use any irrigation.[23]

I'd been in some very poor rural areas in the world, but this may have been the poorest, at least in terms of agricultural development. It showed in the national statistics. Cereal yields are among the lowest in Africa, with maize yields a fraction of those in Malawi and showing little improvement over the last decade. Rural poverty is estimated at over 50 percent.[24]

The Monapo District Peasants' Union hosted us and gave us a briefing on the land conflicts that have come up just in the last year or so, since the leak of the Master Plan. Alberto Locote, the charismatic union president, told us proudly that the union claimed 6,582 farmer-members, who were farming 59,814 acres. Two comrades joined him to describe three recent land conflicts, in Nacololo, Kanakwe, and Itoculo. They were instructive both for their relatively small scale, compared with ProSAVANA's ambitions, and their blatant disregard for local farmers.

Miranda Armando, from Nacololo, told us his community's story. A South African farmer came in the previous year with little warning and started putting up fences right through land farmers were cultivating. He wanted to farm soybeans on a large scale, just as ProSAVANA promises. Like much of the land that is producing conflict, this had belonged to a Portuguese plantation owner until independence. The owners abandoned the farm in 1977, and peasants from the region moved in and began farming. The Mozambican Land Law, revised in 1997, recognizes occupancy rights in such cases, even if a farmer does not have a DUAT.[25] Foreign farmers and companies are not so quick to respect occupancy rights, and neither are many local Mozambican authorities, I came to find out.

The peasant union sought help from the local authorities, but they got little response. They didn't wait for government action: 150 peasant farmers tore down the fences and reoccupied their farms. The South African farmer continues to farm other land in the region, but the peasants have maintained control of their land. Some had DUATs, which perhaps gave them a little more security. Miranda showed us his, beaming. It gives him rights to 50 acres of land, four of which had been part of the South African farmer's land grab.

We set off with Locote down a long dusty road to Kanakwe to investigate a more recent and still unresolved report of land-grabbing. We met with seven farmers who told us in their native Macua language that businessmen had come to the leaders in nearby Patakwe saying "they were from Brazil and Japan" but giving no names. And now they claimed they controlled some land. I was surprised when Locote took us with a community representative to speak to Zeferino, the leader from Patakwe who had given permission for this mysterious land grab. Zeferino walked slowly from his modest home, clearly not pleased to receive unannounced visitors. Zeferino, an appointee from the ruling Frelimo Party, had power. Known locally as a *lider comunitario* (literally "community leader"), he is something like a local party boss with formal authority.

Locote made his case on a makeshift bench in Zeferino's dusty yard. He made some respectful and deferential references to Zeferino, pulling out his Frelimo membership card to show his loyalty to the ruling party. He was firm on the land takeover.

"Farmers are now to be respected," Locote said passionately. "They can't just be ignored and displaced!"

Zeferino nodded, tired, but he would have none of it, even though he admitted that he had personally been hired by the invader to clear some of the land. Locote was persistent. What is his name? "I don't know, you will have to ask the district council."

What nationality is he? "I don't know, they have all the information in the district office."

How much land has been given to him? "I don't know, you will have to ask the land registrar in town."

We left with no answers, but Locote promised he would be back the next day because another "delegation" was coming and they wanted answers. (That was when Mariana and I realized we were Locote's "international delegation," to give him extra weight in such negotiations.)[26]

Was this ProSAVANA at its nefarious worst, with foreigners grabbing land through deals with local leaders, with no public consultation, and with such a dismissive lack of transparency? Or was this just routine power politics in the Mozambican countryside? After all, despite all the public controversy since the megaproject was announced—or perhaps because of it—precious little foreign investment had come to the Nacala Corridor. According to one recent account, as of early summer 2014 there was only one investment up and running, and only three others in the planning stages.[27]

"It's ProSAVANA," Locote said when I asked him. "They don't always use the name ProSAVANA, but we know it is." He said these conflicts were new, coming after a long period of relative calm, a period in which a number of other large farms had been operating in the region without conflict.

ProSAVANA Speaks

Americo Uaciquete, at the Nampula ProSAVANA office, struck anything but a conciliatory tone. A plant biologist by training, Uaciquete was the formal "focal person" for the project in the province. Uaciquete knew how to act like a focal person. So much so that he had become something of a lightning rod in the storms engulfing ProSAVANA. He denounced civil society groups on television as being against development, and he had a run-in with peasant organizations that caused them to end their meeting and call for his resignation. Focal indeed.

Uaciquete is an opinionated man, and we heard a lot of his opinions. He "clarified" for us the problems with civil society organizations and their rejectionist stance on ProSAVANA. Those crazy civil society groups overreacted, he told us, inflamed by their international comrades campaigning against "land grabs." ProSAVANA has always been about small and medium-size farmers. "Development will be very slow if we follow the path civil society is advocating," he warned.

I asked if any investment was coming in. He admitted there was very little. He said the Brazilians came wanting 40,000 hectares each (100,000 acres). "That won't happen here," he told us. "The investors who come can get 2,000 hectares [5,000 acres] and work with out-growers in the community."

I was surprised. This was tantamount to surrender in Pro-SAVANA's grand plan. "Surely the Mozambican government can find a way to bring in the large farms," I said.

"Only if they have a gun," he said. "We are not going to impose the Brazilian model here. Only those who accept the new reality will succeed in the new world," he replied. "When it comes to Mozambique, the Mozambicans will decide." His nationalism was infectious even if his bluster was off-putting.

Later, in Maputo, I got the straight party line from the Pro-SAVANA directorate, the formal tri-national body that coordinates the program. As is ProSAVANA's protocol, I submitted my questions in advance, and they arranged a meeting so that each of the country representatives would be present. Jusimere Mourao, a Brazilian working for JICA, Japan's cooperation group, seemed to act as spokesperson. She gave a long apologia for the "misunderstandings" about ProSAVANA's intentions, then described the new, peasant-friendly ProSAVANA. After taking civil society concerns into account, she reported, the Master Plan was under revision. It would now focus on small-scale farmers and getting them better inputs to improve their productivity. It would emphasize respect for land rights of the communities.

"Agricultural development cannot go just through the private sector," explained Mourao, "or the benefits will remain just with the private sector. Small and medium producers are the main beneficiaries of ProSAVANA. We have no intention of promoting the taking of their land. It would be a crime."

I asked if they were at all worried that foreign investor interest had waned. The representative of the Mozambican government ticked off some companies that had come in—Matanusco, Frango King, one of the main poultry operations. "And a South African soybean farmer in Monapo who has begun farming."

This was the land-grab-in-waiting that we had been told about in Monapo the week before, in Nacololo. I explained that this had caused conflict. He wasn't aware. I explained the story, and they all seemed surprised that it ended with the community tearing down the fences and running the farmer off the stolen land. The government official defended the concession, saying the land was former state farm land, so the government had the right to give the concession to the South African farmer. I asked if it wasn't true that farmers who farm land for ten years, under the Land Law, have use rights to that land. He said no, the state can do what it wants with those farms.

That certainly explained why the three conflicts we heard about in Monapo all had to do with former state-run farms. I confirmed later with André Calengo, a Land Law expert, that the official was just plain wrong about the law. I asked him if it surprised him that someone that high up in the agriculture ministry and in ProSAVANA would be so misinformed. He sighed. He provides training in the Land Law to members of the judiciary and other government officials. "Probably only 30 percent of public officials understand the Land Law."

That needed some follow-up. But it was clear that ProSAVANA was actively and skillfully burnishing its image. Land grab? What land grab? This is a small-scale development project.

This was no accident. It would later come out that JICA, Japan's aid group, in 2013 had led a secret effort to develop a "social communication strategy" for ProSAVANA to weaken civil society opposition to the program. I was getting a dose of that communications strategy. No one knew it at the time, but civil society organizations were getting far more than that. They were being "mapped" by a consultant into "hard-liners," softer opponents who had left the "No to ProSAVANA" campaign, and those who might be persuaded to work with the government. In a classic divide-and-conquer operation, individual organizations were approached about what it would take to get them to work with ProSAVANA, to split from the hard-liners. The strategy was to neutralize the influential Maputo-based NGOs, such as Oxfam and ActionAid (who had declined to sign on to the "No" position), isolate the hard-liners (Justiça Ambiental, Livaningo, ADECRU, and Nampula Peasants'

Union), heavily lobby UNAC (which had just lost its president to a freak illness), and woo local organizations in the Nacala Corridor to dialogue with the program and split from the national "No to ProSAVANA" campaign.[28]

Revelations of the secret campaign would later create further mistrust of ProSAVANA, particularly in Japan, where such meddling in the internal affairs of another country was not as readily accepted as it is in the United States. Parliament would freeze the budget for the program pending an independent assessment, leaving the program in a state of suspended confrontation.

A Land Grab by Any Other Name . . .

I introduced myself to Luís Sitoe, economic adviser to Mozambique's minister of agriculture, and explained that I'd spent the last two weeks in his country researching the ProSAVANA project. I was curious if I would hear the same talking points from this highly placed adviser to the project's most ardent promoter, Agriculture Minister José Pacheco.[29]

Mr. Sitoe smirked. "Did you see ProSAVANA?" I told him I really hadn't. "So far there is no investment in ProSAVANA," he said, with surprising satisfaction. He told me he wouldn't be surprised if the project was completely abandoned by the end of the year. I was shocked; he was talking from a different playbook.

Foolishly, I grew hopeful. I asked Sitoe if the lesson of ProSAVANA was that agricultural development needed to be based on Mozambique's 3 million small-scale food producers. He smirked again. No, he assured me, the government is fully committed to foreign investment, with its capital and technology, as the path to agricultural development. He went into his office and came back with a two-inch-thick project proposal for a 600,000-acre foreign-funded scheme for irrigated agriculture along the Lurio River, on the northern edge of the Nacala Corridor. Was this part of ProSAVANA? No, he reassured me with another smile.

The Lurio River project is enormous, as large as any ProSAVANA initiative. With a budget of $4.2 billion, it includes two dam projects and a series of agricultural development schemes covering more than 240,000 hectares (some 600,000 acres). Irrigation infrastructure is to be built to support a mix of large, medium, and smaller farms producing a wide variety of agricultural commodities—cotton, corn, sugar, ethanol, livestock.[30]

According to an analysis by the Mozambican research group ADECRU and the international group GRAIN, the proposed project area would affect some 500,000 people across nine districts in three northern provinces. They estimated that 100,000 people would be displaced by the Lurio River project, as it crosses some of the most densely populated regions of rural Mozambique.[31] Had farmers and communities in the region been consulted? Sitoe said they had.

"Absolutely not," said Vicente Adriano, of UNAC, over dinner that night. The project remained shrouded in secrecy, even as the Council of Ministers considered approving it in May 2015. ADECRU researchers asked the government for a copy of the project proposal, in accordance with Mozambique's information laws, but they never got a reply. They visited eight of the affected districts. Residents and community leaders reported that not only had they not been consulted about the project, they had never heard of it.[32]

Was history repeating itself? Wasn't one of the fatal flaws of ProSAVANA the project's secrecy and belated consultations with affected communities? Mozambique's progressive land laws call for public access to information and prior consultation with the populations most impacted by the project. Some investors have followed those laws, and many have found communities willing to work with them. Many have not. With the Lurio River project, ADECRU's investigations could not even identify the investors involved, though they identified a consortium created to manage the project, the Companhia do Vale do Rio Lurio (CVRL).

Free, prior, and informed consent is a fundamental principle in international human rights. Affected parties must be informed prior to the initiation of a project, and they must give their consent in a process free of coercion or intimidation. The principle is en-shrined in nearly all the guidelines and standards developed in recent years, such as the Committee on World Food Security's "Guidelines on Responsible Agricultural Investment" and the "Nai-robi Action Plan on Large-Scale Land-Based Investments."[33]

What makes a large-scale agricultural development project a land grab is the lack of consent. On the Lurio River project, the Mozam-bican government had chosen not to provide information in advance of approving a large-scale project, and it had failed to consult or in-form the affected communities, never mind get their consent. An AfriCane consultant told me such consultations were ongoing, but no evidence of that has been reported along the Lurio River.

Meanwhile, belated consultations on ProSAVANA, held the month before with some of the Nampula-based groups JICA had split off from the No Campaign, were denounced as manipulated, unrepresentative, and in violation of the country's information laws. ADECRU and the Nampula Episcopal Commission on Justice and Peace monitored twenty-four of thirty-eight sched-uled consultations and found community members excluded and intimidated, meetings stacked with government officials, and information on the new Master Plan not readily available. The consultations did not involve the many affected communities en-visaged in the project plan. The advocacy groups denounced the process as a sham.[34]

Large-scale foreign land projects will be controversial even when they are introduced in accordance with the law. When the princi-ple of free, prior, and informed consent is ignored, they are bound to generate serious conflict. Revelations about the Lurio River Val-ley Project caused enough of a stir that the Council of Ministers didn't take it up. It joined ProSAVANA in hibernation.

Seeds of Climate Resilience

Nearly two years later, in 2016, I was back in Mozambique, still looking for ProSAVANA. I didn't find much. Government officials wouldn't talk about it. Japanese development cooperation representatives spoke only of pathetically small extension services to a few small-scale farmers. Private investors were scarce. Civil society groups debated whether it was worth cooperating in the wholesale redesign of the program. I wondered why anyone would bother. Like many of the grand schemes hatched in the wake of the food crisis, this one was a bust, by any measure. Still, ProSAVANA remained the Mozambican government's agricultural development strategy for the region. While farmers defended their hard-won land rights, it seemed they would have to look elsewhere for agricultural development.

I decided to look elsewhere as well. I didn't have to go far. I arrived in Marracuene, forty-five minutes outside Maputo, just after the rainy-season harvest in April, and just as the irrigation-fed winter season was beginning. I'd been brought there by ActionAid to see what cooperatives of small-scale women farmers there were doing to grow more food, not with foreign investment, green-revolution seeds and fertilizers, or even much government support. They were doing it with agro-ecology.[35]

Marracuene didn't get much rain that year or much of a harvest due to the drought that had parched most of Southern Africa. One farmer in the village of Bobole told me he'd earned barely one-quarter what he had the previous year from farm sales, and almost none of that was from maize, the Mozambique staple. Across the region production was down, prices were up, and hunger was widespread. In Mozambique, 1.5 million people were facing food insecurity, according to UNICEF, with 192,000 children expected to be severely malnourished in the next twelve months.[36]

In Marracuene, the maize harvest was almost a total bust. Fortunately, the farmers there grow a wide variety of crops, for home consumption and for sale. And they have irrigation, rehabilitated from an old colonial plantation, so they have a second season. I saw healthy crops in the fields—cabbage, carrots, onions, potatoes, sweet potatoes, and cassava. And I saw young maize plants on what turned out to be the association's collective plots, the small portion of the community's 250 acres that this 280-member association agrees to set aside and farm collectively. They work it together every Thursday morning. I watched as women, and a few men, prepared fields, watered new plants, and sprayed for pests.

Women tended most of these farms and ran the association as well. And the maize they were growing was for seed, because the summer harvest was so bad that many farmers had no seeds for the next season. They save, exchange, and recycle seeds, because they don't grow commercial hybrid maize, which they would have to buy every year. They rely on their own preferred native yellow maize. And they keep their community seed bank just for times like these.

In the district farmers' union office, Mohammed Obulialia Cheng'wi, the Kenyan volunteer who is the local agro-ecology promoter, showed me small jars of seeds, explaining that this was now all that was left of their seed bank after the drought. The rest was planted on those collective plots. Mohammed was confident they would grow enough maize seed to get farmers back on their feet.

This was one self-reliant, climate-resilient bunch of farmers. Many bunches, actually, with 7,000 members in nineteen active Marracuene-area associations, all affiliated with UNAC, the national farmers' union. Their drought preparedness was no accident. ActionAid had been working with the alliance of Marracuene farmers' unions, through UNAC, to promote agro-ecology, sustainable agriculture, and climate-resilient farm management.

I was most struck by the community's commitment to its native yellow maize, which reminded me of Malawian farmers' affinity for their orange maize. It predated ActionAid's promotion of alternative cropping strategies. Farmers in Marracuene had simply decided that hybrid white maize offered them no significant advantages over their local saved variety, which produces small cobs but is dependable (if not that particular year) even under conditions of sporadic rains and limited fertilizer applications.

They were apparently so committed to rescuing this local variety that they followed the lead of a volunteer from Brazil, who showed them how to better select seed for purity and performance. As with many so-called local varieties, the quality had eroded over time due to uncontrolled cross-pollination with other maize varieties, including hybrids provided by international donors or the government. By selecting the best cobs and the purest kernels from those cobs, growing them out in the fields, then repeating the process, farmers restored the purity and performance of a preferred food crop. One they did not have to purchase every year.

It is the kind of participatory plant breeding that is rarely considered when governments and international donors—and the neo-Malthusians predicting the end of food supplies—call for urgent investment in improved seeds. They generally mean one thing when they talk about improved seeds: hybrid or genetically modified maize sold by national and multinational seed companies. It is part of the new green revolution for Africa that, like the old one for Asia and Latin America, depends on purchased seed every year, from companies such as Monsanto, and heavy applications of inorganic fertilizer, supplied by multinational firms such as Yara.[37]

As I'd seen in Malawi, on their own these do nothing to improve the fertility of soils. Think of a trout pond stocked every year by the authorities so fishermen can catch fish.

Give a person a fish, goes the adage, and he eats for a day. Teach him to fish . . . Well, teach him to fish from a stocked pond, and he won't eat for a lifetime, he'll eat for as long as someone can afford to keep stocking the pond. Teach him to create and maintain a healthy pond that sustains life—*then* he will eat for a lifetime. The soils are farmers' ponds, and Marracuene's were being fed by crop diversity.

Intercropping is great for soils, building organic matter, adding needed nitrogen for maize and other crops, and reducing input costs. But it also diversifies risk, including nutritional risk in a drought. Mohammed told me that very little maize came out of the fields in that year's extreme conditions, despite their drought-tolerant, homegrown variety. But drought-resistant crops like cowpeas, cassava, sweet potato, and okra survived, providing needed food. Judite

Manhiça, the tall, strong woman who leads the association, said she didn't expect a food crisis in her community after the drought. She farms just an acre of land, but she says it sustains her family.

Agro-ecology was by no means the norm yet in Marracuene; Mohammed estimated that maybe 40 percent of farmers were now employing the practices, or some of them. But he showed the patience of a true agricultural extension agent. He said farmers saw their neighbors do well with the new methods and they slowly were coming around. I asked if the government was supporting their efforts in any way. Mohammed was charitable, pointing out free bags of organic fertilizer the provincial agriculture department gave them. But he couldn't name another serious government contribution to sustainable agriculture. Neither could anyone else I spoke with.

I've seen little evidence, in fact, of any serious agricultural policies aimed at the 3 million small-scale maize farmers across Mozambique who eke out a living, with eroded local seeds, rudimentary tools, no credit, no irrigation, and no extension agents like Mohammed showing them how to put life back in their soils and food on their tables. Instead, their government promotes large-scale foreign investment that threatens their lands and their livelihoods.

And the international community, led by the Bill and Melinda Gates Foundation, pressures African governments to adopt restrictive seed laws that threaten farmers' rights to save and exchange seed, as they do in Marracuene, while promoting the patented varieties being sold by Monsanto and other seed companies.[38] In fact, the day I was in Marracuene, African leaders were gathered in Harare, Zimbabwe, to advance the so-called Arusha Protocol on "Plant Variety Protection." That is the catchphrase for measures to guarantee the intellectual property rights of commercial plant breeders.

The Alliance for Food Sovereignty in Africa (AFSA) denounced the effort in a statement. "AFSA is committed to ensuring that farmers, as breeders themselves as well as users, remain at the centre of localised seed production systems and continue to exercise their rights freely to save, use, exchange, replant, improve, distribute and sell all the seed in their seed systems," said coordinator Dr. Million Belay.[39]

Thus far, the government of Mozambique has dutifully reformed its seed laws to conform, even opening the door to the introduction of genetically modified maize.[40] Such measures create obstacles to the kinds of real solutions—to hunger, poverty, and climate change—farmers in Marracuene were creating for themselves.

Surviving an Angry Climate

Those homegrown solutions seemed all the more urgent when I returned to Marracuene in early 2017. The drought of the previous two years had broken the previous October, but with a vengeance born of climate change. While much of the country received normal rains, Marracuene and the southern part of Mozambique got intense storms. The first, with thunder, lightning, and hail, hit just as farmers were bringing in the last of their irrigated winter crops and beginning to plant maize and other rainy-season crops for the coming summer season. The second hit in late March, taking down trees, maize, and other ripening crops in the community of Bobole, again flooding one of the area's more productive associations in the lowlands along the river.[41] The irrigation system wasn't well maintained, and blockages caused the floodwaters to overflow the banks of the ditches into farmers' fields. Even their nicely cultivated raised beds, constructed to keep waters from directly covering crops, succumbed to the rush of water.

"There has been a big change," Mohammed told me, "in rainfall patterns and in temperatures." From the relative comfort of the temperate United States, it is difficult to appreciate just how punishing climate change is for small-scale farmers in developing countries. It is not just a future risk, it is a present calamity.

Mohammed detailed the recent history in his time there, pointing out the dizzying range of impacts climate change was having on vulnerable farmers. When he arrived in 2010, he said the rainy season was what people were used to, with rains arriving in late

September or October and lasting into the Mozambican summer, when temperatures rose into the low 90s. Crops could tolerate that with enough moisture. The first change he noticed was in 2012. The area got an unusually heavy first rain in early September, well before the rains usually came. That cost farmers some of the irrigated winter crop, which was still in the ground.

In 2014, the rains didn't come in September or October, so crops went in late, and temperatures in the summer rose dramatically, reaching 100 degrees. Maize plants baked in the dry heat, reducing harvests. The winter season, which relies on irrigation, was affected as well, and in ways I wouldn't have imagined. The Incomati River, the source of their irrigation, fell so low in the drought that the Indian Ocean downriver, with sea levels rising from climate change, flowed four miles up the dried riverbed. Salt water flooded the irrigation canals, poisoning the rich land.

The next year was even worse because of the well-documented El Niño weather pattern that parched much of Southern Africa.[42] Mohammed said there were no rains at all in much of the area and temperatures reached 106 degrees, unheard of in the region. Drought-tolerant crops like sweet potatoes, cassava, peanuts, and cowpeas fed farm families when maize harvests failed. They regrew their yellow maize seeds successfully that winter season, under irrigation, resupplying farmers with seeds for the rainy season. Along came the floods, first in October 2016, then again in late March. To add insult to injury, Mohammed said they saw record temperatures in January and February, searing heat over 110 degrees.

"Crops actually burned," Mohammed said, shaking his head. "The leaves of maize plants were brown and dry, and farmers had to plant their maize all over again."

Drought and flooding are the evil twins of climate change for farmers in much of the global south. Across Southern Africa, farmers have seen rainy seasons shorten, rains fail, and extreme weather bring catastrophic flooding. Add record-breaking heat to that destructive mix, and it is a wonder farmers still till their fields. In large part, these farmers survive because of the resilience born of agro-ecology, a conscious strategy of their national farm association, and supportive NGOs like ActionAid, to help farmers adapt to the changing climate.

In the fields of the farmers' association called Popular, we found a strapping middle-aged woman working with her son and a hired hand to hoe her raised beds into shape for winter planting. Florentina Samuel took time out to talk with us, wiping sweat from her brow. Her farm hadn't been wiped out by the floods, though they had destroyed her cassava crop. She didn't seem daunted by the waves of bad weather, and she attributed some of her optimism to the agro-ecological farming she has adopted. "The soil is better now, softer, and good for different crops." She reached into her newly turned soil and showed us the organic matter from last year's crop residues. "We are still suffering, but if this next crop is good we will be okay."

Adaptation Funds Lacking in New Climate Finance

Farmers could certainly use more international support. In the last decade, rich countries have begun contributing to global climate funds to help developing countries mitigate climate change by reducing emissions and adapt to climate changes as they occur. Up to that point, though, farmers like those in Marracuene have been short-changed as the tens of billions of dollars in climate financing are disbursed. Emerging economies such as China, India, Brazil, Indonesia, and South Africa have captured the majority of the funds, for efforts to reduce emissions.[43] Meanwhile, only a small share has made it to the most vulnerable and poorest developing countries to help them adapt their farms for the changing climate. How small a share? According to a recent report from the International Institute for Environment and Development, just 10 percent of climate funds had reached the most vulnerable people in developing countries.[44]

Such assistance can't come soon enough. In response to the latest crisis in Mozambique, UNAC is responding with a national campaign to build emergency stockpiles of native seed varieties for key food crops.[45] Marracuene's maize seed bank saved many area farmers last year after the drought.

"The Marracuene farmers showed us this could work," said Bartolomeu Antonio, UNAC's director of rural development. "We saw how effectively peasants could rescue and improve native seeds."

UNAC and its farmers have mapped and identified key native seeds. They selected cassava, sweet potato, maize, and onion varieties from Zambezia Province, for example, and now plan to collect and grow out seeds, in collaboration with government agricultural experts, to create their own national seed bank. The vast majority of Mozambican farmers depend on seeds saved from crop to crop or exchanged with neighbors. When climate change calls, farmers can lose their seeds as they lose their crops, and they scarcely have resources to purchase replacements.

"We have to protect farmers from losing their seeds," warned Bartolomeu. "Our seed bank can prevent climate change from becoming a climate disaster."

"Go to Xai-Xai—You'll Find a Real Land Grab"

When I was back in Mozambique in 2017, still researching ProSAVANA, a Mozambican colleague who studies large-scale agricultural projects encouraged me to stop looking for ProSAVANA, stop grasping for the ephemera of promised investments. "Go to Xai-Xai," he advised. "You'll find a real land grab."

Indeed, I did.

The rice fields of Xai-Xai, three hours up the coast from Maputo, are vast, coming into view as we descended onto the alluvial plain from the villages that dotted the hills above. They stretched across the plains toward the Indian Ocean as far as the naked eye could see, in the flat green monochrome of a rice plantation. This was indeed a large-scale agricultural project, unlike ProSAVANA, which seemed to grow only rumors, threats, government proclamations, and community resistance.

On May 20, 2014, 400 community members marched to protest
the Wanbao rice project in Xai-Xai, Mozambique. *Justiça
Ambiental Mozambique*

Like ProSAVANA, this project had its share of those, too. A Chinese company had gotten a 50,000-acre concession to grow rice on
this colonial-era farm, and the Chinese had been accused of
land-grabbing, of taking community members' land without autho-
rization and without warning.[46] The company had developed 17,000
acres of its own rice fields, rehabilitating the colonial-era irrigation
system.[47] And it had trained about seventy local farmers to grow
rice on contract on a portion of the company land. Heavily

promoted by Mozambique's president at the time, Armando Gue-
buza, the rice was on the market under his recommended brand
name, Bom Gusto—Good Taste.

I found a sprawling rice plantation and plenty of community
resentment—from contract farmers, from women who had lost
their land. But land-grab accusations aside, the Wanbao Africa
Agriculture Development Limited (WAADL) promised what
large-scale foreign investment in agriculture might offer to a poor,
hungry, underdeveloped country like Mozambique.[48] Here was
desperately needed capital investing in largely unused fertile land,
rebuilding productive infrastructure and bringing in modern agricultural practices.[49] Wanbao was training local farmers in its modern farming methods and setting them up as contract farmers with
a stake in the project. What's more, the project wasn't growing cash
crops, it was growing food. And it wasn't growing food for its population back in China, as the land-grab stereotype suggested, it was
growing rice for the domestic market.[50]

What's not to like about a project like that?

What's Not to Like

Well, at the beginning there was a lot not to like if you were a
farmer using the lands allocated to the Wanbao project. Some
7,000 farmers had moved onto the irrigated lands along the Lower
Limpopo River in the 1980s after the state farm ceased operations.
The irrigation infrastructure had been installed in the 1950s by
Portuguese colonial rulers, producing rice and other cash crops.[51]
With independence in 1975, many colonial farmers fled, some
destroying infrastructure on their way out. The new government,
following the nationalist development policy prescriptions of the
times, tried to turn the Xai-Xai irrigation scheme into a state-run
operation. Most such initiatives, in Mozambique and many other
countries, have failed, as Joseph Hanlon and Teresa Smart argue
in their book, *Chickens and Beer*. They point not simply to the
inefficiencies of state-run farms but to difficulties inherent in

plantation agriculture in Mozambique, from the colonial era to to-day's foreign-investor-driven farms.[52]

It was no surprise that farmers moved onto the irrigated lands once the state abandoned the centralized farm. In fact, farmers there told us they were encouraged to do so by the local government, which even built a small bridge to facilitate community access. Many crossed that bridge and began farming rice, maize, and vegetables, or grazing their cattle, taking advantage of the poorly maintained but still functional irrigation ditches through which water from the Lim-popo River still flowed. Many had been farming the land for more than ten years, which should have given them rights to the land.

No such luck. The government gave a small amount of the land to a Chinese "friendship farm," initiated in 2007 on just 750 acres. When it failed to take hold, the Wanbao Grain and Oil company took over in 2011 with new Chinese financing and management, contracting the production to four Chinese farming groups.[53] The government then gave them a fifty-year lease on 50,000 acres in Xai-Xai, part of the Lower Limpopo Irrigation District (RBL for its Portuguese name), which had been founded in 2010 to manage the scheme.[54] Wanbao's plan was to invest $289 million in the project, with financing from the Chinese Development Bank under a fund for cooperation with Portuguese-speaking countries.[55] The initial goal was to increase rice productivity to meet domestic demand in Mozambique.

The companies wasted no time. The bulldozers were there by early 2012. Gizela Zunguze, gender coordinator from Justiça Ambi-ental (JA), the Friends of the Earth affiliate in Mozambique, took us to meet some of the farmers affected by the project. For five years, JA had been supporting community efforts to get their lands back. Remarkably, nearly all grabbed land had been returned, but it had taken a long time and the affected farmers were still waiting for compensation for lost crops and other damages.

In the dusty courtyard under the shade of a mango tree in the neighborhood of Brutela, Meldina Matsimbe told us she and other farmers had gone down to their lowland fields in January 2012 to find tractors opening roads and irrigation ditches across their fields, fully planted in maize, cowpeas, and vegetables. "They plowed right through ripe maize," Matsimbe told us in Changana, the local language. Two other women from the village nodded. There had been no consultation with the community, no warning, no environmental impact assessment, as required by Mozambican law. Just the sudden appearance of Chinese tractors clearing land for roads and irrigation ditches. Wanbao officials there said they had been given the land, that it was unoccupied.

With JA's support, the community protested to the company and the local government authorities. The bulldozers stopped, and the RBL irrigation district authorities acknowledged it was a mistake. Matsimbe, a widow raising children and grandchildren, said they returned most of the land, some 250 acres used by about sixty families in the community; she said 5 acres still had not been returned. Zunguze told us that neither the company nor the local authorities responded to demand letters for compensation. What did these women eat that year after their crops had been destroyed?

"We had nothing to eat," Matsimbe said. "We had to ask our neighbors for food."

Angelica Moyane, tall and strong, told us a similar story in the neighboring village of Kana Kana. One Sunday in July 2013, she recalled, a tractor came in unannounced and plowed under the community's fields. "Mama" Angelica grew lettuce, maize, onions, and cabbage in the lowlands, sharing irrigation with neighboring farmers. Mama Angelica said she'd had half her land in garlic, a productive cash crop. It was all wiped out, along with the ripe crops of some 500 other farmers who had food planted there.

Maria Gabriela, another Kana Kana farmer, shook her head. "They destroyed everything. The Chinese themselves were eating our crops as they destroyed them."

Gizela said she had found Mama Angelica and other farmers camped outside a government office in Xai-Xai demanding answers. The two of them went to the fields and took photos. They persuaded the local administrator to return with them the next day, and the conflict almost erupted in violence. When an RBL technician came

Angelica Moyane: "We could not even identify our own farms after the Chinese came through." *Justiça Ambiental Mozambique*

to the land ahead of the administrator, Mama Angelica and other farmers surrounded him, farm tools in hand. Someone took the keys from his car so he couldn't flee. Mama Angelica said he was scared. He told them he was sorry and he would get them their land back.

Wanbao withdrew its machines a few days later and farmers returned to their ravaged fields. As in Brutela, the company offered no compensation for the destroyed crops, so crucial to small-scale farmers who live from one harvest to the next. They had to restore the land themselves from the tractor damage.

"We lost crops. We had to buy seeds," said Mama Angelica ruefully. "I have not gone back to garlic."

The company eventually backed off after JA and a local NGO helped the communities submit a formal petition to get all land back and get compensation for their losses. They organized a march from the communities past the Wanbao offices and through the town on May 20, 2014, to present their petition. Zunguze said the protest was tense, with some 400 angry community members marching toward the provincial offices behind a "No to Wanbao" banner. Placards, most handwritten, demanded an end to land-grabbing. "We demand respect for our rights" read one woman's simple plea.

At one point the police stopped the march, telling organizers they didn't have a permit. Zunguze told us things could easily have gotten out of control. "If JA hadn't been there, there would have violence," she said. "Farmers were very angry." After a three-hour standoff, the marchers were allowed to proceed as long as they stayed off the major road through town. When they reached the government offices, Mama Angelica presented the petition to the governor's representative.

Zunguze said they never got a formal response to the petition, but the company land-grabbing slowed, at least in that area. Still, according to Rosa Maringue, a farmer and traditional healer in the village, the local government went after some land in Baixa Fome the next year, some of the same land Wanbao had taken and returned.

The community forced their latest invaders to withdraw, and they again were left to assess the damage. While it was encouraging to hear that community members had mobilized to assert their land rights and get back their farms, it was difficult to celebrate those victories. These women were worn out from the struggle. Sure, they had their land back, but that land lay in the lowlands, far from their homes. Wanbao had the best irrigated land. Worst of all, as each community resisted the land grab, Wanbao just moved on and grabbed land from another community.

I was told that Kana Kana means "don't be doubtful" in Changana, but it was hard not to have doubts about these valiant farmers' prospects with a government so blindly committed to giving away its best irrigated land to foreigners.

Failure to Yield

The other thing not to like about Wanbao was that it seemed to be failing. In April 2017, the only rice being produced was by contract farmers and some Indians who were subcontracting land from the company. What had happened to this model farm?

The Chinese came in with their technology, equipment, and know-how, but none of that worked quite as well in the lowlands of Xai-Xai as it had back home. One longtime rice farmer, who remembered the colonial era, told us their plows didn't work well in the local soil, and they were uninterested in learning from local farmers like him why that might be true. Their high-yield rice varieties produced decent yields, but the rice they sold in the domestic market wasn't as tasty to locals as other available varieties.

Wanbao's contract farming got mixed reviews. The company had formed the Association of Farmers and Irrigators for Agri-Livestock Development and Mechanisation in Xai-Xai (ARPONE) in 2007, to facilitate the training of local farmers.[56] The group was dominated by members of the local political elite eager to get a piece of the project. Wanbao trained sixty-eight local farmers and got the more successful of them producing on 7–10 acres each. But they ran the outgrower scheme as a commercial operation, charging for services like plowing. They provided credit but required a 50 percent up-front cash payment that was difficult for many farmers to afford.[57] Farmers were obligated to sell to the company. And they paid a fixed and low price for the farmers' rice, regardless of market prices. After the remainder of their loans were taken out of the proceeds, farmers had small profits. Some farmers were satisfied with the arrangement, we were told, but many were not.

Boavida Madonda, of Chimbonhanine, a community in the lowlands, was not. A muscular and relatively prosperous farmer in his fifties, Madonda complained that Wanbao paid well below market prices, was unreliable in getting seeds and inputs to them on time, and even expected farmers to arrange their own transportation to get seeds and fertilizers to their farms. "It really isn't worth it," he said. In addition to his Wanbao rice land, he has another 50 acres, which he plants in maize and other food crops. He has a good herd of cattle. He says he wouldn't care if the project failed. "It was better before. I was my own boss. We had enough to eat."

In any case, the contract growers represented a small share of the area's farmers, most of whom were on the outside looking in. Sure, some got jobs on the farm; at its peak in 2014 Wanbao employed about 2,700 people.[58] But much of its technical staff came from China. Few Mozambicans gained technical skills through the project, and in theory that is supposed to be one of the benefits of bringing in foreign expertise. Some 2,000 Mozambicans may have worked for the company, as farmworkers or in construction, maintenance, or company kitchens.[59] But Gizela said they worked without contracts and few came from the villages.

A final complication, not unique to Wanbao's Chinese owners, was cultural. Most couldn't speak Portuguese, let alone the local language. And they mostly didn't think they needed to learn. The arrogance locals complained about reminded me of so many stories I'd heard over the years about U.S. agricultural development experts who came with all the answers, asked few questions, and ended up walking away wondering why their projects didn't work. Or just blaming the local farmers and authorities for their backwardness. Wanbao's project leaders seemed to have an emerging-market hubris every bit as blinding as that of their colonial predecessors.

Ultimately, the project failed because it had run out of money. In 2013, just as Wanbao was bringing more of its acreage into production, floods destroyed 12,500 of the company's 17,000 acres of rice.[60] The company blamed the government for poor maintenance of the irrigation system, which they said had worsened the flood damage. No matter; the Chinese government canceled a loan in 2015 after concluding that the flood risks were too high to keep farming on this floodplain. A World Bank official I spoke with confirmed the assessment, saying that no lender with any sense would put money into such a risky project. Climate change added insult to injury when a 2016 drought slowed the recovery from the flooding.

When I returned in October 2017, Wanbao still had not secured financing and its farming operations were at a standstill. The company said it was still buying and processing rice from its contract farmers, but Boavida reported that he hadn't been paid for his last harvest and he was quitting the project. Zunguze said the company store was still selling a small amount of rice, but the Wanbao offices were closed. The company still claimed it was looking for financing, and we heard rumors the Bill and Melinda Gates Foundation might step in. The Chinese government continues to show interest in investing in Mozambican agriculture, and that could include new financing for Wanbao. But the project seemed to be failing.

So now, after all the promises, government support, and conflicts, this model farm might fail. That would be a victory of sorts—a successful defense against land-grabbing—but a hollow one. What would the community have to show for another failed project?

Let Farmers Grow Food

Zunguze was quick and firm when I asked her what the people want: "Give all the land back to the communities."

Lost in Wanbao's struggle to finance the project and make it viable, and the Mozambican government's continued commitment to it, was an obvious question. Wouldn't the land feed more hungry Mozambicans if the company left and local farmers were organized to grow rice and other food crops on this irrigated land?

I'd seen exactly that in Marracuene, just two hours down the highway toward Maputo. There I saw 7,000 mostly women farmers, organized into cooperatives, use rehabilitated colonial-era irrigation to grow food and cash crops year-round. Why not here in Xai-Xai?

Wanbao was a failing enterprise. Instead of giving all the best land and infrastructure—particularly irrigation—to foreign investors who then displace local farmers, why not give the land to those farmers? Help them organize into marketing cooperatives, and into water use associations to maintain the irrigation system. Help them get credit. Send crop breeders to work with them (not around them) to improve the quality of their seeds instead of displacing their seeds with commercial varieties. Help them plant a diversity of crops, not just rice or maize, to diversify their diets and improve their soils. All of which will help them prepare for the next flood or drought.

Zunguze told me proudly in October 2017 that was exactly what JA and the communities were trying to do. She said they had formed a farmers' association and submitted bylaws to register the group with the government. The farmers' association was formally approved in March 2018 as "Associação Tsakane," which means "happy" in the local language. Mama Angelica was expected to be the president of the association, with Meldina as vice president. As in Marracuene, the vast majority of the members are women. They would soon petition for a collective land title to 750 acres of land for their 400 members.

"If the associations are registered and the farmers have collective rights to some land, maybe the land-grabbing can stop," Zunguze told me. She asked for contacts in Marracuene. She planned to take Xai-Xai farmers there, or to a similar cooperative in nearby Maniça, to learn from their experiences.

4

Land-Poor Farmers in a Land-Rich Country: Zambia's Maize Paradox

When I saw the photo of the little girl in Mutanga, Zambia, I cried. There she sat in the dirt, knees tucked up to her chin, head in her hands, barefoot, maybe nine years old. She looked down into the red dust in front of her, expressionless. She wore a green skirt and a secondhand hooded sweatshirt. She looked poor, but worse than that, she looked abandoned.

It was the kind of photo that passes for "poverty porn," the sort of image that unscrupulous aid agencies use to tug at Western bleeding-heartstrings to loosen their purse-strings. It had that emotional effect on me, which was incongruous because, in fact, I'd taken the photo myself. And the girl was no orphan in a refugee camp. She was one of seven children on a relatively successful small farm in Zambia.

Her name was Machila. Her father, Wilfred Monga, was showing us his farm, and he had a lot to show. He was a successful crop and livestock farmer, small-scale to be sure, but not by Zambian standards.[1] He had 12 acres of land, which he'd planted in a mixture of crops—maize, sweet potato, peanuts, vegetables—with some left for pasture for his 100 cattle. In the dry season, he even had access to village lands for grazing. Goats and chickens roamed

Young girl, Mutanga, Zambia. *Timothy A. Wise*

his compound, which had several small buildings, some with concrete floors and walls, around a dirt courtyard. Paddocks for his cattle lay just outside the perimeter, their soils rich in manure to spread on his crops.

Monga said the family mainly ate the crops and used the animals for milk and cash. He told us they didn't slaughter the cattle for beef. "For us, a cow is milk and money." When the family needs cash, he sells a cow, or maybe a goat. His daughter presumably got a regular diet of milk and perhaps eggs, in addition to the usual *nshima*. She probably also got "village chicken" (a local breed, highly valued over supermarket poultry) and maybe some fresh goat meat, too. Those protein-rich products may have gone to market instead of to the family, but she was no poster child for Zambian poverty.

Still, the stark photo made me wonder what that poverty looked like if this was, for Zambia, a relatively healthy child. A mind-boggling 78 percent of small-scale farmers are estimated to be in extreme poverty, below the $1.25 per day poverty line. Rural poverty overall is 78 percent, one of the highest rates in Africa, and in the world. Some 40 percent of children are considered stunted, short for their age. That is more than 1 million children. Stunting is considered one of the most telling—and unfortunately predictive—of hunger indicators, since the developmental effects last a lifetime.[2]

The high rates of rural poverty are particularly appalling in a country that is considered a green-revolution success story, one of the African countries that has increased maize production dramatically in recent years. Seed and fertilizer subsidies encourage small-scale farmers to adopt high-yield farming methods. The Zambian Food Reserve Agency (FRA) buys surplus maize at a premium price. Since 2002, national maize production has more than tripled, making Zambia a regional exporter in many years.

That hasn't done much for most Zambian farmers, particularly the 70 percent of them who have access to fewer than 5 acres of land. Yields are poor, even with the subsidized seeds and fertilizers. Most don't produce enough of a surplus to sell, so they don't benefit from the government-subsidized prices. That leaves many small-scale farmers with too much land planted in maize, too little in complementary nutritious crops like pigeon peas and vegetables, and harvests that run out in December, 3–4 months before their next crops come in.

Monga himself seemed happy and healthy, right there in the depths of the hungry season in late February. Standing close to six feet tall and with a seemingly permanent smile of healthy teeth, Monga was thin, but he seemed fit rather than malnourished. No doubt the family suffered from the micronutrient deficiencies that plague rural Africa, as the lack of cropping diversity undermines diet diversity.

Machila led five cows out to pasture, stick in hand, smiling with confidence. I was confident in her present, but I wasn't so sure about her future. Her father has enough land, but would she? Monga wasn't so sure. He told us his ancestors originally had 45 acres of land, but generation after generation had divided the land among family members. His 12 acres could become fewer for each of his children, too little land to sustain their own families at anything above a subsistence level. As a girl, would Machila get her own land? Many don't, as the majority of farmers on customary land have no formal title and traditional landholding practices often exclude women from inheriting land.

Zambia is one of the least densely populated countries in the region. Unlike Malawi, good lands are available in some parts of the country, but not in densely populated areas like Southern Province. Monga's farm is on customary land, in the chiefdom of Hamusonde in Southern Province. Chief Hamusonde himself, a successful rancher, told us that he was running out of land in the chiefdom for Monga's children, for the next generation.

Researchers have referred to the paradox as one of land-poor farmers in a land-rich country.[3] The obvious question was why a government with 78 percent rural poverty couldn't find a way to make some of the good, unused land available to land-poor food producers. That would be called land reform, or redistribution, or resettlement, and it has been the precondition for economic development in countries from South Korea and Taiwan to China and Vietnam.[4]

Land reform is nowhere on the agenda in Zambia at this point. Instead the government is reserving vast tracts of land—250,000 acres at a time—for "farm blocks" in the hopes of attracting foreign investors. Foreign exchange from exports of copper, long the mainstay of the country's economy, have fallen with world copper prices, and export agriculture is expected to fill the gap. Few investors have come. The German Amatheon Agri was slowly expanding its maize, soybean, wheat, and groundnut operation near Mumbwa, in Central Province, with the goal of producing on 100,000 acres. But much farm block land sits idle, and many question the development impacts of even successful projects like Amatheon.[5]

According to a 2016 report, the project had generated about 250 permanent farmworker jobs and somewhat more seasonal work. But there were complaints about the pay, hours, and working conditions for both seasonal and permanent workers. Some local farmers were working as "outgrowers," with credit and inputs from the company to grow crops on contract. Depending on the fairness of the contract, outgrower farmers can see improvements in their livelihoods and food security, particularly if they are still growing food crops partly for home consumption. One survey claimed the company had trained 3,500 farmers with the goal of contracting up to 8,500 by 2018.[6]

I hear those numbers, and all I can think of is Monga and his children. Researchers have estimated that the optimal landholding for small-scale farmers in Zambia would be 10 acres, not too much land for a family to farm but enough to produce a significant surplus, sell on the market, and earn cash to invest in the family and the farm.[7] That's what rural development looks like. Each of those farm blocks, with its one big investor and a few hundred workers and outgrowers, could instead put 25,000 land-poor farmers on 10 acres of good farmland. If the government would also invest in irrigation, like it is doing to woo foreign investors, those farmers would be downright prosperous, getting a coveted second harvest during the dry season. That would make the hungry season history for those farmers, and you can bet Zambia's rural poverty rates would plummet.

Monga led me out into his fields in search of one of his goats, which were out foraging in unplanted fields. We walked past a freshly turned quarter-acre where a woman with a hoe was planting sweet potatoes. Monga proudly showed me his maize, a local variety called *Gankata*, which means "resistant" in the local language. He said it does well, not just in terms of yield but because it is the kind of maize his family needs, a flint variety that produces good grain and resists pests and diseases in storage. That's not the high-yield maize variety promoted and subsidized by the government. Monga saves *Gankata* seeds from one year's harvest to plant the next. He gets input subsidies, but he doesn't need a subsidy for his *Gankata*, and his animal manure makes the state-subsidized fertilizer an afterthought, an optional soil amendment.

Monga found the goat he was looking for, a healthy gray breed, fully grown. He threw it to his shoulders, the legs draped around his neck like a scarf. We needed to get back before a sudden drizzle turned into the usual midday downpour. We beat the rains, and while we waited in the shelter of our car Monga slaughtered the goat. He'd made another sale, to one of the city-dwellers who knows the value of fresh goat meat straight from the farm.

Machila weaved her way back up the path toward the homestead, cows at her command. Maybe that goat would pay for her school expenses. That would be a pretty picture. Prettier still would be one in which her land rights were secure and she had the resources to overcome Zambia's paradoxical combination of rich land, rising food production, and persistent hunger and poverty.

Africa's Breadbasket

When optimists point to Africa as the world's "next breadbasket," they point to countries such as Zambia. Feeding a "crowded world," as the narrative goes, will involve improving productivity on existing farmland—"sustainable intensification"—while bringing good un-cultivated lands under the plow. And parts of Africa, with relatively low population densities, high-quality land that has not yet been cul-tivated, and low productivity on lands that have, look like one vast orchard of low-hanging fruit in the noble quest to feed the world.[8]

Most of that imagined fruit now hangs on lands controlled by traditional leaders, and therein lies the problem. Zambia, like many African countries, has a dual system of land tenure: statutory land developed in the colonial era for estate or plantation farming, mainly for export crops, and customary land left under the control of traditional leaders, or chiefs, to whom the colonial masters del-egated local rule. In Zambia, the government has claimed (incor-rectly) that 94 percent of the land is under customary rule.

When development experts talk about bringing new land under cultivation, their eyes are clearly fixed on land controlled by tradi-tional leaders. Very few of the people farming there have any for-mal title to that land even if their families have been farming it for generations. That tenure insecurity has allowed local chiefs to cut deals with investors, and investors to trick chiefs into signing deals with them, which feeds land-grabbing and displaces local families, who are left with no legal recourse. But it also undermines productivity on customary lands. Without tenure security, farmers will not invest in long-term improvements to their farms. Without titles, they can't easily get credit for things like tractors. Without the right to buy and sell land, the more productive farmers can't gain economies of scale by buying or renting land from less productive farmers, because customary land is not a tradable commodity. And bribery aside, there is no incentive for the chiefs to grant land to agricultural investors when such transactions involve the titling of land (as statutory) and its transfer out of the chiefs' control. Why would any traditional leader negotiate away parts of the kingdom?

The surge in land-grabbing with the food crisis sparked community resistance on the ground, as I saw in Mozambique, along with national and international efforts to protect the land rights of farmers who lack secure tenure. Internationally, that has produced landmark agreements on guidelines for land tenure, "responsible agricultural investment," large-scale land-based investments in Africa, and even proposals for a UN Declaration on the Rights of Peasants and Other People Working in Rural Areas.[9]

The neoliberal answer to tenure insecurity, however, is property rights, not peasant rights. For such "modernizers," from the World Bank to the Gates Foundation, the problem—as always—is the lack of effective markets, so the answer is to give all those farmers formal titles to the land, in effect privatizing what for centuries has been community property. That will spur investment while freeing farmers to plant their land, rent it to another farmer, or willingly sell it to a foreign investor. This approach has spurred a wave of land mapping and titling projects, sponsored by the World Bank and international donors such as USAID, along with active efforts to reform national land policies to allow more private land ownership.

As I saw in Zambia, many could agree on the need for a new national land policy, but consensus was elusive when it came to agreeing on the final text. Traditional leaders initially resisted any proposal that encroached on their dominion over their kingdoms, while national leaders and the donors who backed them wanted access to those lands for development. Both showed a willingness to compromise. For their part, community members wanted protection from arbitrary decisions by both the chiefs and the national government. They knew that private land titles wouldn't protect small-scale farmers from displacement, they would only give title-holders one tiny bargaining chip when the time comes to negotiate their dispossession.

Zambia's National Land Policy

In the dimly lit offices of the Zambia Land Alliance (ZLA), the Land Policy Subcommittee gathered in early 2016 to discuss the latest government draft. They were not enthusiastic. There had been some recent movement in a process first initiated ten years earlier, but the policy was still too focused on private property rights.

"The draft policy is still pro-investment, not pro-poor," said Kalalam, coordinator of ZLA's District Land Alliance for Lusaka, the capital. It is one of eight regional organizing centers that educates community members on their land rights, provides paralegal support for land claims, and organizes for reforms within the customary land structures. In the peri-urban areas surrounding Lusaka, they are particularly focused on securing land rights for women.

ZLA's strategy, beyond participating in the technical committee developing the land policy, was to promote the use of Traditional Landholding Certificates in the chiefdoms. Piloted three years earlier in Southern Province, the certificate demarcated family plots and gave community members a document signed by the chief, a middle ground between the privatizers and the status quo.

"It gives security of tenure, even when corrupt people come in," added Agnes, from the Caritas Justice and Peace Program. "It says: 'I belong here, I have the right to be here.'"

The next day, ZLA's Nsama Nsimiwe and Jesinta Kunda took me to see how the land certificates were working in one chiefdom.[10] Chief Ndake received us in the community land rights office of the small compound that constitutes his "palace." As one of Zambia's traditional authorities, he reigns over a swath of Nyimba District in the country's Eastern Province. The only thing traditional about Chief Ndake was the formal greeting we were expected to offer, on one knee. He greeted us casually and warmly, smiling from beneath his glasses. Perhaps in his fifties, the chief wore a polo shirt emblazoned with the slogan of the day: "We use a toilet—do you?" The chief explained that they had just installed a lot of toilets across his kingdom, a major public health initiative.

Chief Ndake was as down-to-earth as could be. He apologized profusely for delaying our meeting. He explained that one of the chieftainesses (yes, there are many women chiefs) was delayed on the road when her path was blocked by elephants. Being a traditional leader in rural Zambia is clearly not for the faint of heart.

Chief Ndake, a traditional authority in Zambia's Eastern Province, at his community land rights office. *Timothy A. Wise*

The chief got quickly to the point. His chiefdom consists of 405 villages, according to a recent census, with 17,868 households and 79,505 people. Until recently, none had title to their lands, which had been apportioned at the discretion of the chiefs or their local deputies (known as "headmen") over centuries of customary rule. After independence, colonial land became state land, and a 1995 land law declared all land to be under the authority of the president. But customary land remained under the control of the chiefs. Over time, pressures had grown on traditional authorities to give up their lands, for conservation areas, mining, game parks and other forms of tourism, urban expansion, and agricultural development.

Without documentation of their landholdings, villagers had been subject to arbitrary displacement, be it from the national government, their own chiefs, or both, as private investors curried favor to gain access to good land. Large-scale foreign investments—land grabs—had grabbed headlines, but most arbitrary land deals were smaller and came from domestic investors.

Either way, villagers had little protection. Chief Ndake told us that he and other chiefs did not want to see the kinds of formal land titles the national government initially proposed as part of its new land policy. It wasn't just that the chiefs would lose much of their power, he said. If one's land can be freely bought and sold, it is likely that financial pressures, such as unpaid debts after a bad harvest, would cause many to lose their land. Indeed, research highlights precisely that danger.[11]

The ZLA's traditional landholding certificates were the perfect answer, Chief Ndake told us. They demarcate boundaries and register the land claim with the traditional authority. The land then cannot be bought, sold, or rented outside the family without the chief's consent. Chief Ndake had issued some 1,300 traditional landholding certificates, and more villagers were applying all the time. And why not? They took one month to get, compared with up to five years for formal land titles. They incorporated greater transparency than national government processes, as the local leaders knew the lands and visited them before signing off. And they alleviated regular conflicts due to their simple design, which required the consent of all neighboring landholders to the demarcation of any plot.

"If the entire chiefdom had certificates, we would have very little conflict," the chief told us. "We would have peace."

Securing Land Rights for Women

In the village of Mulongu Ndiye Chinundi, twenty residents received us in a small community building. Sitting on benches, they sang the praises of the land certificates. One woman said she had gotten better consideration for a loan because of her land certificate, even though the document is not yet considered "bankable"—it is not accepted as collateral. Conflicts over boundaries had indeed been reduced.

Perhaps the most popular benefit of the certificates was that they designated an approved list of heirs to the land. This is critical to women's right to land, as widows often struggle to secure an inheritance. As Chief Ndake told us, in his chiefdom the matrilineal family of a deceased husband (his mother's family) has rights to the land over his widow and children, who are often shipped back to their home villages, where they have scant opportunities to get decent land. He said women were most enthusiastic about the certificates, realizing their importance as de facto wills. Men spoke in favor as well. If land is one of the only things a man has, one man told us, he wants it to go to the family he leaves behind.

Chief Ndake indicated that the certificate system was gaining traction, particularly as a response to the national government's disappointing initial land policy proposal, tabled in 2015. Other civil society organizations and donors were working with traditional authorities in different parts of Zambia on even more ambitious efforts to document landholdings, using remote sensing and other mapping systems.[12]

Matt Sommerville was working on one of those efforts as part of a USAID-funded project. He was critical of the more piecemeal documentation efforts such as ZLA's, arguing that complete areas needed to be demarcated for any system to work. "You can't give one person land rights without giving all her neighbors land rights too," he told me. "It just doesn't work." Still, all told there would soon be thousands of certificates issued, the kind of "facts on the ground" that could move policy-makers to accept the practice.

More recent drafts of the land policy were encouraging, ZLA's Nsimiwe said, accepting the integrity of customary lands, withdrawing the demand for formal titles, and promoting the use of traditional land certificates. In part, that was thanks to ZLA's community consultations on the policy in late 2015. The national government had scaled back promised consultative meetings, holding just one meeting in each of the country's ten provinces, mostly with political leaders, not the community. ZLA filled the void, with support from USAID, organizing twenty district-level consultations across all ten provinces, involving 743 people, including some traditional leaders and their headmen. The recommendations were unambiguous, rejecting the national government's moves toward private land titles outside the customary land system. Instead, they wanted the power over customary lands vested still with traditional authorities, and with tenure security documented for families, villages, and chiefdoms through some form of traditional landholding certificate.

Squandering Natural Wealth

As it turns out, Zambia is far less land-abundant than the government claims. According to a study by Michigan State University and Zambian researchers, the estimate that 94 percent of Zambian land is under customary rule dates to surveys from the 1960s. With the creation of national parks, game reserves, and erosion to statutory land through private investments, the figure drops to 54 percent. And much of the remaining land is far from roads and marketing centers, creating obstacles for any sort of development, large or small. According to the study, farmers are heavily concentrated on the 5 percent of land that is nearer to roads and market centers.[13]

There certainly is some unused land, but what shows up on satellite images as unoccupied is often common land used for timber, fuel, forest products such as medicinal crops, and grazing for small livestock such as goats. Some of those unfarmed agricultural plots are actually fallow lands, intentionally left unplanted to preserve their fertility. Such "shifting cultivation" is common where land is relatively plentiful, and it represents sound ecological management, at least it does when population densities are low. Often, what passes for unused land is land without clear title, and in Zambia that is a lot of land.

Many large-scale land deals have gone sour all over the continent when a big company has signed a sweetheart deal with national leaders and the local chiefs only to find that the land they've been given is by no means "unoccupied." As I saw in Mozambique and Tanzania, the resulting land conflicts after the Great Land Rush of 2008 only highlighted the land-governance failures of the current setup.

But there is underutilized and undeveloped land, and the obvious question was why Zambia still had so many farmers going hungry for lack of land. Researchers found that most Zambian farmers live in relatively densely populated chiefdoms, as I'd seen in Hamusonde. Just as Monga had explained, as communities have grown with each generation, land has been allocated to young adults, and then their children, to the point that many chiefs have little land to give. Plots are now often subdivided among family members, leaving many farmers with plots too small even to grow a subsistence never mind a surplus to sell.

Having a surplus puts a farmer in the market as a seller, not just a buyer, which everyone agrees is the first step toward creating a commercial farm economy. The researchers calculated that in Zambia the difference between having no surplus and having some to sell was the difference between one and two hectares. Two hectares (about 5 acres) brings farmers into the market as sellers and offers the chance that they can earn enough cash to invest in their farms. They estimated that the optimal small-scale landholding was about 4 hectares (10 acres), a farm size that could

facilitate the development of commercial farms capable of investing in productivity-enhancing technologies.[14]

In Zambia, one-third of farmers have plots of 2.5 acres or less.[15]
These are the land-poor farmers in this somewhat land-rich country. Nearly all of them grow food, precisely those foods that nourish most Zambians—maize, groundnuts, potatoes, sweet potatoes,
cassava, tomatoes, legumes of many varieties. And those same
farmers are the majority of Zambia's malnourished population.
According to one estimate, giving such land-constrained farmers
2.5 acres more land would reduce poverty rates among them from
86 percent to 53 percent, and the overall poverty rate for smallholders as a group would fall to 48 percent.[16]

On my first visit to Zambia in 2014, I saw one small project that
showed the value of giving farmers control over more good land.
The Chanyanya Smallholders Cooperative Society of 126 households in Kafue, south of Lusaka, was well connected enough to get
secure title to about 1,250 acres of statutory land. They irrigated it
with European donor support, set up small garden plots for themselves on some of it, and sublet the majority to a commercial soybean and wheat farming business in which the cooperative retains
a significant equity share.

The farmers get more food from their garden plots, with year-
round production of cash and subsistence crops thanks to the
irrigation. And the subletters develop the land through capital-
intensive investment, with cooperative members sharing in those
profits and retaining title to the land. They seemed enormously
better off, though I wondered if they might do even better if they
each had 10 irrigated acres and they were shown how to become
midsize commercial farmers.

Still, the benefits of giving land-poor farmers more land seemed
clear. Confronted with this obvious solution to persistent rural poverty, the Zambian government has gone in the opposite direction.
The government has been creating an "agricultural land bank,"
transferring large tracts from customary to statutory land. Leaders
then auction it off to large-scale investors, some foreign, some from

Zambia's urban elite. The Farm Block Program is the national government's initiative to create 250,000-acre modern farms.

The Hollow Promise of Agribusiness

There is nothing particularly original in Zambia's farm block scheme. I'd seen much the same everywhere I'd been in Africa. Malawi had its Green Belt Initiative, Tanzania its SAGCOT Corridor program, and Mozambique its ill-fated ProSAVANA scheme for the Nacala Corridor. All tried to secure agricultural land to lure large-scale private investments, promising publicly funded infrastructure to fuel the new wave of "public-private partnerships" (PPPs) that were all the rage following the food crisis. After a notable surge in donor support for publicly funded agricultural development in 2009, U.S. president Obama backed off in 2012, ushering in the G-7 countries' New Alliance for Food Security and Nutrition.[17] At best, the New Alliance lacked ambition. It was only for Africa, and it lacked public financing—just $6 billion, compared to the previous three-year commitment of $22 billion. Instead, it relied heavily on private investors to bring serious money for agricultural development. The public sector had done its part, Obama implied, now it was time for the private sector to take the lead.

At its launch, the New Alliance boasted a private sector that looked like a who's who of global agribusiness—Monsanto, DuPont, Yara (fertilizers), Cargill. If these were countries, many would rank in the top fifty by GDP. Were cash-strapped African governments really supposed to partner with the likes of Monsanto, with annual revenues larger than the GDP of many countries?[18] Were desperately poor farmers going to "partner" with multinational grain traders? Wasn't there a danger that the partnership would look a lot like the relationship between a hammer and a nail?

UN Special Rapporteur on the Right to Food Olivier De Schutter warned that small-scale farmers were being left out of such arrangements. Africa represents the last continent for industrial agriculture to conquer, he told the *Guardian* in 2014. "There's a struggle for land, for investment, for seed systems, and first and foremost there's a struggle for political influence."[19]

At best, you could have a managed process such as the Farm Block Program, which planned one 250,000-acre farm in each of Zambia's ten provinces. This is the now-popular strategy of the "anchor farm," a commercial operation that brings in technology and infrastructure, then contracts with farmers in "outgrower" schemes designed to modernize peasant agriculture and integrate them into "value chains."

In theory, each farm block would attract an agribusiness investor to establish a "nucleus farm" of 25,000 acres around which the government would try to install up to three large commercial farms (2,500 to 12,500 acres), with a priority on export crops. The plan envisioned unspecified numbers of medium-scale farms (250 to 2,500 acres), so-called emergent farmers (125 to 250 acres), and small-scale farms (60 to 125 acres), that would grow crops for the agribusiness firm's processing facility. (That the program defines "small-scale" farmers as those with more than 100 acres of land gives some idea how divorced the policy is from Zambian reality, in which 70 percent of farmers have fewer than 5 acres.)

At worst, investors don't wait for the national government. They go straight to local leaders and cut deals that displace local farmers for the large-scale production of palm oil or some other cash crop, often for export. More large-scale Zambian projects are outside the farm blocks than inside them, as investors have been impatient about negotiating through the national government.

The dangers were highlighted in a detailed report by De Schutter. "If they are not careful, farmers end up as disempowered labourers on their own land."[20] De Schutter put the onus on governments to ensure that such arrangements are fair to smallholders, that land is not taken from them for such projects, and that small-scale farmers are allowed to grow food in addition to cash crops. This, he argued, is to ensure that their basic food needs are met if international markets buffet the core business, as they so often do.

I'd always been skeptical of programs to get peasant farmers to grow cash crops for export instead of food for local markets. Export markets are erratic and usually offer only a tenuous lifeline to small-scale producers. Food production leaves you with, at the least, food. And if population is growing, so is the local demand for food. As Willard Cochrane, one of the architects of U.S. farm policy coming out of the Great Depression, quipped, "Agricultural demand is inelastic because the human stomach is inelastic." All human beings require a certain minimum to sustain themselves, no matter how high the price. And no one eats five meals when prices go down. So demand for food grows reliably, basically at the rate of population growth. Harness that for domestic production, and you've got the first prerequisite for economic development: growing demand for something you can produce.

Neoliberal economists have spurned that sound logic for decades, promoting their theories of "market-led" development based on assumptions largely untethered from the real world. The promotion of large-scale agribusiness-led projects as the solution to local food insecurity rests on such shaky assumptions, now empirically proven false by the Land Matrix and other monitoring efforts:[21]

- Assume that land grabs produce staple food. (Mostly, they don't.)
- Assume that such food is consumed domestically. (It's more likely to be exported.)
- Assume that the calories they might produce go to hungry people. (They don't; they go to people who have the cash to buy them.)
- Assume that calories are all that's needed to nourish someone. (They aren't; micronutrient deficiencies are prevalent.)
- Assume that the grabbed land didn't displace anyone from producing food. (Most projects have displaced farmers.)
- And last, what I call the "field of dreams" myth: If you build it, they will come. If you make land available, investors will invest. (Unlike in the hit Kevin Costner movie, they haven't come.)

Zambia's large-scale land schemes seemed to suffer from all of these flawed assumptions. As I'd seen in Malawi, Tanzania, and Mozambique, government promises of land and infrastructure are often inadequate to convince an investor, especially a foreign investor, to come. Land taken from farming communities may never get developed, or a project may fail, as I saw in Xai-Xai, Mozambique. In such cases, hungry farmers sit landless on the outside looking in. The only permanent jobs the failed SunBiofuels project created in Tanzania were a few security guards hired to keep displaced farmers off their former land, which lay idle.[22] And there is rarely a legal process, or any incentive, for the national government to return unused "leasehold" land to the chiefs and communities who had given it up.

The Land Matrix documented thirty-four land deals in Zambia by 2016, with more than 1 million acres under contract. Most of that is outside the Farm Block Program, whose goal is to put 2.5 million acres under intensive cultivation. But most of Zambia's farm blocks still lack a stable anchor farm. That is the case on the Nansanga farm block, one of the oldest in the country.[23] Frustrated by the lack of interest, the government in 2015 installed the quasi-governmental Industrial Development Corporation to stimulate large and small investments. The government installed much of the promised infrastructure, but by July 2017 there still was no anchor farm, just a few smaller operations. In any case, the land was neither idle nor unoccupied, as proponents of such schemes often suggest. Estimates vary, but government documents suggest at least 427 households lived on the Nansanga land; many had indicated they did not want to be moved or swallowed up by the larger project.[24]

In 2017, Human Rights Watch issued a scathing report, " 'Forced to Leave': Commercial Farming and Displacement in Zambia." Decrying the government's obsession with commercial agriculture as a "panacea" for combating rural poverty, researchers found poor regulation of agribusiness investments and limited protection of the rights of residents, many of whom had been displaced from ancestral lands without compensation or legal recourse. They found little upside from most of the commercial ventures they studied in Serenje District, including Nansanga.[25]

Human Rights Watch concluded that their study "illustrates broken promises, governance failures, and human rights abuses connected with commercial farming."[26]

More Maize, No Less Hunger

If Zambia's surge in maize production isn't coming from large-scale schemes such as the farm blocks, where is all that maize coming from? Could Zambia be that elusive green-revolution success story, using commercial seeds and fertilizers to "sustainably intensify" maize production on existing small-scale farms? If so, why hasn't all that maize reduced the country's alarming levels of rural poverty and malnutrition?

Those were the questions I posed to some of the agricultural development experts in Zambia, and there are many, which just makes the country's food insecurity even more confounding. For years, Michigan State University has teamed with researchers in several African countries. In Lusaka, the Indaba Agricultural Policy Research Institute (IAPRI) is one of its partners. Their efforts had produced some of those studies that identified the constraints on customary land and the problem of land-poor farmers in a land-rich country.

Nick Sitko, a Michigan State researcher who had spent eight years in Zambia, briefed me by phone on what he generously called the "unreliable policy environment" for maize production. Others were not so charitable, decrying the national government's "policy incoherence." Like Malawi, Zambia has an input subsidy program, which has had more success than Malawi's in putting hybrid maize seeds and fertilizers into the hands of small-scale and so-called emerging farmers. Some 65 percent of farmers use commercial seeds, and 50 to 60 percent use inorganic fertilizer, a key goal of the green-revolution strategy. Fertilizer use has increased 70 percent since the input subsidies were introduced in 2002. Subsidy recipients are twice as likely to use commercial seeds, with adoption rates over 80 percent.[27] This is the kind of technology adoption that the Alliance for a Green Revolution in Africa dreams of.

The other major policy driver of maize production is the country's Food Reserve Agency (FRA), which is mandated to buy maize at subsidized prices. The FRA purchases the vast majority of its maize from farms no larger than 50 acres, mostly from a relatively small group of midsize farms.[28] The input subsidy targeted those same small- and medium-scale farmers, though the smallest-scale farmers—those with less than 1.25 acres—are excluded from subsidy programs, some 15 to 20 percent of farms.[29] Sitko explained that the FRA was then mandated to sell its maize reserves to national millers at below-market prices, the goal being to give poor consumers a steady supply of cheap maize meal, the staple for *nshima*.

On paper, at least, the policies sounded quite coherent and potentially pro-poor. What could go wrong? Pretty much everything. Maize productivity on small farms hadn't increased very much, in part because they couldn't afford the copayment for seeds and fertilizer required by the government. So midsize farms were getting the vast majority of the subsidized inputs. But because the standard fertilizer mix was wrong for a lot of the country's soils, productivity had not increased very much. Farmers were putting more of their land into monocultures of subsidized maize without getting a lot more maize. In the process, they were losing access to the complementary and nutritious crops they used to grow—groundnuts, legumes, and other staples. And other drought-tolerant staple crops, such as cassava, millet, and sorghum, had seen production stagnate or decline. With subsidies favoring maize, the area planted to maize rose 77 percent nationwide from 2004 to 2014, while the area in millet fell 40 percent and sorghum area declined 47 percent.[30]

So much for the pro-poor input subsidies. Small-scale farmers saw declining crop diversity and not much maize productivity.

The Food Reserve Agency's subsidized prices had certainly driven midsize farms into maize, and much of Zambia's increase in maize production had come not from productivity increases on existing maize land but from bringing new land into maize. That expansion, though, was putting pressure on small-scale farmers as richer farmers and urban elites bought up customary land. Zambia Land Alliance members had told me that rich Zambians were a greater source of land-grabbing than foreign investors. The FRA also drove large-scale farms out of maize production, since they could not get a reliable price for their maize, and local millers, the remaining commercial buyers for their maize, were getting subsidized grain from the FRA and wouldn't pay a decent price to the large-scale farmers. To make matters worse, the government would periodically, and somewhat unpredictably, ban exports in the name of food security, eliminating one last potential market for commercial farmers' maize.

Sitko explained that the FRA preferred selling to large mills in each province rather than to the local mills prevalent throughout rural Zambia. "The policy favored a small number of large mills, undermining small-scale local mills," Sitko told me. This added insult to injury for rural communities, as a lot of small mills went out of business, leaving local farmers with few places to sell their grain. Worse still, "it sucked the maize out of rural areas," said Sitko, leaving rural Zambians not only with limited productivity gains, fewer markets for their maize, and more pressure on their land, but also less milled maize in local markets.

Even worse, that FRA price cut for the millers, which was supposed to ensure low-priced maize meal, was barely passed on to Zambian consumers, the supposed end beneficiaries of this elaborate set of policies. Those large millers in effect had the market power to keep most of it for themselves. Urban food prices were kept moderately low, but rural Zambians saw little cheap maize to buy when the hungry season descended on their villages.[31]

I was reeling from this relentless volley of policy failures, but Sitko had one more punch to throw. He reminded me that the input support program and the Food Reserve Agency consume 98 percent of the government's budget for "poverty reduction."

I was floored. Zambia's maize policies seemed more like "poverty enhancement" programs. Somehow, Sitko was surprisingly optimistic about Zambia's prospects. "Land constraints can be overcome," he reassured me. And many in government understand that what they are doing isn't working. He encouraged me to speak with his boss, IAPRI Research Director Antony Chapoto, the next time I was in Zambia.

Chapoto, a Michigan State graduate, welcomed me into his spacious office with a smile. The institute was large and clearly well funded, and it quickly became clear that he had ready access to high-level government officials. Chapoto apologized for being late, saying that he was preparing for a meeting with an International Monetary Fund mission, trying to figure out what policy reforms he could get away with proposing there. He was not shy with me about his dissatisfaction with the ineffectiveness of current government policies.

"There is a commitment to smallholder farmers," he said of government officials, "but they miss the mark." He said half of Zambian farmers still did not produce a surplus to sell, so it was the wealthier farmers who were reaping the benefits, and the programs were very expensive. "We really aren't getting the bang for the buck."

Chapoto was particularly critical of the input subsidy program. He said that seeds and fertilizers are distributed with no attention to the actual condition of the soils. The standard compound of nitrogen, potassium, and phosphate was the wrong mix for most Zambian farms, which was the reason for such lackluster productivity gains despite the country's massive increases in fertilizer use. He confirmed that Zambia suffered from the same sort of yield plateau I'd seen in Malawi, where farmers need more fertilizer every year just to get the same yield. Soil testing showed that Zambian soils have grown acidic, in part from excessive fertilizer use. So they need lime, which is nowhere in the input program. Acidic soils dramatically reduce the productivity of fertilizer, by half or more. According to one economic study, "fertilizer use on maize is not profitable at commercial prices for the majority of Zambian farmers (under current practices)."[32]

He told me he'd like to recommend that 10 percent of the input subsidy budget be used for soil testing, which isn't cheap at about $33 per test. Still, he thought the improved response to more carefully selected inputs would more than pay for the high costs. He pointed to a planned fertilizer blending plant, which would allow a diverse mix of fertilizer blends for different soils rather than the off-the-shelf compound multinational firms sell in Zambia now. That was clearly a waste of money, but one the government kept approving.

Chapoto was also excited about the introduction of e-vouchers as a replacement for seed and fertilizer coupons. Farmers kept buying seeds and fertilizers even though they weren't productive, because that's what the coupons gave them. But e-vouchers could be spent on any of a wide variety of inputs. In a pilot program, 15 percent of purchases went for something other than maize seeds and fertilizers, items such as legume seeds, other inputs such as lime, and veterinary drugs for farm animals.[33]

I imagined the multinational seed and fertilizer companies weren't as enthusiastic as Chapoto about those e-vouchers. It was easy to see that farmers and consumers weren't the main beneficiaries of Zambia's "poverty reduction" programs in agriculture. As far as I could tell, the winners were commercial farmers with land; large millers, a powerful national agribusiness lobby; and multinational and national input suppliers. Those diverse constituencies readily congeal into the powerful lobby that clogs the pipeline for innovation and policy reform.

"If we start talking about agricultural diversification, moving away from maize, we can start talking about food security," Chapoto told me candidly, knowing he was stating the obvious. "Starch can only fill your tummy. My grandmother gave us a diverse diet, never the same thing every day." He clearly hoped that one day his incremental reform efforts could produce a break with the monoculture model.

I wished him luck with the IMF. His reform recommendations would not include crop diversification. Not yet. He told me he was going to advocate a universal school feeding program such as Brazil's. And expansion of the e-vouchers. As I wrote this chapter six months later I was pleased to see that the e-voucher program was indeed going national.[34]

In Diversity There Is Strength

At the Kasisi Agricultural Training Center outside Lusaka, the innovation pipeline was flowing freely, and Kasisi's innovators had long since shifted their focus to organic agriculture. As Kasisi director Henrietta Kalinda explained, it hadn't always been that way. The Jesuit center had been founded in 1974 to promote green-revolution technologies, trying to avoid having Africa miss out on the agricultural boom. Kasisi would give young farm families plots of land and train them in the new high-input techniques, until they noticed something in the 1990s.

"We saw that they were not selling enough to pay for the inputs," explained Kalinda. "And the land was becoming degraded—they needed to use more inputs for the same output." Their farmers, like so many others, were running to stand still. Kasisi gradually made the shift to what Kalinda calls sustainable organic agriculture. ("Organic can be unsustainable too," she cautions.) Kasisi is now the premier sustainable agriculture training center in Zambia.

"We are finding that organic production works much better, it is much more resilient," she added. "Farmers have done much better in erratic rains."

We got a tour of the demonstration farm, which is used to experiment with new techniques, to train farmers in the transition to organic practices, and to support the center from the sale of produce. It is an impressive operation, featuring a large pivot irrigation system feeding a rich diversity of crops. The day we visited, farmers weeded plots of squash, amaranth, cowpeas, and pigeon peas in the quarter of the crop circle devoted to training. Farmers pay a monthly fee for the irrigation but get to keep or sell the produce they grow. Farmers work with Kasisi extension agents to learn how to multiply seeds, bring small animals into the farm, compost manure, intercrop effectively, harvest and manage water, and control pests.

The wide range of biological pest control practices was mind-boggling. It included push-pull methods, with Desmodium legumes intercropped with maize, naturally repelling pests while Napier grass borders drew them away from food crops.[35] Other natural insecticides included lemongrass, oregano, mint, and marigold. They teach farmers to create sprays from neem leaves, aloe, and even raw milk, which is a natural fungicide when mixed with manure. The scourge of maize farms in Southern Africa in recent years is the fall armyworm, but Kalinda said their farmers had suffered little damage thanks to such practices.

The majority of the irrigated crop circle is devoted to cash crops, which pay for a significant share of the center's operating costs. The day we were there, one large section was planted in soybeans to be used and sold as fodder for animals. The largest section was in barley, which Kasisi was growing on contract with a local beer-maker. Kalinda said there still was no price premium in Zambia for organic produce, but there was definitely demand. Kasisi's vegetables are coveted in Lusaka, and the center is supplying organic vegetables to two clinics for their cancer patients.

Gloria Musowa works with the Chongwe Organic Producers and Processors Association (CHOPPA), a group of nineteen cooperatives several miles from Kasisi where many Kasisi farmers put their training to work. Musowa said most farmers have between 12 and 35 acres of land, though some have just 5. All farm organically, selling through the cooperative in local markets.

I had to ask about maize, though it was interesting that the crop seemed to have no privileged status at Kasisi. Musowa acknowledged that farmers very much wanted to grow maize, and the center helps them do so in a more sustainable and productive way, without chemical inputs. Is there a loss of productivity? Just the opposite, she said. In one two-year project, they found that organic farmers using improved open-pollinated maize seeds that they had multiplied themselves got double the yields compared to conventional farmers using green-revolution inputs, 2.4 tons per hectare compared to 1.2. With input costs lower, their farms were far more profitable. And those advantages increased over time as soil quality improved.

Needless to say, they were more food-secure as well. Musowa said it was common to find twelve to fifteen different plants growing on one farm. "With more diversity on the farm, they can compensate for a bad year for maize," she told me, and their diets were far healthier even in good years.

Kalinda was optimistic about changing government policies. "FISP is expensive to farmers and to the nation. It is not sustainable. Alternative systems are needed. Slowly the government is moving away from the FISP." Kasisi is contributing to that. Some of their training and educational programs are with government extension agents who see firsthand what Kasisi saw in the 1990s. "They see their farmers are poorer at the end of the season using the current approach."

"We are trying to force a revolution from below," said Kalinda with a smile.

Promoting the Right to Food

That revolution can't come soon enough for many of Zambia's hungry farmers, nor for Hilal Elver, the current UN Special Rapporteur on the Right to Food. Elver was in Zambia in May 2017 at the invitation of the government to assess the country's progress in the realization of the right to food. She was diplomatic, praising government officials for their openness, but she clearly was alarmed by what she saw.

"The push to turn commercial large-scale agriculture into a driving engine of the Zambian economy, in a situation where the protection of access to land is weak, can risk pushing small-holder

farmers and peasants off their land and out of production with severe impacts on the people's right to food," Elver said in Lusaka at
the end of her ten-day mission. In her short statement, Elver called
on the government to adopt "a gender-sensitive, inclusive National
Land Policy" that "protects the rights of those living on customary
lands." The UN envoy concluded with a call to reconsider policies
that overemphasize the production of maize on larger farms.[36]

"The agricultural sector has failed to make a dent on poverty levels in the rural areas and as such the model for the strengthening
of the agricultural sectors needs to be altered," Elver said.

Like many of the experts I spoke with, I found myself hopeful,
if not optimistic, about Zambia's prospects. Zambia has a functioning, if imperfect, democracy. Juliana Nnoko-Mewanu, the Human
Rights Watch researcher who wrote the hard-hitting report on
large-scale projects, told me that she'd found many government officials to be quite responsive to the report's calls for improvement.
Some had taken immediate steps to remedy glaring abuses. Key
advisers at IAPRI and elsewhere are providing sound analysis and
advice. Maybe the expanding use of e-vouchers will indeed show
that farmers don't want just maize seeds and fertilizers; maybe they
will create markets for drought-tolerant seeds like millet and sorghum, or even for compost instead of chemical fertilizer.

As I write this, the government is still struggling with traditional
leaders over a national land policy draft that incorporated most of
the recommendations from traditional authorities, farm leaders,
and civil society groups. Customary land would not be privatized
with titles but recognized with some form of traditional landholding certificate after a national effort to map landholdings. Wom-
en's land rights got particular attention in the policy. The policy
would be followed by a customary land bill that formalizes traditional leaders' role and the rights of their subjects. This still seemed
not to have satisfied the chiefs, at least as of mid-2018. The negotiations went on.

I was struck, though, by one telling omission from the land policy. There was no right or process to return land to communities

when large-scale projects fail. The government remained intent on liberating land from the customary system, and once it is pried loose the government is loath to give it back. This reflects its obsessive commitment to large-scale export agriculture. With revenues from copper low, the government is looking for foreign exchange more than it is looking for food security, and that does not bode well for Zambia's millions of land-poor farmers. The government's much-ballyhooed 2016 National Agricultural Policy, which charted a path to 2030, declared its first principle to be "The right to adequate and nutritious food," but there was nothing in the policy to make me think the government was ready to reconsider its fixation on agribusiness-led development.[37]

Achieving tenure security would certainly be a major achievement, and a prerequisite for realizing the right to food for Zambia's small-scale farmers and their families. But it doesn't solve their land shortages. Only meaningful land reform can do that. And it doesn't help farmers make more sustainable and productive use of the land, to grow food for the people who most need it, the farm families themselves.

I imagined Monga's granddaughter, Machila, twenty years from now, with title to a nice plot on one of those irrigated farm blocks, as part of a cooperative working with Kasisi to grow a diverse and healthy mix of organic crops. Wouldn't that be a beautiful picture?

Part II

The Roots of Our Problems

AFRICA WAS CERTAINLY REELING from a wide range of challenges in increasing food production and reducing hunger, and as I'd seen in Malawi, Mozambique, and Zambia the solutions to those problems were consistently blocked or diverted by agribusiness and big agriculture. The notion that technology would allow them to grow the food they needed, and that all the industrial-scale food would feed the hungry, seemed absurd. They weren't growing much more food, and the hungry weren't much better fed. The roots of their problems, it seemed to me, were as multinational as the firms that were pushing their way into the continent. Those tangled roots led back to the United States, where we are repeatedly told our highly productive farmers are feeding a hot, hungry, crowded world.

Within the United States, the roots are deep in Iowa, the heart of the U.S. corn belt and the home of Norman Borlaug, father of the green revolution and founder of the World Food Prize, the self-proclaimed Nobel Prize for agriculture. Since the inaugural prize in 1987, the World Food Prize has become an ever-more-elaborate ceremony, with a carefully staged State Department announcement of the year's winner and a three-day conference in Des Moines, Iowa, in October around World Food Day. It has also become dominated by agribusiness, not surprising given the technology-obsessed visions of its founder.

By all accounts, Norman Borlaug was remarkable, a dedicated, indefatigable, creative crop breeder whose efforts to develop high-yielding wheat varieties, and his determination to make those seeds available to farmers in India and other countries facing hunger, won him the Nobel Prize in 1970. He was also incredibly stubborn. From what I could tell, his single-mindedness about technology as the key to feeding the world left him quite impaired when it came to understanding how the real world worked.

According to biographers, two formative events profoundly shaped his view of the world, and he clung to the deep impressions they left even though he had misinterpreted them at the time and continued to do so throughout his long and storied career.[1]

The first was his deep disdain for farming or, more specifically, the "drudgery" of small-scale farming. He came from a poorly endowed area of Iowa. According to biographers, he grew up hating farmwork, and part of his motivation in promoting technology in agriculture was to liberate farmers from such drudgery. The problem, of course, is that many farming communities view such labor as dignified, even as they seek to make it more productive and less physically demanding. Borlaug's vision of capital-intensive farming has certainly come to pass in the U.S. heartland, reducing drudgery but leaving depopulated rural areas with the few remaining farmers earning very little after agribusiness firms have taken their cuts. In developing countries like India, where Borlaug's green revolution took hold, freeing family members from the drudgery of farm labor sent them into the country's sprawling urban slums because there were no jobs waiting for them. With underemployment so prevalent in every developing country I studied for this book, Borlaug's commitment to giving farmers, in his words, "relief from endless drudgery" seemed quite obviously to be the wrong prescription based on a flawed diagnosis of the problem.

More damning, though, was Borlaug's faith in the spurious conclusions he drew from a violent milk strike he witnessed in 1933 at the age of nineteen while a student in Minneapolis. He happened upon a confrontation between police protecting a milk truck from protesters trying to stop the milk from being delivered and sold. The standoff turned violent, and Borlaug reportedly emerged shaken at seeing so many desperate, hungry people in the Great Depression. He reportedly vowed to dedicate his life to preventing what his biographer summarized as "the terrible fathomless hunger" he saw in the street that day.

What he failed to realize at the time—which is perhaps forgivable in a nineteen-year-old—was that the problem wasn't a lack of food, it was too much of it. Dairy farmers were on strike because overproduction had undercut the prices for their milk to the point that farms were going bankrupt and farm families were losing their livelihoods. The organized response of remaining dairy farmers was to withhold their milk from the market and stop its sale in the cities, both to raise the price of milk and to force government action to reduce the oversupply. The "fathomless hunger" Borlaug saw around that milk truck were mostly farmers who were victims of overproduction, and some of them were now penniless with no way to feed their families. In short, he got it completely wrong.

What seemed less forgivable was Borlaug's deep commitment to such an erroneous interpretation of this searing experience. He seemed incapable of learning that more food does not mean less hunger, that it can actually cause hunger. And policies that simply promote ever-higher levels of farm production fail to address the complex reasons we see hunger in a world of plenty.

His World Food Prize suffers from the same disconnect with reality. I first traveled to Iowa when the 2013 prizes were awarded to three scientists for their pioneering work developing genetically modified seeds. One was from Belgium, the other two were U.S. scientists from Monsanto and Syngenta. The event was surreal. Cardinal Peter Turkson was there from the Vatican to report that after careful theological study the Catholic Church had ruled that genetic modification was not a sin. World Food Prize president Kenneth Quinn had earlier unveiled a spectacular renovation of the Hall of Laureates, the grand World Food Prize building on the banks of the Des Moines River. Unmentioned in the unveiling was

One thing was clear: Iowa is a God-fearing state, but Agribusiness is all-powerful, ordaining that farmers tame and dominate every inch of Eden, all to achieve their manifest destiny to feed the world. Behold, ye who doubt, its most hallowed temple: the glorious World Food Prize Hall of Laureates on the banks of the well-fertilized, algae-choked Des Moines River.

As near as I could tell, Agribusiness's genesis story went something like this:

In the beginning—1926—Agribusiness created corn, or it liked to think so. It hadn't, of course: 7,000 years earlier, the Mesoamerican gods had beaten them to it, creating corn and then humans from that corn. Even if you didn't buy that creation story, there was no doubt that observant and purposeful Mesoamerican farmers had domesticated corn from its ancestor, *teosinte*, whose grain looks nothing like corn, in one of the most anonymous yet momentous strokes of human ingenuity. What Agribusiness actually created those thousands of years later was hybrid corn, and it declared that hybrid corn was the only corn that mattered. And Agribusiness saw that it produced a lot and, most important, farmers had to buy it every year. And it was good, for Agribusiness.

On the second day, Agribusiness separated the land from the water, expanding drainage tiles under millions of acres of farm-belt swampland. And the land was good, especially for long straight rows of hybrid corn. Actually, Agribusiness got the federal government to pay for much of the drainage, under the New Deal's Civilian Conservation Corps and other government programs.[2] And Agribusiness saw that the drained cropland was good; getting taxpayers to pay for it was even better.

On the third day, with way too much corn, Agribusiness created pigs to eat some of it, right there on the farm. Actually, it just created a new diet for them. Pigs had already been created by that other God, and farmers the world over kept these animals as insurance policies, since they could eat just about anything, their manure was good for the land, and they could be sold for meat. Agribusiness saw that they would get fatter faster eating corn and soybeans, which farmers began growing instead of oats and hay to feed their animals. They didn't need oats or hay because Agribusiness gave them tractors to replace their draught horses, substituting oil for horse feed, "horsepower" for horse power, and the simple corn-soybean rotation for its more soil-enriching three-crop rotation. Agribusiness saw that more corn and soybeans were good, and that meat was even better, because it took 5 pounds of grain to create a pound of meat. Or even 10.

On the fourth day, Agribusiness created animal prisons, which it called hog farms even though they were factories. And it created commercial feed to fatten the animals. It moved the animals into the hog farms. The new feed companies would buy all the cheap corn and soybeans, and the hog farms would buy the feed, creating two commercial transactions where before there had been none. And they would spread far and wide, and lo, so would chicken prisons. And so would the millions of gallons of their concentrated manure. It would be sprayed on the fields of crop farmers, who now needed to purchase manure, since their animals were in the prisons. And Agribusiness held its nose at the putrid odor, like everyone else, and said it was good, proclaiming its own genius for creating such a costly commercial nutrient cycle from the natural one it had destroyed by moving animals off the farms.

On the fifth day, Agribusiness created an army of lobbyists, and it would be called the "farm lobby" even though it lobbied for corporations. The army persuaded the U.S. Congress to pass the Freedom to Farm Act, the 1996 farm bill that officially outlawed government measures to ensure fair prices for farmers, decent prices for consumers, and controls on production so supply would not exceed demand and agricultural land would not be farmed to exhaustion. Those policies—support prices, government procurement and grain storage, land set-asides and conservation—had been the foundation of U.S. farm policy, long eroding since the Great Depression. Agribusiness, all-powerful in the neoliberal nineties, thus bequeathed unto itself the lowest prices on the highest production possible. And it was good, the low prices for Agribusiness processors, the high production for Agribusiness seed, chemical, and other input suppliers.

On the sixth day, laden with way too much corn fetching rock-bottom prices, Agribusiness created ethanol to power our cars. And it commanded that the fuel be made from corn even though corn was the least efficient crop to make it from. And behold, with Congress providing subsidies and mandating ethanol use in gasoline, one-third of that corn was suddenly used to make fuel instead of feed or food. And it was good, for Agribusiness.

On the seventh day, with the corn-surplus problem temporarily solved by the invention of a new agribusiness, with corn prices at record highs and wreaking havoc with poor people overseas, and with every inch of even marginally farmable Iowa land brought into production, Agribusiness rested. Agribusiness surveyed its good works and ordained that a temple should be anointed to honor its wisdom and good fortune. And so the World Food Prize Hall of Laureates was transformed into that temple, with offerings from the faithful. Forevermore, they would gather, on World Food Day no less, for an annual ritual of worship and adoration.

Now, so deep into such a profound devolution, it was difficult to say which part of that genesis story was the real problem. Factory farming of hogs, which creates concentrated pools of toxic—and nutrient-rich—manure? Corn and soy farmers who misapply or over-apply that manure, along with chemical fertilizers, to their land, creating runoff? The elaborate tile drainage system that makes the state's farmland farmable but adds subsurface nutrient streams to the surface runoff without the interference of soil or roots to clean it? The ethanol-drunken surge in crop prices that prompted farmers to pull some 500,000 acres out of the successful Conservation Reserve Program, substituting corn and soybeans for the grasslands that helped filter the water? Or was it the abandonment of government policies that had kept in check such unsustainable overproduction?

For many Iowans, the immediate problem was their polluted drinking water, and to deal with it they had created the world's largest nitrate removal plant to protect Des Moines's drinking water from the nitrates, *E. coli*, and potassium-laden sediment that flowed downstream.[3] These flowed all the way down the Mississippi to a "dead zone" the size of Connecticut in which all the sea life created on the Hebrew God's fifth day had been asphyxiated.[4]

No one I asked in Iowa could really tease out the causal connections. Hugh Espey, of Iowa Citizens for Community Improvement, may have come the closest. "We grow more corn to grow more pork to grow more corn to grow more pork," he told me in his Des Moines office, "and so on."

I decided to start at the beginning, in Coon Rapids, where Agribusiness's creation story began, with seed entrepreneur Roswell Garst and the invention of hybrid corn. His granddaughter, Rachel Garst, sent me there, pulling out a map in her Des Moines living room and running her finger up the Middle Raccoon River to Coon Rapids and beyond. "The Dead Zone starts here," she told me.

"The Dead Zone Starts Here"

I wouldn't have known it when I checked in at the historic Garst farmhouse, which has been turned into a combination museum and bed-and-breakfast. It sits on the edge of the Garst Farm, which the family has transformed into the 5,000-acre Whiterock Conservancy, a beautiful multiuse trust where much of the land is actively farmed. They're still growing granddad's hybrid corn, but Whiterock, set up to demonstrate conservation farming and ranching, is an oasis in the corn-soy desert of west-central Iowa.

The next morning I walked one of the nature trails, past the original Garst barn where the last sheep were being herded into a nearby field to graze. Up the trail, sections of native prairie grass broke up corn and soybean fields to reduce soil erosion, improve water quality, and restore native habitat. Monarch butterfly–friendly milkweed, undisturbed by the Roundup herbicide decimating its feeding grounds across the state, glistened brightly in the low morning sun. Bald eagles nested in a nearby tree, a set of beehives hummed in a glade down the hill. Cows grazed on a high pasture, part of White-rock's rotational grazing plan. No feedlot here. A small harvester augured fresh corn into a waiting wagon, leaving the residue in the fields to return nutrients and organic matter to the soil.

I descended the path toward the farmhouse, wondering where exactly that dead zone began. I was seeing a lot of life. That's when I spotted the modern building off to my left: Garst Seed, the company Roswell Garst had founded.

Roswell Garst didn't invent hybrid corn. It's a little hard to say who did; Agribusiness would probably give that award to Henry A. Wallace, founder of Pioneer Hi-Bred Seed, because his was the first hybrid seed to go commercial on a large scale.

Charles Darwin is actually credited with discovering in 1850 that crossing two different varieties of corn could produce a stronger offspring. Michigan State University botanists, encouraged by Darwin, documented this process of "heterosis" in field experiments in 1881, an effect that came to be known as "hybrid vigor." Further work in the early twentieth century by George H. Shull and Edward M. East laid the groundwork for Henry A. Wallace, who began experimenting with the technique in a small plot in his backyard in Des Moines.[5] He started entering his hybrid corn in state yield competitions. It didn't hurt Wallace's research effort that his father had been named secretary of agriculture in 1921 and had put public money behind the hybrid corn research.[6]

At first, Wallace's corn failed to outperform the most popular farmer-saved varieties. But then in 1924 his Copper Cross won first prize, with a modest yield advantage. The victory, widely proclaimed—and self-proclaimed in his family's popular *Wallaces' Farmer* magazine—begat his first sales in 1925, which begat the Hi-Bred Seed Company in 1926. Commercial hybrid seed corn was born.

Wallace produced only a few bushels of Copper Cross in 1926 and sold it at a loss.[7] The yield gains were small and the price was prohibitively high. Before long, though, his company would become Pioneer Hi-Bred (and later DuPont Pioneer), which would for a time stand as the largest seed corn company in the world. But not without Roswell Garst.

Garst was a bit player in the genesis story, but he was a key acolyte in spreading the gospel. A serial college dropout, Garst had gone into real estate in Des Moines until the 1929 crash laid waste to his venture. He returned to Coon Rapids thinking he could partner with Wallace, producing seed on franchise. When Garst and a partner founded the Garst and Thomas Hi-Bred Corn Company in 1931, few farmers had even heard of this new-fangled seed, and few breeders were betting that those hidebound farmers would buy it.[8]

It was a tough sell, in part because farmers were not accustomed to paying for something they were used to getting for free; most saved their traditional open-pollinated seeds, selecting their best corn from the last harvest. It was a particularly tough sell in the 1930s. With the Depression, crop prices had fallen 60 percent. The promised yield gains didn't come close to covering the cost of the seeds.[9]

But the new seed companies loved the proprietary nature of the new hybrid corn, which had the valuable quality (to them) that kernels from the new crop could not be planted as seed without losing their hybrid vigor. With hybrids, farmers had to buy new seed every year, something the new seed prophets proclaimed to be a small and inevitable price to pay on the path to progress.

Critics, however, claimed the hybrids were more like drugs, the seed companies the dealers looking to hook users then make a killing off the addicted farmers. Some argued that the particular hybrid program developed by Wallace deliberately chose a form of crop improvement that would create just such addictions, that comparable yield gains could have been achieved with an investment in scientific breeding focused on improving the productivity of open-pollinated varieties.[10] Hindsight is 50/50, to butcher a phrase, but in this case that might be appropriate: we'll never know what kind of innovation we might have seen from such investment. We do know that improvement of open-pollinated populations has produced yields up to six times those of the pre–hybrid era averages, and that the yield potential and rate of progress of this method is comparable to that of hybrids.[11] We also know, with 20/20 hindsight, that such investment would not have come from the private sector, which would have seen little profit in improving seeds only to watch farmers replant them. Where's the market in that?

For the hybrid cause, Garst was a private-sector evangelist, traveling thousands of miles of country roads to promote the bountiful seeds. He famously would fertilize a large "N" in the middle of a field so farmers would see at harvest time a vigorous N of tall corn demonstrating the value of nitrogen fertilizer. As creative and persistent as Garst was, he probably would have failed if President Franklin D. Roosevelt hadn't tapped Henry A. Wallace, Garst's erstwhile collaborator, to be his agriculture secretary in 1933. The hybrid crusade, and the market for Wallace's own company's seeds, saw massive funding and promotion, with seed handouts boosting private-sector sales.

Those sales jumped when researchers discovered in their experimental fields a particularly vigorous hybrid that survived a devastating drought in 1934. In the resulting Dust Bowl of the 1930s, dry topsoil blew off overfarmed land. Sales of the new seeds soared with a second drought in 1936, in part because many farmers had seen their crops of open-pollinated corn wither—so they had no seed for the next season.[12]

To Henry A. Wallace's eternal credit, he saw the Dust Bowl for what it was: the rampant extension of unsustainable farming practices that created both overproduction and poverty, for farmers starved by low prices and for consumers too poor to buy food in the Depression. His supply management policies made the federal government the "CEO of agriculture" with the power to set minimum farm prices, enforce them by buying crops and storing them for sale when harvests were low, distribute surplus food to the poor, and limit production by giving farmers the incentives to take land out of agriculture. At one point fully 20 percent of cropland would be kept out of production through conservation or set-aside programs.[13] Wallace saw clearly that unregulated market forces would lead to booms and busts, and to the kind of soil erosion so dramatically evident in the Dust Bowl. With his seeds and their supporting technologies he was contributing to overproduction, but his federal policies limited the damage. By and large, those policies worked, well into the 1960s and even 1970s, with agribusiness always lobbying to eliminate those restrictions. After all, they wanted maximum production for sales of seeds, fertilizer, and machinery, and cheap prices for processing industries such as livestock.[14]

But the productivity campaign went full tilt. Public works projects dramatically expanded tile drainage, opening more land to cultivation. Synthetic fertilizer, to which the seeds were bred to respond, began to develop as a major input industry. Tractors came to replace horse-drawn equipment, allowing more densely planted corn. The seeds, bred for high yields in long uniform stands, had just the conditions for which they had been created. By 1940, nearly 100 percent of Iowa's corn farmers were buying and planting hybrids—from Garst and Thomas, Wallace's Pioneer Hi-Bred, or one of the other companies that had sprung up to capitalize on the new seed market.

Still, the yield gains were quite modest. By 1940, corn yields in Iowa had increased by about one-third, but according to field tests, the new seeds were responsible for only a fraction of those gains.[15] Crop research at the time put the yield advantage at just 9 percent. But Wallace, Garst, and the other seed prophets hailed hybrid genetics as the savior, while promoting its companion technologies—tractors, synthetic fertilizer, tile drainage. Whatever the actual cause, by 1960 no one could deny that there had been a productivity boom. Nationally, hybrids accounted for 96 percent of U.S. corn acres, and yields had more than doubled. By 2002, corn yields were more than five times their 1933 levels.[16] How could that not be a tribute to genetic improvement? None of the prophets bothered to explain how yields for many other key crops—wheat, cotton, oats, potatoes, barley—which had seen seed improvements but not new hybrid varieties, still experienced yield increases comparable to or better than those for hybrid corn.

In the end, it is impossible to apportion credit among the individual factors that contributed to the boom. Most credit plant breeding (not just hybridization) and mechanization, which allowed for closer rows and increased planting density. And perhaps most important, the growth in synthetic fertilizer, particularly after World War II when all that ammonium nitrate produced for munitions could instead provide the nitrogen needed to fertilize those densely planted rows of industrial crop production.[17] The Garsts were part of that innovation too, with Roswell's brother Jonathan helping develop and promote the conversion of munitions to fertilizer.

The seed prophets saw bountiful seed profits, as the transition to purchased seed took hold in the corn belt. With most of the United States awash in corn after World War II, Garst took his salesmanship abroad, most famously in his overtures to the post-Stalin Soviet Union. In Coon Rapids, Garst is now most famous for hosting Soviet premier Nikita Khrushchev and his entourage right on his Coon Rapids farm in 1959. Garst personally had made at least three trips to the USSR before that to promote the use of hybrid corn. He considered himself an agricultural innovator and a citizen diplomat. "He really thought he was going to feed the world," his granddaughter Rachel Garst told me, "and he thought that would bring world peace."

The memorabilia from this bold effort to thaw Cold War tensions filled the Garst farmhouse where I stayed. Grainy black-and-white photos covered the walls, a scrapbook collected the newspaper clips from the unusual visit, which put Coon Rapids on national and international maps. Bookshelves brimmed with chronicles of Garst and his exploits. Garst's official biographer, in his understated way, captured the man's unique zeal, describing him as "an evangelist in pursuit of his conviction that great national and world problems could be solved—or at least alleviated—by new technology—specifically, by new farming techniques."[18]

Solving Problems, and Creating Them

Roswell Garst's granddaughters are both ardent environmentalists, and Whiterock, with its working lands and cutting-edge environmental practices, is their proud family legacy. Rachel, who in

2008 organized a grand fiftieth-anniversary commemoration of the Khrushchev visit with his son and thirty Russian agribusiness leaders in attendance, saw Whiterock as a practical, visible challenge to industrial agriculture. Liz, her older sister, inherited the agricultural bank the family started. She lived in Coon Rapids and saw Whiterock's innovations as practices that could and should be widely adopted to clean up agriculture's environmental mess, demonstration projects for others to emulate. They certainly agreed that Iowa had a lot of problems and that the industrialized agriculture their grandfather had so effectively promoted was a big part of the reason.

Following the corn boom ignited by their grandfather's work, Iowa had gone all-in on soybeans, which farmers could grow in rotation with corn. Soybeans offered a high-protein oilseed for which agribusiness had created a booming demand in the state's concentrated animal feeding operations (CAFOs), mostly to feed hogs. By the time I was there, some 8,000 CAFOs dotted rural Iowa, many feeding 2,000 or more hogs at any one time and creating more manure than their owners knew what to do with.[19] Altogether, Iowa had about seven times as many hogs as people. Battles raged across Iowa over the siting of new hog facilities, as the stench often rendered communities unlivable, at least for those unfortunate enough to live downwind. The factory farms sold manure to grain farmers to spray on their fields, but atomizing the toxic goop created its own pollution problems. The pig farms spread across the state to be close to grain farms; it was too expensive to ship manure in these volumes long distances. Because the manure was oversupplied it tended to be over-applied, adding to the water problem. *E. coli* was one of factory farming's leading "externalities"—the sanitized economic term for the costs imposed on others by one's activities.

Excess manure from farmlands added to massive fertilizer runoff. With crops consuming less than half of the nitrogen fertilizer applied to them, the rest either went into the air as nitrous oxide, a major contributor to global warming, or flowed down the tile systems into streams and rivers. Excess phosphorus joined the toxic flotilla, unleashed by erosion not only from agricultural land but also from streambeds overfilled with water the land could no longer absorb.[20]

Iowa soils were absorbing even less water than they had ten years earlier. Somehow, agribusiness had managed to make this deplorable situation worse with the rise of corn ethanol, which consumed nearly 40 percent of the state's crop.[21] The ethanol boom, which began in earnest in 2005 thanks to government subsidies and incentives, had helped create the price spikes of 2007–2008, which came to be known as the global food crisis. Those high prices gave farmers an economic incentive to put even more land into corn. Some 500,000 acres came out of conservation land in Iowa as farmers put every inch into production, no matter how marginal or environmentally sensitive that land might be.[22] (Nationally, some 25 percent of conservation land had been brought back into production.) The planting surge didn't just add more agricultural chemicals to the overflowing toxic soup, it sped their delivery. Farmers plowed up the grasslands and buffers that had helped filter the water and reduce erosion near waterways.

To make matters worse, genetically modified crops accounted for nearly 100 percent of the corn and soybean acres in the state. Beyond the debates about the safety of eating GM foods, one impact since their introduction in 1996 was the large rise in herbicide use, specifically Monsanto's Roundup.[23] The crops were engineered to survive extensive spraying, which eliminated the need for farmers to weed their fields but massively increased the use of Roundup. That brought health concerns about glyphosate, the herbicide's active ingredient, and those concerns only grew when farmers started spraying Roundup on non-GMO crops such as wheat, an off-label use as a desiccant before harvest.[24]

Monarch butterflies and other wild species had their own concerns about Roundup. As the acreage grew, their habitat— especially the perennial milkweed in which they lay their eggs after their long migration from Mexico—was rapidly disappearing, as the weed-killer took out every unprotected plant in its path, including the perennials. Research had assuaged earlier fears that the cause of monarch declines was the other GM product, corn engineered to kill the European corn borer, which may have also been killing monarch butterfly larvae. But it now seemed likely that the culprit was Roundup's habitat-destroying domination of the countryside.[25]

The Working Lands of Whiterock

Liz Garst and her partner Darwin Pierce offered hope grounded in the hard, cold realities of Iowa's landscape. For them, it was all about changing the economic incentives, internalizing the environmental costs of the harmful practices.

"Farmers don't know their soil is eroding," Garst explained in her living room, which looks out on Whiterock land. She explained that Iowa had lost 50 percent of its topsoil and 50 percent of the organic content in its soils. "If you can show them how much topsoil they are losing, they will take steps to care for the soil."

Harvesting corn from the working lands of Whiterock Conservancy, the former Roswell Garst farm in Coon Rapids, Iowa. *Timothy A. Wise*

She was clearly proud of Whiterock, but she is a hard-nosed realist, just as one might expect from a banker. Iowa has the least public land of any state in the country, she told me, and not a single national park. "We need private landowners to become environmental stewards. Right now, there are no incentives to make people truly value soil and water. There is no cost to farmers of water pollution."

She was critical of the state's voluntary Nutrient Reduction Strategy, which was controversial because it set relatively low targets for getting farmers to dump fewer chemicals and it left compliance voluntary. Liz said it was having some impact, making farmers realize they can plant cover crops in the off-season to reduce erosion and runoff. But she clearly thinks more regulation is needed and current economic incentives are perverse. She told the story of Whiterock receiving a donation of a 70-acre farm on which the land was terraced, to slow erosion and allow water to filter into the soil. When the appraiser came to value the land, for tax purposes, he was impressed with the terraces, saying he'd found very little erosion. "He then lowered the appraisal," Garst reported, "because the terraces made the land less 'farmable,'" less amenable to highly mechanized agriculture.

Pierce was more openly critical of prevailing farming practices. He is a proponent of "high-density grazing," carefully managing livestock to restore grasslands, as they are doing at Whiterock. "Twenty-two percent of pasture has been lost in Iowa since 2002," he told me, plowed under for corn.

Liz Garst thought technology could solve at least some of the problems it had created. She was particularly encouraged by "precision agriculture," the use of new technologies to better manage the land. She sent me to the other side of town to see George Johnston. She wanted Johnston to show me the future, which she assured me was better than I expected.

Johnston welcomed me outside the warehouse that holds his small office, introducing me to his son, who he said was the college-educated brain behind the GPS and sensing technologies that closely map the land for the highest returns. What could that technology do? It boggled the mind. The sensors allow him to closely align his seed and input use with the varying types of soil and water conditions on different parts of his farm.

He mocked up a farm map for me, drawing curving lines through the square 600-acre plot, one of several rental plots that he farms, leaving it looking like a jigsaw puzzle. These are his soil types, and each needs different treatment for maximum yield. He can vary planting density—a key determinant of yield. He can adapt the levels of fertilizers and pesticides depending on the precise needs of the given plot, and he had readings of each sector's needs from the sensors in the new combines. Johnston told me each GPS-guided system costs $25,000, and he needed one for every one of his many machines. They can guide a planter down straight mile-long rows, amending the soil as they plant the seeds.[26]

How does this help the environment? "We're going to get higher yields with fewer inputs," he said matter-of-factly. The soil analysis had him planting cover crops more than he used to, and he left residue from corn and soybeans on the fields. Both are practices long encouraged by environmentalists to slow erosion and build organic content, but they are scarcely adopted by farmers. Johnston saw the soil improve.

Johnston pointed back to his jigsaw puzzle of a farm map, identifying one small area. "We realized that these 27 acres are not profitable to farm." The sensors allowed him to closely calculate the costs and returns on his different sections of the farm, and some were losers. He was leaving those fallow, letting some go to wetland, and planting some in prairie grass, driving his huge combines around those acres. That was about 5 percent of this particular farm, and it made perfect business sense to him to pull those out of production. He ticked off the seed and input savings, which he had ready at hand. He was not so quick to quantify the environmental benefits, but he was aware there were some—wildlife habitat, wetland preservation, erosion reduction, and, yes, reduced water pollution. But that's not why he was doing it. This made sense even in the short-term view of a businessman.

Unfortunately, so does over-applying fertilizer. It's not all that expensive, and it is seen as "yield insurance" by farmers: they never want to lose yield, so putting on too much is entirely rational. Put more on high-yield land to maximize the high output, put more on low-yield land to coax more from the poor soils. So far, there is very little evidence to suggest that precision farming has lowered the environmental impacts of corn-soy agriculture. The input usage just keeps climbing in the U.S. farming business.[27]

Agriculture Without Farmers

Johnston, though, is less a businessman than a full-service contract farmer, and he is one of the reasons people in rural Iowa worry about the future of farming. The real businessmen are not farmers; in fact, they know next to nothing about farming. They are investors, and when the bubble burst in 2007 on all their intangible financial assets many of those investors turned to agricultural commodities and farmland. With the average age of the U.S. farmer nearing sixty and with few heirs in sight—at least few who want to farm—literally millions of acres of farmland are expected to change hands.[28] Land values skyrocketed with the speculative frenzy and the high crop prices. And it provoked two worrying trends. First, many of those heirs don't want to farm but they want to keep the land as an investment, and for sentimental value too. So they rent it out, maybe to a neighboring farmer, maybe to a high-tech contract farmer like Johnston.

The other group looking for people to farm for them is the city slickers who've come in as speculators, including equity funds looking for a fast buck.[29] I can't say I get it. The farmland prices sure look and smell like a bubble waiting to burst, and the returns are terrible, and unlikely to be made better by smart-ass city managers. There's no one to lay off; they're almost all gone already. Until the drones start managing the GPS-guided machinery through the fields, it looks like low margins and high risk as far as the eye can see. And that's a long way on the corn-soy fields of northern Iowa. But for those absentee landlords, Johnston represents a new kind of ultra-efficient "custom farmer" who can manage vast tracts of farmland for a fee. Rental markets are almost as inflated as land markets, and in Iowa cash rents were running more than $250 per acre. For the owner of the 600 acres Johnston showed me, that's a tidy $150,000. For farm kids who inherit land, that rental income is their retirement fund. For the city-slicker speculators, it's the income on an asset that they are betting will keep appreciating. In either case, the owners need a custom farmer like George Johnston to pay the rent.

For farmers like George Naylor, that's a big problem. I'd first met George, a firebrand in the finest tradition of the prairie populists, when he was president of the National Family Farm Coalition, a DC-based advocacy group that tries to counter the overwhelming pro-agribusiness lobbying by the American Farm Bureau and other faux-farmer groups. I told George when I saw him at his farm in Churdan that I'd just been to Johnston's farm because Liz Garst told me, "Everybody talks to George Naylor, go see a modern precision farmer."

"I guess that makes me an 'imprecision farmer,'" he laughed. "It feels that way sometimes, with all the changes around here." We went to dinner at 209 Main, the local burger joint in nearby Paton, with his wife, Patti Edmundson, and her brother Jerry. They persuaded me to get the Tool Bar burger, named after the world's largest planter from John Deere, which spanned 120 feet. Naturally—or unnaturally—the huge burger was half beef and half bacon.

George and Patti farm 460 acres in Greene County; Jerry's got 3,000, most of it rented. All three nodded ruefully as I told them about my visit with the hyper-efficient custom farmer. "They're just letting the non-farmers control all the land," Jerry said. In their sixties, they could all remember much better times, before agribusiness drove many farmers out of agriculture. "We had 150 acres," said George of his youth, "and it was plenty. No one worked Sundays, Mom didn't have to work off the farm."

They could see their neighbors' houses, they rode the bus with the other kids to the school in the nearest town, a town that had banks and seed dealers and hardware stores and groceries. "It was

Iowa farmer George Naylor displays his non-GMO corn.
Timothy A. Wise

a decent living," added Patti, who grew up in nearby Guthrie County. "No one got rich, no one was poor. We had communities and neighbors." Now Greene County has only two schools, down from seven in their day.

"We all had livestock to sell," added George, "not like now." Jerry said his grandparents' mantra was, " 'Don't let anything leave the farm unless it walks off.' We knew that everything that was sold from the farm was embodied nutrients." Jerry was particularly concerned about the huge environmental impacts of the current farming model. He should know, he was previously with the state department of natural resources. "There are two places you just can't compromise," he said. "One is the environment, the other is food."

Compromise would be a kind word for what's happened in Iowa to both food and the environment. It looked more like an agribusiness offer neither food nor the environment could refuse.

Neither could local farmers. As Liz Garst had said, the economic incentives mostly go the wrong way. The high-yield seeds, inputs, and machinery allowed one farmer to cover more acres. Prices were usually low, so margins were low, and the only way to stay in business was to "get big or get out," as U.S. secretary of agriculture Earl Butz had said back in the 1970s. A lot of them got out, and their rural communities were disappearing around them. Greene County had lost 44 percent of its residents since 1940, the biggest drop coming in the 1980s.

A Hard Row to Hoe

George Naylor was not one to quietly accept offers he wasn't supposed to refuse. As Patti explained at their farmhouse the next morning, she was helping him diversify. They showed me an apple orchard with an impressive forty different varieties. Patches of native prairie, their gift to the monarch butterflies and other native species, grew around the house, which George's grandfather had built in 1919 and which George had inherited along with the land.

Still, George mainly grew corn and soybeans; there was no market for anything else. But he refused to grow GM crops. That was partly why filmmakers Trace Sheehan and Scott Kennedy were there that day to interview George for a film they were making on the polarized debate over GM food. George told them as the camera rolled that he didn't necessarily believe GM crops were poison (their ears pricked up). He just didn't believe in extending corporate control, on the farm and in the food system.

The filmmakers clearly wanted to get George to say more about how he thought GM foods were safe to eat. They tried to get me in on the act too, interviewing the two of us together. When we found out the film was commissioned by a pro-industry group and Shee-han and Kennedy were on a mission to find GM critics who would say something nice about GMOs, George and I sniffed the rat and George sent them on their way.[30]

George tucked me into his 1988 tractor to harvest some of those premium non-GM soybeans. No GPS guided the tractor, just George, his own HPS—human positioning system. Over the din of the combine, George explained that he got the combine used for $12,000 and paid $75,000 for his tractor, also used. It was the most he'd ever paid for anything. He said the main way he stayed in busi-ness with only 460 acres (a small farm by current Iowa standards) was that he owned most of that land, it was paid off, and he didn't jump at the next shiny thing John Deere had in its showroom. The newest equipment can cost up to $1 million, which a farmer can get with a five-year loan. As long as crop prices were high and interest rates were low, as they had been until recently, this seemed to make sense for the bigger farmers. In 2014, the situation reminded George of the 1980s farm crisis. Crop prices were starting to crash; corn fetched barely half its price of two years earlier. And interest rates were threatening to climb.[31] That could set off a whole new wave of debt problems and farm foreclosures, particularly if the land bubble burst and farmers couldn't cover their rents. While George's combine doesn't get many compliments, he usually gets the last laugh.

In a good year, George said he made between $75,000 and $100,000; prices had been high in recent years, and he'd done well. Still, that's only $150 to $200 per acre, a piss-poor return on invest-ment. In more typical years, George said he'd clear just $25,000 to $50,000. He was lucky: he'd inherited 320 acres, free and clear. "Personally," said George, "I have no idea why an investor would buy land at this level."

Over dinner around George and Patti's small kitchen table, I asked George what it felt like to be a millionaire. He laughed as I did the calculations out loud. Just in the last fifteen years, his land had soared from about $2,500 per acre to about $10,000. So the 380 acres he owns outright were worth nearly $4 million. "You're rich!"

I announced. "Yeah," he said, "too bad I don't have any money."
He would, if he sold the farm, but no young farmer could afford
to buy it. His two sons stood to inherit the farm from George, but
he wasn't sure if either was interested in farming. Maybe they'd
just hang on to it and hire George Johnston's whiz-kid of a son to
custom farm their inheritance. Or they'd sell. "Investors with no
connection to the land or the community are showing up at farm
auctions and paying multimillion-dollar prices," George said with
disgust, "in cash." The big guys were set to keep getting bigger, and
everyone else was going to get poorer.

When More Is Less

George wasn't just feeling sorry for himself; the research backed
him up. According to a detailed study by Food and Water Watch,
"The Economic Cost of Food Monopolies," agribusiness expansion and consolidation, with fewer companies providing inputs and
buying the bulk commodities farmers produce, were sucking the
wealth from Iowa. Researchers looked at the recent expansion of
factory hog farms in the state, which had come in the last three
decades, as George's pigs walked off his farm for the last time into
the new factory farms.

From 1982 to 2007, the number of farms selling hogs declined
from 49,000 to 8,700, most of them housing 2,000-plus hogs, often
owned outright by a shrinking number of meatpackers. Nationally,
the top four packers in 2007 controlled 65 percent of all purchases,
up from 36 percent twenty-five years earlier. That gave them the
kind of market power that let them push down prices paid to hog
farmers while keeping consumer prices high. In Iowa, the top four
packers—Smithfield, Tyson, JBS, and Cargill—controlled 90 percent of the market.[32]

Over that twenty-five-year period, the number of hogs produced
in Iowa doubled, and agribusiness hailed the efficiency of large-
scale production. Meanwhile, hog prices fell by more than half,
meaning that altogether Iowa hog farmers were earning 12 percent

less than they were in 1982 for producing more than twice as much. But think of all those packinghouse jobs, says agribusiness. Over the same period, the number of jobs barely increased, with automation eliminating almost as many jobs as the new demand created. And the same monopoly power that drove down prices did the same to wages. Overall worker earnings, adjusted for inflation, declined 16 percent over the twenty-five-year period. Researchers showed that in recent years the more hog production a county added, the lower residents' personal income would be; on average, for every 1,000 additional hogs a county produced personal income was reduced by $592 per year.

It would be one thing if consumers saw lower food costs thanks to our great efficiency. But according to the U.S. Department of Agriculture, even though the cost of production went down between 1992 and 2004, pork prices actually rose. So why, exactly, are we producing so much more pork? Demand in the United States has been flat for years. But we have to feed the world, cries agribusiness. As if the hungry in the world can afford imported pork. "We are producing pork for China's middle class," said Mark Rasmussen, of the Leopold Center for Sustainable Agriculture. "Why does the U.S. have to incur environmental damage to produce China's pork?"

"Growth in the consolidated hog industry became a mechanism for draining value from, and not adding to, Iowa's rural economies," concludes the Food and Water Watch report.

Concentrated economic power is what sucks value from a community, and the meatpacking industry has not been shy about exercising that power. Iowans, for their part, haven't been shy about demanding an end to such classic abuses of monopoly power. Just four years before my 2014 Iowa visit, the Obama administration's Department of Justice seemed ready to do something about it. On March 12, 2010, Obama's chief trust-buster came to Ankeny, just ten miles north of Des Moines, and 800 Iowans packed a small community college to demand action to ensure fair competition and relief from monopoly power. It was one of five hearings convened around farm country. By all accounts, the outpouring was overwhelming. But the economic power that comes with monopoly control also brings political power. Agribusiness lobbyists swarmed the halls of Congress, and Obama's incipient antitrust effort was quietly shelved.[33]

Back in Des Moines, Hugh Espey, at Iowa Citizens for Community Improvement, made clear that the state's 8,000 hog farms were draining not just economic value; they were literally draining pollutants into the local water. Some of them come from the lagoons of waste that accumulate under each CAFO. Air pollution from the stench has made some areas unlivable, and the pits are supposed to be sealed, but leaks occur all too often. The toxic stew flows off the surface or down those clever drainage tiles into the water, sometimes carrying E. coli to Des Moines. Espey told me the state's official list of "impaired waterways" had grown from 200 to more than 750.[34]

By this point in my research, I'd started asking people to rank the causes of Des Moines's water crisis. Everyone had their own rankings, but most had the same basic list—fertilizer runoff, hog manure, tile drainage, poor soil conservation practices on the farm. Espey's was longer than most, based on his organization's history working on a wide range of campaigns. His included "corporate concentration," reflecting the organization's willingness to confront agribusiness in a way few in the state would.

Espey added one cause no one else had mentioned: ethanol. I'd been surprised not to hear it until then. After all, water pollution had gotten much worse in the last ten years, and that was the period when corn ethanol grew sixfold in a few devastatingly short years.[35] Iowa is one of the nation's largest producers of ethanol, and the industry was consuming some 40 percent of all that hybrid and GM corn from Iowa's farmers, a huge increase from just ten years earlier. It wasn't that the refineries directly polluted the water. The increased demand for corn did, indirectly.

Espey explained how the surge in demand encouraged two trends detrimental to Iowa's waterways. First, it pushed farmers to plant more corn on the land they had. Second, much of that was marginal land—grasslands, wetlands, conservation land. Some of the state's most sensitive land came out of conservation and into corn. Espey told me this was way worse even than it sounded. The new corn land was of course drenched in fertilizer, and the runoff didn't have far to run, since many of those sensitive lands were close to waterways. Worse still, the deep roots of those uprooted perennial prairie grasses had filtered the runoff coming from the contiguous farms. No more.

His organization was campaigning to slow factory-farm expansion and fight for clean water. With so many culprits working in such toxic harmony, he knew his was just a finger in the dike that barely contained agribusiness's overflowing externalities.

Bill Howell, at POET's Coon Rapids ethanol refinery, didn't see ethanol as a cause of anything but progress. "Everything about it is good," he gushed to me before I got a quick factory tour. He blamed the price spikes on speculation in the oil industry, which ethanol could reduce by cutting demand for oil. We shouldn't limit ethanol to just 10 percent of gasoline mixes but should push ahead to so-called E-15. "NASCAR is using E-15," he told me, assuming I'd agree that specially designed race cars would be a good indicator of what would work well in the U.S. car and truck fleet. He was bullish on ethanol exports. "The international market is a fantastic playground right now." He was optimistic about next-generation biofuels, and POET had the most advanced cellulosic ethanol facility in the state, up the road in Emmetsberg. They were using corn stover as the feed stock, and Howell saw no problem with taking those nutrients off the farm for the higher purpose of ethanol, oblivious to the fact that doing so reduced the intended environmental benefit of this "advanced biofuel."

"That's just doubling down on the current soil problem," Leopold's Rasmussen would say later when I told him about our conversation. I pointed out to Howell that many were now calling for reductions in U.S. federal subsidies and mandates because of ethanol's contributions to the food price spikes. Not so fast, Howell told me. Prices are low now. Take away ethanol and corn markets would crash. "Ethanol is now stabilizing agricultural markets."

Kind of like a fix of heroin "stabilizes" an addict. But in a sad way, he wasn't wrong. Iowa was pretty well addicted to corn, hogs, and ethanol. Pulling the plug on any of them would no doubt trigger devastating withdrawal symptoms. Take away 40 percent of the demand for Iowa corn, and a third of national demand, and we would no doubt see a wave of farm bankruptcies that would make the 1980s farm crisis look like a mild recession.

"It Will Take a Crisis"

Linda Kinman was all about fixing problems. She was a public policy analyst for the Des Moines Water Works, the last line of the city's defense against farm-generated water pollution and an unlikely radical in the fight for the future of Iowa.[36] The Water Works runs the world's largest de-nitrification plant, a water treatment facility on the Des Moines River, right where the Raccoon River comes in from Coon Rapids. It uses an ion exchange process to remove nitrates and other pollutants from the water so the city's residents can drink it. She and her boss, Bill Stowe, were also trying to remove the pollutants at the source, or significantly reduce them, and that has made them a target for farmers and agribusiness groups that don't want to be blamed for Iowa's deteriorating water quality. They blame golf courses and suburban homeowners for over-fertilizing their grass.

"The argument that the cause is anything but agriculture is ridiculous," Kinman said firmly. "Eighty-five percent of our watershed is agricultural land use. For us to say we need to work anywhere else but the agriculture community is crazy." You couldn't miss the urgency in her voice, and the frustration. The year before, nitrate levels hit 9.6 parts per million (ppm), just below the Environmental Protection Agency's limit of 10 ppm. "This year, most days in September we were over the 10 ppm limit." Climate change is making it worse. "We now get more frequent events of intense rainfall, so it has a tendency to flush the system."

Kinman goes out of her way not to vilify farmers, blaming

absentee landowners who won't invest in conservation practices. That is a growing problem. She noted that more than half of Iowa's farmland is now rented. And she blamed the factory farms, not just for water pollution from their manure but for air pollution. "Those guys deny they create air quality issues," she laughs. "They say their shit doesn't stink."

The Water Works leaders are a lightning rod for criticism because they have been uncompromising and aggressive in confronting the polluters. They filed a lawsuit against three upstream drainage districts accusing them of polluting the water that Des Moines was paying to clean up. Such contamination is considered "non-point-source" pollution, on the specious argument—from guess who?—that the farmers don't live on the waterways so the pollution has no specific source. But those handy tiles run right under their land, draining water from the topsoil through underground perforated pipes, creating the streams of polluted water that end up in the river. Kinman said the Water Works had opposed the 2013 Nutrient Reduction Strategy. She said the science was good (even if it fails to identify the pollution as "point-source"), admitting that agriculture was contributing to the problem, but it had no specific goals, no timeline to meet them, and it was voluntary. "We opposed it because there was not enough urgency in it." Proponents claimed it would reduce nitrate and phosphate pollution by 45 percent, but Kinman thought there was little chance it could do anything close to that.

The solutions, she says, are simple, at least on paper. Improve soil quality to keep the rain where it lands, adopt more diverse cropping systems to reduce the nutrient load, which comes heavily from corn, and put in cover crops and plants with deeper roots to cut the amount of nutrient runoff and leaching. Then there are the less simple solutions. "We never talk about the other entities that should be part of the solution," she told me, "the Monsantos, the DuPonts, the ones who are part of the problem. Why aren't they providing funding where we need it?" She knew the answer to that one. Agribusiness was fighting every move to better regulate water quality. Can things change?

"It will take a crisis, like when the rivers caught fire in Ohio," she said. "You need that to wake people up. When was the last time you saw a case of blue baby syndrome?" You mean when babies turn blue from low oxygen levels in water contaminated with nitrates? "That could happen here."[37]

"We make cities treat their waste," said Marian Gelb, of the Iowa Natural Heritage Foundation, at a Des Moines coffee shop. "Why don't we make CAFOs treat their waste?" Duane Sands, longtime agricultural policy adviser for the organization and our companion for coffee, said what Gelb already knew. "The concentration of land and wealth is a huge issue, and it's a food security issue. Agribusiness can write ten-to-twenty-thousand-dollar campaign contributions. It's just a cost of doing business."

Mark Langgin, longtime environmental campaigner, agreed. "Farm Bureau and agribusiness are the center of right-wing power in the state," he explained. The Farm Bureau, which presents itself as representing farmers, "is really a property rights organization." The membership they claim counts their commercial insurance business, which includes property, liability, and some crop insurance. That business is huge, and it makes them more a financial firm than a farmer organization.

It is difficult to overstate the power the Farm Bureau holds in Iowa, and its willingness to use it. When I started my research one Iowan told me, requesting anonymity, "Good luck getting anyone to talk to you on the record. Everyone's afraid of the Farm Bureau." With the Iowa Pork Producers Association, the Farm Bureau stifles meaningful action on factory farms and water pollution, and on a host of other agricultural policy issues. Someone I spoke with lost a position on a local corporation's board after advocating prudence in the siting of new hog farms.

Another Iowa Is Possible

Everyone told me I had to talk to agricultural ecologist Matt Liebman, at Iowa State University. They told me he was showing what could be done to change, if not reverse, the state's intense path dependence on agribusiness-driven economic development. After my journeys through the corn-soy-pork-ethanol industrial complex, I had the feeling that path had already been paved over, in corn. I was starting to make sense of that strange path, but I had no clue how anyone was going to shift the state's dependence. According to an old saying, "If we don't change direction, we'll get where we're going." Iowa had gotten there and now seemed committed to following agribusiness's lead into an unsustainable future.

Liebman was indeed a breath of fresh air. He's been working with Iowa farmers for twenty years, and he's clear-eyed about the barriers to change. "We have several decades of data to show that corn and soy leak a lot of nutrients. No mystery there," he told me in his office. With a million miles of tiles, the nutrient-laden water gets where it's going, faster than ever with climate change. "There have been three 500-year floods in the time I've lived in Ames.

"But you're never going to get anywhere if you tell farmers that they aren't good farmers, that they're polluting the water and

Iowa State agricultural ecologist Matt Liebman at the university's Marsden Farm.
Timothy A. Wise

poisoning the land," he went on, clearly frustrated with the way most environmentalists deal with agriculture. "Most every farmer thinks he or she is working to be a good steward of the land. But if you tell them that you can increase the value of their farming operation while simultaneously increasing the value of their land by slowing erosion and restoring soils, you're telling them how to leave their kids a much more valuable asset."

He's equally frustrated with the anti-technology bias of most foodies and environmentalists. "Ignoring the potential contributions of technology is stupid. Blatant acceptance of technology is a poor idea, but so is blanket rejection." He was encouraged by the potential for precision agriculture to reduce input use and put unproductive land back into prairie or wetlands. One of the most successful projects he's involved in, Science-based Trials of Row-crops Integrated with Prairie Strips (STRIPS), works with farmers to do just that. Results of the project have shown that planting as little as 10 percent of farmed land in carefully positioned native prairie can keep the water and soil on the farm, improving soil fertility while cutting water pollution by up to 95 percent.

Liebman has little patience for biotechnology advocates, but perhaps less for its critics. Herbicides are convenient (not necessary) for no-till agriculture, which is good for mitigating climate change and reducing soil erosion. But glyphosate overuse is not. "We could control weeds with massively lower chemical use, which would make the resistance issues much less challenging." Instead, he says, agribusiness is bringing in additional herbicides, like dicamba and 2,4-D, to deal with the weed resistance to glyphosate, the active ingredient in Monsanto's Roundup herbicide.[38] "Why do we think that this will solve the problem? It's stupid for environmental quality and stupid for dealing with resistance."

"I'm not saying this technology is evil, I'm saying there are ways to use less of it." Like many true agricultural scientists, Liebman was frustrated with everyone's obsession with GMOs, industry and critics alike. He clearly saw it as an unfortunate but passing phase. "We are living in the rubble of the Roundup age," he told me, one of the most depressingly optimistic things I'd heard in Iowa. He seemed to think the Roundup age had run its destructive course, but it left us living in rubble.

We climbed in his car and headed to his experimental fields. He had a lot going on. One project showed that prairie grasses could produce as much energy in the form of advanced cellulosic ethanol as harvested corn stover. But because stover was a byproduct of corn, it was more profitable, so his prairie grasses were not likely to get much uptake—not yet, anyway.

His longest-running project was the one I'd read about, known as the Marsden Farm Study. Over eight years, he had shown that adding a third rotation of oats or another feed crop, with cover cropping, to the usual corn-soy rotation could yield huge benefits. A fourth rotation added alfalfa for hay, and animals to eat it and contribute their manure. He walked me through it, literally. The alfalfa had deep roots, unlike corn and soy, so it stabilized the soil while replenishing nitrogen far more effectively than soybeans did. He'd shown that with the added rotation, herbicide use went down 88 percent, fertilizer use dropped 85 percent, and water pollution dropped to near zero. What about productivity? He said there was no loss in yields. In fact, corn yields went up 4 percent while soybean yields went up an impressive 9 percent because it turned out the added rotation reduced the incidence of a fungal disease known as "sudden death syndrome." And profitability? Input costs dropped and the more diverse farming system was as profitable as the traditional plot. And it got more profitable over time as soil quality kept improving.[39]

What a finding! This was the proverbial win-win solution, disproportionate environmental benefits from relatively small changes to farming practices, with huge upsides for farmers in terms of soil quality and rising productivity. No onerous regulations, no government subsidies needed. It had been four years since his paper was published. How many farmers in Iowa are doing this now, I asked, reveling in the hope I hadn't found anywhere else in Iowa.

"Relatively few," Liebman said with a sigh, bringing me back down to Iowa's eroded earth. "There would be some losers if farmers adopted the three-crop or four-crop rotation systems." The losers were mostly a who's who of the state's agribusinesses. Fertilizer dealers and manufacturers would lose 85 percent of their market. Pesticide companies would lose sales, because fewer chemicals would be needed to control pests. Seed company sales would fall because they'd see one-third of the land go out of corn and soybeans. (Yes, they could sell alfalfa seeds, but the patents aren't as lucrative, and alfalfa is a multiyear crop that only needs to be planted once.) Grain dealers would see a decline in total corn and soybean volumes. Corn and soybean prices might go up slightly with the reduction in supply, which would mean higher prices for industrial livestock producers on their main cost of production, feed. Finally, ethanol refineries might have to pay a few more cents per bushel for their corn.

"Basically," mused Liebman, "I couldn't have devised an innovation that offended more of Iowa's powerful agribusinesses." Even though the study wasn't actively suppressed, as had been rumored, he told me the university and the USDA "ignore it."

George Naylor told me to "ask Matt what I'm supposed to do with the alfalfa." Liebman admitted that there is currently no available market, but there could be. Hay from alfalfa is good fodder for cattle, according to Liebman. But Iowa innovated its way right out of cattle, and it has relatively few decentralized, medium-scale feed lots to take up the hay. It would be good for Iowan agriculture if it did. Liebman noted that alfalfa could be used to produce cellulosic ethanol, but that would hit corn agribusinesses doubly hard, replacing demand for corn ethanol and for cellulose-derived fuel from corn stover. Still, a study by the Union of Concerned Scientists documented how and where added rotations could be profitable for farmers.[40]

I felt for Liebman. I asked what it meant for his research. "I'm still interested in rotation work," he told me. "It's important. But it's been difficult to have that conversation here." He remained buoyed by the responses he'd gotten to the paper, even if it didn't result in much change. "People wanted to hear that another world *is* possible. We can do this if we want to. It's not that we can't, it's that we won't."

Another World Is Possible

Liebman's words would echo in my head as I traveled the world trying to understand what was keeping us from doing what we need to
do, to grow more and better food in a way that doesn't destroy the
natural resources that we need. Not just to eat today but to eat tomorrow, when a changing climate will present far more challenges
than we face now.

I found it hard to leave Iowa with much hope for the state, despite
the tireless and creative efforts of its reformers. They weren't having
much luck when I was there in 2014, and agribusiness had struck
down reform after reform since then. Iowa's devolution continued.

That case the Water Works brought against agricultural polluters upstream? Dismissed by a court dominated by agribusiness interests.[41] Meanwhile, the dead zone in the Gulf of Mexico by 2017
had grown to nearly twice its size in 2014.[42] The voluntary Nutrient Reduction Strategy was not meeting its weak targets, and new
water-quality legislation has been slammed for making taxpayers,
not agricultural polluters, foot the bill.

The federal government continues to back corn ethanol, maintaining the Renewal Fuel Standard that mandates the use of ethanol in gasoline despite its questionable impacts on greenhouse gas
emissions. The Trump administration is leaning toward raising the
blending limit to 15 percent, which could trigger a new wave of corn
price spikes. The 2018 U.S. Farm Bill is under negotiation, with
no hint that Congress will consider any of the obvious failings of
the current legislation. The cornification of the world may get even
worse, as Monsanto is working on a short-season corn variety they
claim will allow corn to be profitably grown in parts of Canada and
other regions that up to now have been too far north for the crop.

Climate denial sits in the White House, meaning that farmers in
Iowa, other parts of the United States, and especially overseas will
see worsening heat, drought, and extreme storms, making it hard
to eat today and harder to eat tomorrow. A Republican Congress
is rolling back financial regulations that have limited dangerous

speculation on commodity markets. We've seen no serious anti-trust action despite the clear demand for protection. Meanwhile, a new wave of agribusiness megamergers—Bayer-Monsanto, Dow-DuPont, ChemChina-Syngenta, Smithfield–China's WH Group, Brazil's JBS–Cargill's pork, Archer Daniels Midland–Bunge—threatens to further narrow choices for both farmers and consumers, giving agribusiness even more market power. Remember Garst Seed? Bought by Syngenta in 2004, the Garst brand was dropped in 2014 and the seed facility next to the Garst farm was sold and closed just after I was there in 2014.[43]

To add local insult to injury, the Iowa legislature voted to cut all public funding for the Leopold Center, leaving the future unclear for one of the few consistent voices of agricultural sanity in the state. Leopold's project budget had long been considered untouchable, funded by a small and sensible surcharge on fertilizer and pesticide registration fees.

I thought back to Roswell Garst and his seemingly well-intentioned effort to feed the world with hybrid corn. There certainly was a lot of hybrid corn in the world, but it was often difficult to see how it was doing anything to feed the hungry today. It was surely undermining the resource base that could allow all of us to eat tomorrow.

Agribusiness certainly ruled supreme in Iowa. In the temple of the World Food Prize Hall of Laureates, they could even claim the blessing of God Himself, if they ignored the parts of the message they didn't like. They did.

At the 2013 prize ceremony that awarded three biotech scientists the World Food Prize, one of the featured speakers was Cardinal Peter Turkson. The Ghanaian had come from the Vatican to proclaim that, after much theological study, the Church had concluded that genetic modification did not go against Church doctrine. And the assembled disciples of Agribusiness, gathered for a luncheon remarkably and tastelessly constructed from GM soybeans, did cheer the news. Few seemed to take in the cardinal's further proclamations regarding those small matters of feeding the hungry, and doing so sustainably.

Turkson reminded the faithful that "the problem is not, of course, an overall scarcity of food," it is, "in large part, a problem of distribution of food, or access to it." The disciples shifted uncomfortably in their chairs, picking at the strange soy-custard dessert. "New technologies are promoted with the claim of making more food available for everyone," Turkson went on. "But that is not the whole picture. In reality, the innovations are so designed or implemented as to benefit relatively few interests that are already well-off." I looked around; many had put down their dessert spoons. "Along the way, many small producers will inevitably be excluded and/or moved off their land." Thank you, I said to myself, as we all took sips of our de-nitrified water.

"It should not surprise us if some populations reject certain innovations, not because they are faulty or perceived as such, but because the manner of their delivery entails unbearable costs to those who are supposed to benefit from them," Turkson went on, gently but firmly admonishing Agribusiness and its disciples for bringing down their wrath on those who would resist GM or other technologies. "It is not they who are missing the point." Offering a set of ethical guidelines, the cardinal admonished the flock not to be driven solely by "the motive of profit" and to promote transparency to "guarantee producers' and consumers' right to information" by labeling GM products.

He wasn't through. "Biodiversity is humanity's patrimony. It needs to be protected, indeed privileged. The development of new types should not require, or lead to, the disappearance of traditional species." He concluded with a call to "apply the principle of precaution or prudence by taking every reasonable measure of caution beforehand, to avoid the risk of damaging human health or the environment."

The applause was polite. Agribusiness's anointed representative, Kenneth Quinn, guardian of Norman Borlaug's flame from his pulpit at the World Food Prize Hall of Laureates, thanked the cardinal. Then he went right back to feeding the world the only way he knew how, with more sacrifices at the altar of Agribusiness.

6

Fueling the Food Crisis

I arrived in Rome in October 2013 hopeful that I would be a small part of a historic step in addressing one of the most important drivers of the 2007–2008 food crisis. The recent and rapid expansion of biofuel production, particularly of corn-based ethanol that helped extend corn's dominion over Iowa, was on the agenda of the Committee on World Food Security (CFS), the UN body tasked with coordinating international efforts to monitor and address the crisis. A commissioned report from the CFS's High Level Panel of Experts (HLPE) had reviewed the literature, documenting the various ways biofuel production had contributed to the recent food price spikes by diverting crops and land from food production to the generation of liquid fuels for cars, trucks, and other vehicles. They confirmed that 20 to 40 percent of those devastating food price increases could be attributed to biofuel expansion, particularly in the United States and Europe.[1] Food prices were still high, with the third price spike in the last six years threatening millions more poor people with extreme hunger. The time was ripe for policy action, with a range of proposals on the table to reduce biofuel pressures on food and land by reducing government incentives that subsidized biofuels or mandated their use.

No such luck. As usual, the U.S. delegation led the denial of reality. After the presentation of the expert report, U.S. ambassador

to the FAO David Lane publicly questioned the quality of the
work, suggesting that biofuels were just one of many factors contributing to the price spikes. In private I'd gotten an economist
with the U.S. delegation to admit that it was indeed one of the
more significant factors, but there was no way that simple acknowledgment of reality would be allowed into any formal CFS resolution. Over the course of the four-day session, the delegates from
the United States, Europe, Brazil, and other biofuel producers shot
down every reform proposal. The final resolution would contain no
recognition that such policies contribute to high food prices, no
acknowledgment that any policy that harms food security should
be revised, no call to limit the contribution of northern biofuel demand and investment to food insecurity in developing countries.[2]
With several developing country delegates ready to object in the
final plenary discussion, the chair gaveled through the resolution
without debate and the door closed on another attempt to address
the structural causes of the food crisis. Global leaders, fiddling in
Rome while our food burns.

As my eye-opening tour of Iowa had revealed, those structural
causes are complex and interwoven, and biofuels are a central
thread. The issue goes far beyond the diversion of so much U.S.
corn from food to fuel markets, driving up crop and land prices in
Iowa and contributing to the state's water pollution crisis. What
happens in Iowa doesn't stay in Iowa. Certainly the nitrates and
phosphates didn't, traveling down the Mississippi River and creating the dead zone in the Gulf of Mexico. But neither did the price
impacts, given the dominance of U.S. exports in global markets.
The U.S. corn diverted to ethanol represented 15 percent of total
global production, a demand shock to food and feed markets worldwide.[3] Meanwhile, the European Union had followed similar policies, mandating that 10 percent of liquid land transportation fuel
come from biofuels. They were outsourcing that production—and
its negative impacts—driving land grabs and deforestation as developing countries converted land to the production of palm oil—
or the obscure jatropha—for biodiesel.

But the ripple effects of biofuel expansion not only traveled, they built strength as they did, producing a storm surge of destruction on distant shores. The waves were driven by the ever-closer integration of food and fuel markets. If food was fuel, food prices could be driven not by the supply and demand for food but by ever-volatile petroleum markets. Roiling the waters further, the deregulation of financial markets in the late 1990s had unleashed its own waves of financial "instruments" designed to bundle commodities, including agricultural and energy commodities, into new derivatives that could be more easily traded on global markets. The same Wall Street speculators who produced the 2007 financial crisis had created a safe haven from the housing and stock market storm their speculation had created. In the wake of the financial crisis, speculative capital flooded into this new "asset class" of commodity derivatives that combined oil, food, and other commodities, mostly minerals.

Food became fuel, and both became financial instruments.

The Perfect Storm

The economics of the biofuel boom are mind-bogglingly complex but also disarmingly simple, so intuitive, in fact, that pretty much everyone except global policy-makers seems to get it. If a new market starts demanding significant shares of a food crop, prices will rise, at least until supplies catch up. But even if farmers expand production and demand is met, they will have shifted land out of other crops, reducing the supply of those crops and pushing up prices. Or they might have brought new land into agricultural production, which could be fine if it isn't ecologically sensitive land. Either way, the demand shock of new biofuel markets diverts food, feed, and land from the food chain to the fuel sector and provides incentives and guaranteed markets for crops that can serve as biofuel feed stocks.

At any significant scale, this would not go well for food prices, and it didn't. That was particularly true for U.S. ethanol made from corn. Ecologically, corn is the worst crop to turn into liquid fuel, even if it's also one of the easiest. The production of ethanol from corn yields far less alcohol than from sugar and is quite energy-intensive to produce, not just the refining but the mechanized, fertilizer-fed crop itself. Estimates vary, but there is no question that corn ethanol is one of the least climate-friendly of biofuels.[4]

And it is likely the most disruptive, since, as one of the three most important global cereal grains, with rice and wheat, corn ethanol relies on the feed stock most directly connected to global food markets. The United States is the largest producer and exporter of corn, so what we do transmits quickly to global markets. Even though the vast majority of the yellow dent corn we grow is for feed, not direct human consumption, global corn markets are closely linked across yellow, white, and other varieties. White corn can be (and is) used as animal feed; yellow corn can be (and is) mixed with white corn in some food preparations. Mexico's white-maize tortilla prices are certainly sensitive to rising U.S. prices for yellow corn, especially because post-NAFTA Mexico imports one-third of its corn directly from the United States.[5]

Anyone who doubted that should have been disabused by the "tortilla riots" that broke out when prices for this Mexican staple jumped in 2007. Tortilla prices increased 60 percent or more in some areas. Many decried U.S. biofuel production as the cause.[6] But what came to be called the food crisis wasn't limited to Mexico, and it wasn't only for corn. In fact, sixty similar food-related protests took place in some thirty countries in 2008. A second wave of food price spikes in 2010–2011 was among the key triggers for the Arab Spring, the wave of protests that toppled governments across the region. In Egypt, rising prices for imported wheat threatened to drive bread prices up at a time the government was preparing to decrease consumer bread subsidies, fueling popular unrest.[7]

Nor is there doubt that government policies, in the United States and elsewhere, are largely responsible for the surge in biofuel production after 2005. That was the year the U.S. Congress approved the Renewable Fuel Standard (RFS), which mandated rising volumes of biofuel use in the nation's cars, trucks, and other vehicles. That guaranteed market was backed by a "blending allowance" of 10 percent for ethanol in U.S. gasoline, tax incentives to those blenders, tariff protection against cheaper ethanol imports, and some added incentives. The RFS was expanded in 2007, which only added more renewable fuel to the coming food price fire. It included a mandate for 36 billion gallons of renewable fuel use by 2022, with a nested set of mandates for different types of biofuels. Conventional or first-generation biofuels, such as ethanol from corn, are recognized to have limited environmental benefits, with supposed reductions in greenhouse gas (GHG) emissions of at least 20 percent. The conventional biofuel mandate tops out at about 15 billion gallons, equivalent to about 10 percent of U.S. gasoline consumption. The rest of the mandate was to be met by more "advanced" biofuels, those with a so-called GHG score of 50 percent or better, indicating more substantial climate mitigation benefits.[8]

The assumption when the RFS was crafted and expanded was that those advances would come from good old American know-how, using feed stocks such as corn stover or perennial grasses (as Matt Liebman was doing in Iowa). These not only yield higher GHG scores, they also reduce the food-fuel competition that comes with corn-based ethanol. In fact, the stated rationale for the RFS was to have corn ethanol transition the country into more advanced biofuel use, particularly so-called cellulosic ethanol, made from non-food crops such as perennial grasses or corn stover.[9] To date, cellulosic ethanol remains unprofitable to produce despite significant R&D investments, in part because the RFS subsidized corn ethanol and failed to support the needed transition. Many still hope that those investments will eventually pay off, that the government can get the economics right for a transition.

Until then, it's all corn all the time. Ethanol consumes roughly 40 percent of the U.S. corn crop, up from just 5 percent in the early 2000s. To be fair, a small portion of that gets returned to animal feed markets as the "dried distiller grain" left over after the sugar is extracted in the ethanol refinery. So the net diversion is probably closer to 30 percent. Still, the growth was spectacular precisely during the years that led up to the food crisis.[10]

This was another case of a good initiative at the local level turning sour when agribusiness took it over and took it to scale. Corn ethanol started out in the 1990s as a way for farmers to add value to their own corn, which was getting terrible prices in the market after the elimination of supply management policies. Overproduction was a constant, and there was plenty of surplus corn to refine. In the 1990s, farmers began forming cooperatives to produce ethanol. Their hope was that the chronic surplus could be reduced with an expanded Conservation Reserve Program that could take land out of production, and ethanol could sop up the remaining surplus. The market conditions were favorable. Gasoline prices were high and subject to the whims of foreign oil producers, providing both a market incentive for a cheaper fuel and a national security rationale—energy independence—for the new industry. What's more, the federal government was moving to restrict the use of MTBE, the gasoline additive that added oxygen to gas tanks to raise octane levels, decrease engine knocking, and reduce air pollution. There were legitimate concerns about air and groundwater contamination.[11] Ethanol could become that new oxygenating additive to gasoline.[12]

By 2000, the USDA reported, there were twenty-two farmer-owned cooperatives with some 800,000 members refining ethanol. The agency called the cooperatives the fastest-growing segment of the emerging biofuel industry. Farmers saw it as a way to produce fuel and also animal feed from the remaining parts of the plant. As the USDA put it, "They believe that turning corn into ethanol takes a $2 bushel of corn and turns it into $3 worth of fuel and $1 worth of feed."[13] No one worried too much about impacts on food prices, since farmers were seeing such a steady and price-depressing surplus of corn. The cooperatives were producing around 450 million gallons, and nationally only about 5 percent of corn was going to ethanol.[14]

What started as a good idea for farmer-led rural development turned into another agribusiness-dominated extractive industry in the corn belt. By the end of 2016, five companies produced nearly half of the 15 billion gallons going into U.S. cars and trucks.

Ethanol was consuming not 5 percent of U.S. corn but 40 percent. Grain behemoth Archer Daniels Midland led the industry, producing more than 10 percent of U.S. ethanol, followed by POET and Valero Energy.[15] Cooperative production was largely a thing of the past, and by 2015 so were the higher corn prices farmers saw with the price spikes. For farmers, it was back to selling cheap corn, with agribusiness firms pocketing the value addition from fuel and feed.

The price impacts from ethanol's expansion were dramatic, no matter what U.S. ambassador David Lane told the members of the Committee on World Food Security in Rome. Some estimates suggested that U.S. corn prices from 2006 to 2011 were 27 percent higher than they would have been without the ethanol expansion. Bruce Babcock, at Iowa State, took a more conservative modeling approach, comparing actual prices to what they would have been if biofuel production had not increased over its 2004 levels. He estimated that by 2010 prices would have been 21 percent lower without the policy-fueled ethanol expansion.[16] Those numbers are consistent with the range of global assessments, and with the U.S. National Academy of Science estimate that U.S. biofuel policy was responsible for 20 to 40 percent of the post-2007 global food price increases worldwide.[17]

European Biofuel and the Palm Oil Boom

The other part of the world that mattered most during the price crisis was Europe. Like the United States, the European Union approved mandates for biofuel use in liquid transportation fuel, with a similar target of 10 percent in 2009. Because European vehicle fleets run mainly on diesel fuel, the biofuels of choice came from feed stocks like soybeans and African palm, crops that European countries scarcely produce.[18] These were mostly considered advanced biofuels, showing more significant GHG reductions than corn ethanol. But that all depended on how they were produced; if someone burned down carbon-sequestering rainforest to grow the crop, those climate benefits went up in the smoke. That, of course, is exactly what happened, to a significant extent. Because the EU couldn't grow all of its own biodiesel feed stock, producers had to import it, and no one was producing African palm in volumes great enough to meet the sudden surge in demand.[19] By all accounts, the EU biofuel mandate prompted a wave of land grabs and deforestation as entrepreneurs looked to capitalize on this lucrative new market. Indonesia became ground zero as capital from all over the world marched across the archipelago tearing up peat forests and displacing farmers, mainly to feed the European thirst for palm oil.[20]

Because the impacts were so visible and international in nature, particularly compared to U.S. corn ethanol, campaigners fought the EU mandate more actively and effectively. Reformers introduced the useful and intuitive concept of "indirect land use change," now known in policy circles as ILUC (pronounced "I-luck"). Investors claimed that they weren't part of the problem because they weren't diverting food crops to get their palm oil. ILUC offered a way to estimate the impact such investments still had on food markets. If African palm replaced soybeans on a farm, and one assumed continued demand for soybeans, where would those additional soybeans come from? Often, that road led to the Amazon, where Brazil's soybean behemoths would take over forestland cleared and grazed first by cattle ranchers. ILUC captured the indirect cause of that distant deforestation, putting much of the EU's biofuels sourcing in a harsh light. As a result, reforms in early 2018 set a 12 percent biofuel mandate but capped biofuels from croplands at current levels and limited them to 7 percent of EU 2017 transport fuel consumption. The remaining mandate must come from truly advanced biofuels. The European Commission also called for the phaseout of palm oil in biodiesel by 2021. Notably, both are targets that allow for some continued expansion and do nothing to undo the damage done by the initial surge in EU demand.[21]

A similar ILUC calculus applies to U.S. corn ethanol. Increased corn use for ethanol, for example, takes land out of soybeans in the United States. Those soybeans need to come from somewhere, and Brazil is the most likely supplier, with new soybean land coming at the expense of forests and grasslands. In the United States, though, we have seen no EU-style reforms to the Renewable Fuel Standard, just a relaxing of the wildly unrealistic mandate for cellulosic and advanced biofuels with no real solution to how that quota might be filled. Two perverse answers are on the table. First, why not just fill it with corn ethanol? It's better than gasoline, for GHGs, right? Corn states and agribusiness allies are pushing for E-15, raising the blending limit for gasoline from 10 percent to 15 percent, creating an opening for another price-inflating surge in corn ethanol production.[22]

The other answer is breathtakingly cynical. The law allows the renewable fuel mandate to be met to a significant extent by the use of "other" advanced biofuels, ones that do not have to be produced in the United States. Brazil's sugarcane-based ethanol is considered advanced, with a GHG-reduction score of 50 percent despite widespread concerns about a range of other social and environmental impacts. So the United States has met part of its advanced biofuels mandate by importing Brazilian ethanol, then exporting environmentally inferior U.S. corn ethanol back to Brazil. Talk about perverse. The laudable climate mitigation goals of the RFS are accounted for and scoffed at, with some of those carbon reductions spewed right back into the atmosphere in shipping emissions. The growth of soy-based biodiesel in the United States has reduced this counterproductive commerce, but the United States still relies on Brazil as an export market for its excess corn ethanol. The two countries trade ethanol with one another for no reason other than gaming the RFS to create a market for ever more U.S. ethanol beyond our 15-billion-gallon cap.[23]

Don't Blame China's Growing Middle Class

But why blame our corn when so many other factors contributed to the price spikes? As the FAO's expert panel acknowledged, biofuels were not the only cause, and the list of contributors is indeed daunting: tight inventories; export restrictions imposed by key global producers; rising demand in fast-growing developing countries such as China, particularly for meat; extreme and widespread droughts and other weather events, possibly attributable to climate change; financial speculation on agricultural commodities markets, particularly in the immediate aftermath of the financial crisis; rising oil prices, which push up food prices; population growth; declining growth in agricultural yields, related partly to underinvestment in research and development; a compromised resource base (especially soil and water), related in part to climate change; macroeconomic factors such as loose monetary policies and a weaker U.S. dollar.

Those who continue to deny or discount the importance of biofuel expansion often hide behind this complex array of contributing factors. How can we know which is more important? There are two clear answers to that question, the second less appreciated than the first. First, the evidence is overwhelming that the diversion of food/feed crops and land for biofuel production was the largest demand shock on global markets, because of both its scale and its rapid and unexpected surge, largely in response to government incentives. The United States can't take 15 percent of the corn out of global food/feed markets without serious repercussions. Other factors that could have been demand shocks really weren't. Global inventories were tight, but not that tight. Drought affected wheat production in Australia, but not at a level that would normally have prompted such price spikes. One of the responses to the price spikes—export restrictions by major producers, particularly of rice—certainly made a bad situation worse, but they were responding to price increases already under way.[24]

The most common alternative explanation offered by biofuel's apologists was the rising demand for feed as meat consumption took off in fast-growing economies like China and India. They were a particularly convenient scapegoat, the newly non-poor meat-eaters in developing countries who were expanding their diets to include more animal-based proteins. Rising global meat consumption poses many challenges, particularly for climate mitigation, but to the extent the trend reflects massive reductions in poverty and increases in the effective demand for food the challenges are welcome and the mitigation should come first from fat eaters in rich countries.

The rise in demand for meat-based diets, and the feed demands that result, have generated slow, steady, and predictable demand growth over several decades. China's demand for soybeans was neither sudden nor unexpected, though its reliance on international markets to supply its domestic livestock sector came more recently. China had already reduced its corn stocks, shifting from an exporter of corn in the early 2000s to an occasional importer. An earlier expert report for the CFS showed that the annual global growth rate in demand for cereals, *excluding U.S. biofuels demand*, averaged 1.3 percent from 2000 to 2011, only slightly higher than in the 1990s and lower than in the previous three decades. Biofuels demand just from the United States added half a percentage point to that global growth rate, boosting the growth rate for global cereals demand by nearly 40 percent.[25]

Meanwhile China's imports of soybeans (an oilseed, not a cereal) have increased steadily over a longer period of time, growing an impressive 400 percent since 2000.[26] That certainly added to global demand and put upward pressure on prices, but it was not the same kind of sudden shock to global markets. Economic modelers—and global producers—have been accounting for changing diets and rising demand for feed grains and oilseeds for many years.

The second answer to the question about biofuels' role in the food price increases is intuitive, except to policy-makers: biofuels' demand for food, feed, and land comes from outside the food system, so it represents a new external factor over and above existing dynamics within global agricultural markets. As the High Level Panel of Experts noted in its study, biofuels should be seen "as an additional factor acting on top of these other factors, and independent from them." In some cases "the introduction of biofuels might have had not merely an additional, but an *amplifying* effect with respect to that of another factor."[27]

In other words, agricultural markets will have their ups and downs, due to intrinsic factors such as the weather and long-term factors such as population growth and the increase in the number of meat-eaters, but add a sudden surge in demand extrinsic to the food system and we are bound to get shortages and price increases.

Developing Countries Pay the Price

And those price increases are bound to hit the poorest countries the hardest, particularly the nations that depend heavily on imported corn. I estimated that from 2005 to 2010, the "ethanol premium" cost corn-importing countries $11.6 billion in higher import prices. More than half of that—$6.6 billion—was borne by developing countries, from Mexico ($1.1 billion) to Egypt ($727 million). North African countries, many of which saw serious social unrest, saw corn import bills $1.4 billion higher over those six years.[28] The link between high food prices and unrest in the region is by now well documented; U.S. ethanol contributed to that instability.

The world's least-developed countries are the ones most vulnerable to such shocks. Over the last fifty years, and particularly since the 1980s, these nations have gone from being small net exporters of agricultural goods to huge net importers. The shift came when World Bank and International Monetary Fund structural reforms in the 1980s forced indebted developing country governments to open their economies to agricultural imports while reducing their support for domestic farmers. The result: a flood of cheap and often-subsidized imports from rich countries, forcing local farmers out of business and off the land. By 2011, those countries collectively imported nearly three times as much agricultural produce as they exported, leaving a yawning trade deficit of $22 billion.[29] That trade deficit was significantly higher thanks to the U.S. ethanol premium.

Of course, that ethanol premium didn't just affect importers. Globalization's transmission belt for commodity prices pushed up corn prices even in countries that did not import much corn. In

Uganda, for example, retail corn prices spiked in 2008, more than tripling. Ugandans spend on average 65 percent of their cash income on food, with poor urban consumers getting 20 percent of their calories from corn purchased in the marketplace. More than half of Ugandans were considered "food insecure" in 2007, and the price spikes only made that worse.[30]

Guatemala may be emblematic of all that can go wrong with the biofuel boom. The country saw its import dependence for corn grow from 9 percent in the early 1990s to around 40 percent today. This in a corn-producing country, one of the birthplaces of domesticated corn. Nearly all that imported corn came from the United States, so the U.S. ethanol premium added $91 million to Guatemala's import bill between 2005 and 2010, $28 million in 2010 alone. How big an impact was that? It represented six times the level of U.S. agricultural aid to Guatemala that year, and nearly as much as U.S. food aid to this poor country. It was equivalent to over 10 percent of the government's annual expenditure on agricultural development. This was devastating for a country in which nearly half of children under five were malnourished.[31]

But higher import bills were the least of their biofuel problems, as a brilliant New York Times feature pointed out. Even though Guatemala still grew most of its own white corn for tortillas, soaring international prices doubled the price of tortillas for the average consumer. But the most devastating cost of the ethanol boom was the competition for land. Demand was soaring not just for corn-based ethanol but also for sugar-based ethanol and for biodiesel made from palm oil. Guatemala has good land to grow all three. Only the United States is foolish enough to make ethanol from corn, so the high prices spurred an agricultural boom in palm and sugar plantations, which competed for land directly with local corn producers.[32]

One of the few potential benefits of high corn prices is that if a farmer grows enough corn to sell she can get a good price. Peasant farmers, overwhelmingly from long-oppressed indigenous groups, farm some of the worst lands in the country. With corn prices high, many farmers wanted to grow more. They were having a hard time renting new land, or even just keeping the land they had, with large landowners expanding palm and sugar plantations. Suchitepéquez Province, until recently a major corn-producing region, was taken over by sugarcane and African palm plantations. Palm oil became the country's third-largest export, with sugar being number one. Farmers who used to rent land near their homes to grow corn were now walking miles to find fields they could sow for food. Reporter Elisabeth Rosenthal found José Antonio Alvarado harvesting his corn crop on the narrow median of a highway. "We're farming here because there is no other land, and I have to feed my family," he told her. The land he used to rent is now planted in sugarcane for ethanol exports to Europe.[33]

Félix Pérez told her he used to grow corn, beans, and fruit behind his house, which now sat in the middle of palm plantations. He had to walk about three miles to a hillside plot that he could rent for four months of the year. The palm oil produced on his former land was being exported for cooking oil, not biodiesel, but no one doubted that the high prices were driven by European biodiesel demand.

Biofuel demand is feeding land-grabbing in Guatemala, as in Indonesia and other parts of the developing world. In the Polochic Valley, the Chabil Utzaj S.A. sugar refinery evicted eleven communities from land they had farmed for decades. Guatemalan government forces, the refinery's owners, and private security agents expelled residents, destroying their houses and crops to prevent them from returning. Several people were killed in the conflict.[34]

"There are pros and cons to biofuel, but not here. . . . These people don't have enough to eat. They need food. They need land," Misael Gonzáles, a Guatemalan farm labor union leader, told the *Times*. "They can't eat biofuel, and they don't drive cars."[35]

Members of the K'Quinich community in Guatemala's Polochic Valley survey
the land taken from eleven communities by the Chabil Utzaj S.A. sugar refinery.
Daniele Volpe/ActionAid

Gambling on Dinner

They don't hold any financial derivatives either, the other brave new
commodity roiling food markets. It was bad enough that food was
now fuel, and so was land. It was even worse that Wall Street now
had them conveniently bundled together into commodity funds
that speculators could buy and sell with no knowledge of nor regard
for either food or biofuels. Buy and sell they did, particularly in the
wake of the financial crisis in the United States. Why? Speculative
capital needed a new place to go. They had blown up the subprime
mortgage market, taking the housing market down with it. The
stock market had plunged as a result. Billions of dollars sought safe
harbors in turbulent times. Thanks to the very deregulation that
had caused those disasters, the speculators now had a whole set of
new financial "instruments" that neatly packaged commodities into
a handy "asset class."

Actually, there were no commodities anywhere in sight. What these commodity funds included were "futures," the longtime markets that have allowed sellers (such as farmers) and buyers (such as pork producers) to navigate the inevitable swings in the prices for corn and other raw commodities. Futures prices used to be based on supply and demand, with meticulous market information informing participants about future supplies, demand, and prices. Most of the participants were buyers and sellers, so-called commercial hedgers with a material interest in the commodity, hedging their risks with financial bets on future prices. A farmer could lock in a future price for her corn. A feed company could do the same on the buying side. In the late 1990s, only about one-fifth of futures market participants were speculators. Many followed those markets closely, and their investments helped lubricate those markets by adding liquidity, a larger pool of cash to back all those deals and help sellers reach buyers.

What deregulation did was allow Wall Street traders to make far more risky bets on a broadened array of commodity funds. What the financial crisis did was push all of the traders into those funds at once, theater-goers all running to the same exit after the fire they themselves had set turned into an inferno.

Basically, the speculators ruined the future by distorting those markets. Where before there were four commercial hedgers (those with a commercial interest in the traded commodity) for every speculator, suddenly there were four speculators for every hedger. Some $9 trillion in trades took place in commodity derivatives, with 80 to 90 percent in over-the-counter (OTC) trading, transactions that were conveniently outside of regulators' scrutiny. Five banks controlled 96 percent of derivatives activity, giving a few players decisive market power. And they were almost all betting on higher commodity prices. Not because they knew anything about weather forecasts and harvest projections for key corn-producing areas but because that was the way to bet. And the more they bet the more futures prices were bid up, and the higher futures prices got the more food prices climbed.[36]

But wait, it's worse than that, in large part because of biofuels. Biofuels tied food and petroleum markets together in new ways, both concrete and speculative. Energy prices have been linked to food prices for a long time, since energy costs (tractor fuel, fertilizer, transport) are a major cost of production on the farm. Concretely, the biofuel boom put ethanol in direct competition with gasoline, with one as a substitute for the other. So high prices for one increase demand for the other as fuel blenders switch, increasing its price in turn. On the speculative side, petroleum futures markets are enormous and wildly traded. Researchers estimated that some 20 percent of the U.S. gasoline price drivers paid at the pump in 2011 was due to speculation in oil markets.[37] So speculative bets on Saudi, Iranian, or Venezuelan oil output now transmitted more readily than before to agricultural commodities prices.

Want to tie them even more closely together? Meet the commodity index fund, one of Wall Street's new derivatives introduced after financial deregulation in the late 1990s. Index funds were created by Goldman Sachs and other financial players as a hedge against declining returns in other sectors, based on the observed tendency of commodity prices to hold their value as other assets lose theirs. An index fund is typically a basket of twenty or more commodities, usually with 30 percent or less of its value in agricultural commodities. In July 2008, the ratio for the S&P Goldman Sachs Commodity Index, by far the largest index, used for 63 percent of the market, held 75 percent energy futures and only 10 percent grains futures, with the rest in metals and other commodities.[38]

So the movement of the index funds was driven overwhelmingly by the price of oil, itself a highly speculative market with some 70 percent of futures investments coming from non-commercial speculators.[39] Under such institutionalized structures, the price of oil drove the movement of the index funds and pushed up the prices of agricultural commodities, *no matter what was happening to the fundamentals of supply and demand for corn.* Worse, the index funds were mandated to keep the value of their commodity classes in strict proportion, so that when the prices and value of energy products went up the funds had to buy more corn and soybean futures to maintain the mandated proportions.

This represented yet another institutional impetus to bid up agricultural futures regardless of market fundamentals for those crops:[40] And bid them up they did. Index fund purchases from 2003 to 2007 already were larger than the purchases by traditional futures market participants. In the first half of 2008, index fund investments doubled as speculators sought safe haven in commodities markets. From 2003 to July 1, 2008, such investment rose from $13 billion to $317 billion, *a 25-fold increase.*[41] Finance capital had come to dominate commercial hedging in futures markets, index funds had become huge investment vehicles in uncertain economic times, and the index funds moved with oil and minerals prices, dragging food prices along with them. The emergence of "high-frequency trading" only exacerbated these impacts. More and more, trades were made based on small movements in market indicators triggered automatically by algorithms programmed to buy and sell. To the extent traders followed the same indicators and bet the same ways—surprise, they did!—the herd behavior already built into such speculation got a shot of financial amphetamine and the herd became a stampede.[42]

The resulting connections among food, fuel, and financial markets were complex, to say the least. Leave it to complex systems modelers to put the ethanol and speculation impacts together in a way that illustrated their tag-team impacts on food prices. The New England Complex Systems Institute (NECSI), just down the street from me in Cambridge, had been contracted by the U.S. Army to help explain the food price spikes, the army's interest clearly being the resulting social unrest, in North Africa and elsewhere. As complex systems wonks do, they plotted the run-up in retail food prices and they tested the wide range of suggested causes against that graph, which at the time showed a slow rise starting in 2004 with a spike in 2007–2008 and another in 2010.[43] They found an explanatory model that fit the food price index movements to a remarkable degree. They split the causes into two parts. First, they identified an underlying steady rise in prices related to supply and demand and driven entirely by the expansion of corn ethanol. Not biofuel expansion in general, just corn ethanol in the United States. According to their model, that alone explained a significant part of the rise not just in corn prices but in global food prices. Their explanation was the same as mine: corn is such an important food and feed stock that U.S. ethanol demand had an inordinate effect on food prices.

How did they explain the two price spikes? They modeled the amount of speculative capital untied to other concrete investments. That enabled them to quantify the approximate value of capital available for commodity speculation. They then quantified the outflow of speculative capital from real estate and stock markets in the United States into commodity funds. The model explained the price spikes when combined with the steady upward pressure on prices from U.S. ethanol expansion. Their model tested and rejected other explanations in the process, disproving notions that rising prices were caused by weather, rising demand for meat in China and India, or supply interruptions, none of which correlated much with the movements in food prices.[44]

Their conclusions were quite clear, and in some ways quite encouraging, if you thought U.S. policies were amenable to change. "Both causes of price increase, speculative investment and ethanol conversion, are promoted by recent regulatory changes—deregulation of the commodity markets, and policies promoting the conversion of corn to ethanol. Rapid action is needed to reduce the impacts of the price increases on global hunger."[45]

Why is that good news? Because it is harder to address some of the other drivers, such as the weather or the move to meat-based diets in emerging economies. By comparison, these are simple (if complex politically), and the U.S. government could go a long way to solving them unilaterally: end ethanol incentives and implement stronger regulations to curb commodity speculation. Throw in a financial transactions tax—a very small tax on every financial transaction—which new research shows would most impact high-frequency traders, and we could make important progress on food security.[46]

The UN Commission on Trade and Development made a similar recommendation: "Because of these distortions, commodity prices in financialized markets do not provide correct signals about the relative scarcity of commodities. This impairs the allocation of resources and has negative effects on the real economy. To restore the proper functioning of commodity markets, swift political action is required on a global scale."[47]

The U.S. Congress started down that path of re-regulating the financial sector, with the Dodd-Frank reforms in 2010. Unfortunately, the financial industry since then has managed to use the profits from its speculative trading to weaken regulations and tie them up in court.

Speculating on Biofuels in Tanzania

Villagers near the Tanzanian town of Kisarawe saw the full fury of the integration of food, fuel, and financial markets. They agreed to what turned out to be a speculative land deal to grow jatropha, a little-cultivated African plant, for biofuels. When it failed they were left on the outside of their 20,000 acres looking in. Fittingly, it was Goldman Sachs that first identified jatropha as a good bet for oil for biodiesel.[48]

Britain-based Sun Biofuels had secured a ninety-nine-year lease with promises not just of compensation for the land but jobs, roads, clinics, schools, and wells. The company started by clearing 5,000 acres of mostly forestland and planted jatropha trees. Europe was looking for feed stock to meet its renewable-fuel mandates for bio-fuel use, and jatropha was the new "green gold." Jatropha was supposed to be a biofuels miracle crop. An oilseed native to Africa, it was inedible and therefore would not compete with food or feed crops, and it was advertised as growing on "marginal lands," so it would not compete for cropland. Jatropha was all the rage across Africa in the wake of the food crisis, attracting venture capitalists like the ones behind Sun Biofuels.[49]

As it turned out, jatropha was a bust, particularly for speculators.

Jatropha in Sun Biofuel's Kisarawe farm before it was abandoned. *Tom Pietrasik/ ActionAid*

It took 3–4 years to get a crop, a long time for impatient capital. It hadn't really been domesticated for commercial cultivation, so no one really knew what varieties would grow well and be suitable for biofuel production. Early indications were that to be productive it needed more water than other biodiesel feed stocks.[50] Sure it grew on marginal lands, but only with marginal returns. The last thing investors wanted were marginal returns, so they went for good agricultural lands, setting up the food-fuel competition yet again.

By the time I was in Tanzania in 2014, Sun Biofuels had ceased production, and so had most of the other jatropha projects in Africa.[51] I asked to meet with the company, and I was told that Mtanga Foods had taken over the lease and I could meet with Valerie Fernandes, who was managing Mtanga. She had also worked for Sun Biofuels, which made me suspicious. When she acknowledged that Sun Biofuels and Mtanga had "overlapping boards of directors," this started to look very much like Sun Biofuels was just flipping the land to Mtanga after securing the lease with a lot of false promises to villagers. She was entirely dismissive when I asked if Mtanga would honor the development commitments Sun Biofuels had made to secure the land—the clinics, roads, wells, schools. She was adamant. The company had paid compensation and that was all they owed. And the villagers were presumptuous to think that Mtanga had any obligation even to consult with them about their plans.[52]

I was shocked at her candor. So were the villagers I met the next day in Kisarawe. They'd never heard of Mtanga. They hadn't even been told the lease had been transferred. They just wanted their land back. "We used to fetch water. It was close," explained Salima Nasoro, a brightly clad woman from Muhaga village. "We used clay for handicrafts. We cut poles for construction. We made timber. We got charcoal. We kept bees. We collected traditional medicines." Now, the land was mostly off-limits. They hadn't grown much food on the land before, but they had depended on the forest the way rural communities often do. With much of the forest gone and the land under guard, they had lost even those benefits. They'd even lost one of their burial grounds. Now all they had was a graveyard of scraggly, untended jatropha trees. A 5,000-acre jatropha graveyard.

Tanzanian land minister Anna Tibaijuka called actions like these "equivalent to Ponzi schemes." But a lawyer in the land ministry told me there was little chance the lease would be canceled and the land returned to villagers. The Tanzanian government was committed to the same failing policies as Mozambique and other African countries, betting on large-scale foreign land projects to develop its rural sector, and letting those investors take projects to a scale that made no sense under local conditions.

In the northern city of Arusha, I learned that, much like the early days of corn ethanol, farming jatropha had once been a local initiative to help farmers get cash and useful products from something they were already growing. Jatropha was indeed native to the region. It was commonly used by the nomadic Nyaburu tribe in nearby Singida to mark the graves of those who died far from home. The plant was indeed drought-tolerant; it only needed a lot of water to produce commercial biodiesel oil. It was also a common hedgerow, widely planted by villagers at the urging of former president Julius Nyerere to keep nomadic herds from eating crops. The oilseeds were indeed poisonous so they kept away animals. You could find a lot of jatropha bordering croplands, but no one was doing anything with the oilseeds.

Maybe Goldman Sachs, Sun Biofuels, and all the other specu-lators just misunderstood the word *marginal*, I thought. It didn't mean land that was poor quality, it meant land along the margins of farms.

Livinus Manyanga, who cofounded Kakute, a nongovernmental organization that promotes small-scale development in the area, laughed at my bad joke. He was a mechanical engineer by train-ing. He had helped the Tanzanian government develop its biofuel policies. He said he told the foreign biofuel companies jatropha wouldn't work on plantations. He said it is not as easy a crop as they thought; it needs water, fertilizer, and frequent pruning. "I told them, wait four or five years and you will collapse."

Kakute had been working to add value to local farmers' jatro-pha for years. On the organization's own 75-acre farm they put jatropha as hedgerows, and they learned that the crop was very labor-intensive, not easy to automate. They got good productivity, up to 25 pounds of oil from each tree. But the oil still ended up being expensive for commercial uses. Still, he explained that only one-quarter or one-third of the value of the crop is in the oil. Re-ducing jatropha to just oil was a waste of its potential. In the south, Kakute showed that at a village level the crop could be valuable. The organization developed an inexpensive way to press the oil from the seeds and a generator that could run on straight jatropha oil. Combined with one solar panel, that could give a village that didn't yet have electricity a twenty-four-hour source of power. Even without the new equipment, Manyanga said the oil made soap, which meant villagers didn't have to use scarce cash to buy it. And it was perfect for household lamplight, too.

"You start with soap, which you can make locally," he said, clearly proud of Kakute's useful innovations. "Then you can use the seed cake to make cooking material so you don't cut trees for charcoal.

The jatropha trees last for twenty-five years, and they will make your land green."

Kakute helped start Jatropha Products Tanzania Limited to develop a market for jatropha products, turning farmers' hedgerows into needed cash. The group was working with 2,700 farmers helping them produce, use, and sell a range of jatropha products, including organic fertilizer and briquettes made from the seed cake to use as a cooking substitute for charcoal.

"Many things that are good start very small and grow," Stephen Minja, director of Jatropha Products told me. "But maybe only to medium size."

Jan Gevaert had come the closest to taking that model to a larger scale, but when he met me at Arusha's Impala Hotel he was closing up shop. Under his direction, the Dutch Diligent Energy Systems had tried to expand jatropha markets for small-scale farmers, including for the production of commercial biodiesel. As part of the so-called Trickle Out Project, Diligent was purchasing seeds from some 60,000 farmers for the production of oil for local use and export, briquettes for industrial use as a fuel, and pellets for household cooking needs. Diligent encouraged farmers to plant jatropha as hedgerows, but to avoid competing with food production the company told them they wouldn't buy their jatropha if they planted it on other land. The company was part of the international effort to make biofuels sustainable, with a focus on reducing indirect land use change. Diligent had won some acclaim because its biodiesel had been used in a test flight by the Dutch carrier KLM in 2009.[53]

"It's the only model that can work at this point; you have to have enough farmers," Gevaert told me. Funded by venture capital, Diligent needed 100,000 farmers to make the project viable, buying small amounts from each. They didn't get there, and the patient capital ran out of patience as capital markets recovered from the financial crisis. "I still strongly, strongly believe in that model," Gevaert said, sad to let go of an initiative in which he had clearly invested a lot. He said the project needed just one more year of financing to turn a profit.

Manyanga agreed. "It could have worked." Still, he seemed

relieved that the biofuel-driven jatropha boom had gone bust, saying it had diverted everyone from the crop's true potential. Maybe they could now get back to small-scale development. "You are not going to make a lot of money," he told me. "You will just be changing the local economy."

All Corn All the Time

Tanzania may return to small-scale biofuel development, but we're way past that point in the United States. The only good news about the biofuel boom is that, at least in the United States, the expansion has slowed considerably. It is hard to imagine any easy way to take some of that corn land back from ethanol, but for global food prices it was clearly the rate of expansion—the demand shock—that made prices go up so far and so fast. With demand no longer growing so quickly, crop prices are back to their usual punishing levels as the world is awash in what has been called a "global grain glut." Barring another biofuel boom, we are unlikely to see a repeat of the food price increases we saw between 2007 and 2013.[54]

But we can't rule that out. The United States has hit the blending wall of E-10—10 percent ethanol in gasoline—limiting further expansion, though exports are increasing. But biodiesel from soybeans is still a growing market under the RFS mandate, and the industry is pushing hard for lifting the gasoline blend limit to 15 percent. That could provoke another surge in corn demand and food price spikes. Unfortunately, there is little likelihood the U.S. government will reform the RFS to remove support for corn ethanol and promote meaningful incentives and investments (not just unrealistic targets) in cellulosic technologies. A meaningful transition from corn to cellulosic ethanol is one of the only large-scale measures I'm aware of that could move land out of corn production, and the environmental benefits—reductions in soil erosion, greenhouse gas emissions, and pesticide use—would be enormous.[55]

The European Union is nearing its own blending wall thanks to legislated limits on the use of domestic or foreign cropland for biofuel production, taking indirect land use change into account. We could easily see another financial crisis, made all the more likely by U.S. tax cuts, which put more money in the hands of rich investors, and the gutting of the financial regulations developed to keep them from taking destructive risks with that money. Food, fuel, and financial markets are even more intertwined than they were in 2007, and that only increases the risks that instability in oil and financial markets will take the world's poor on another roller coaster ride of price volatility.

Unfortunately, much of the world has imitated the global powers with their own mandates and incentives for biofuel use. I surveyed the global policy situation in 2015 and found that at least sixty-four countries now have biofuel mandates. The consumption increases implied by full implementation of such mandates in just the most important seven countries or regions project a 43 percent increase in crop-based biofuel consumption in 2025 over 2014 levels. International agencies warn of even greater biofuel expansion, particularly in countries such as Indonesia that are at the center of the palm oil boom.[56]

I thought back to the early days of corn ethanol in the United States, with farmer cooperatives trying to sustain their farms and communities by adding value to their corn. Their cooperative ethanol refineries were swallowed up by agribusiness as ADM and its corporate competitors took the industry well beyond any scale that made sense for farmers, the environment, or the world's poor, who suffered the insecurity that came with the food price spikes triggered by the industry's expansion. I could imagine Iowa farmers pining for days when they might control their own economies and communities with value-added ethanol production. They wanted to grow, but, as Manyanga said, maybe only to medium size. They didn't want to make a lot of money. They just wanted to change and improve the local economy—for farmers.

7

Monsanto Invades Corn's Garden of Eden in Mexico

By the time I arrived in Mexico City in 2014, the corn issue on people's minds wasn't the ethanol-driven spike in tortilla prices, or the apparent return to punishingly low crop prices for Mexican corn farmers thanks to NAFTA. It was the battle to keep GM corn out of Mexico.

In 2009, Monsanto, Syngenta, Dow, DuPont, Pioneer, and other multinational agro-chemical companies petitioned the Mexican government for land in northern Mexico for the commercial production of genetically modified (GM) corn. The government reshuffled its bureaucracy and adjusted its laws to accommodate the agribusiness giants, quickly approving permits for experimental and trial planting, the precursor, they all assumed, for the quick issuing of commercial licenses. Indeed, those commercial license requests would be for nearly 7 million acres. But in September 2013, Judge Jaime Eduardo Verdugo J. issued a precautionary injunction on all further permits, citing "the risk of imminent harm to the environment." A group of fifty-three individuals and twenty-two organizations, in the name of a coalition of farmer, consumer, and environmental groups (La Demanda Colectiva), had petitioned for a ban on GM corn, arguing that inevitable gene flow from GM to native corn would threaten Mexico's maize diversity.[1]

Tractor caravan leaves Chihuahua to join the January 2008 "Without Corn There Is No Country" farmer protest in Mexico City. *Enrique Pérez S/ANEC*

When I arrived in Mexico six months later the injunction was still in place. It was difficult to imagine a more unlikely place to stop the biotech giants. The Mexican government, a subservient U.S. partner under NAFTA, fully backed their requests. Between the companies and the government, they had more than 100 lawyers working to overturn the injunction. The Gene Goliaths had already filed more than sixty legal challenges. Taking them on was a plucky little David of a public interest law firm, and a strong and well-organized group of leaders who had been fighting for Mexico's maize diversity for years. Armed only with legal slingshots, they had beaten back every challenge, relying on new powers that came with Mexico's recognition for the first time of class action suits. Still, with Mexico's well-documented history of government corruption, what chance did David & Co. LLC have of stopping a genetically modified Goliath? Yet another legal challenge, from Monsanto, was pending before yet another judge.

Since it was Easter Sunday, I attended mass at San Hipólito Church in the heart of Mexico's historic city center. Locally, the eighteenth-century church is known less for Saint Hipólito than for San Judas Tadeo, the "patron saint of lost causes," according to the translation at the church entrance. I didn't think the GM lawsuit was a lost cause, but it sure seemed a long shot. I lit a candle and said a prayer. I'm not Catholic, nor even very religious, but it seemed the least I could do. The next day, the judge denied Monsanto's request, leaving the injunction in place.

I told René Sánchez Galindo, the public interest lawyer on the case, that I'd said a prayer to San Judas. He laughed a knowing laugh. He told me that he is not very religious, but when he was nine years old he fell off his bike, hit his head, and went into a coma. His family didn't know if he was going to survive. He came out of his coma on October 28, the day the church devotes to San Judas Tadeo. "My aunt is a firm believer," he said. "She told me that she had prayed to San Judas when I was in the hospital and that he had saved my life."

Sánchez Galindo thanked me for my prayer but offered a different explanation for defeating the latest legal challenge. "The judge surely eats tacos," he smiled. "Everyone here eats tacos. They know maize is different."[2]

A Question of Contamination

Adelita San Vicente, lead plaintiff in the class action suit and director of Semillas de Vida (Seeds of Life), a nonprofit organization working to promote and conserve seed diversity, explained the stakes in the legal fight. "It is difficult to imagine a worse place to grow GM maize than Mexico." The country, with its neighbors to the south, had been part of the Mayan civilization, whose Mesoamerican ancestors domesticated maize some 9,000 years ago. As a "center of origin" for the crop, Mexico has among the greatest diversity of maize types—known as landraces—in the world.[3] The crop evolved with human civilizations as part of the distinctive *milpa* system of intercropping, taught in the United States as the "three sisters" of maize, beans, and squash, which sustained the soil while providing a nutritionally diverse diet.[4] Maize is one of the world's most important food crops, as I'd seen in places as far away as Southern Africa, so the agricultural biodiversity is a vital global natural resource. The distinct landraces, each evolved into myriad local varieties adapted to the ecological and cultural needs of a region and its people, served as the raw material for modern crop breeding. "Mexican maize is a gift from Mesoamerica to the world, which they are trying to privatize with patented GM seeds," said San Vicente.

The legal case is complex, but the core issue couldn't be simpler. Maize is an open-pollinated crop: the pollen that sprinkles from the tassels at the top of the plant falls or blows onto the silks of any ear of maize, near or far, pollinating the crop kernel by kernel, each having generated its own silk. Cross-breeding—human-directed or wild—is particularly easy with maize, which is why it developed into such a wide diversity of varieties. But uncontrolled cross-pollination can result in unwanted varieties. Over millennia, farmers learned to protect the integrity of their best varieties by isolating plots from one another, then selecting the purest, best kernels to save as seeds for the next year's crop. The fear about transgenic maize is that its pollen, borne on the wind, could unintentionally pollinate native maize varieties, undermining the genetic purity of the crops.

The issue of transgenic gene flow was not hypothetical. In 2002, transgenic traits were found in native maize varieties in the southeastern state of Oaxaca. The discovery, by two U.S.-based scientists, Ignacio Chapela and David Quist, sounded alarms throughout Mexico. Not only had the transgene migrated on the wind, through maize's open pollination, it had done so despite a nationwide ban on the planting of transgenic maize. That 1998 moratorium was based on scientific advice of the National Agricultural Biosafety Committee, convened by the government to help develop policies and regulations to deal with what was then a very new technology.[5]

Obviously, transgenic maize had been planted, though not on a scale at all comparable to the commercial farming now being proposed. But even in such low densities gene flow had occurred.

Though it was impossible to confirm the source of the contamination, evidence strongly suggested that it came from the inadvertent planting of a GM seed by a farmer who had received a ration of maize, in kernel form, from the rural anti-poverty program DICONSA. At the time, the agency included imported U.S. maize in such distributions, with no labeling that such grain likely contained GM kernels and should not be planted. (That practice has since been discontinued.) The peasant farmer most likely did what peasant farmers do—experiment with new seeds in their fields.

Local farmers did not call the finding gene flow, they called it contamination, genetic pollution, and they demanded an investigation. In concert with Greenpeace and other advocacy groups, they filed a citizen petition for a high-level study of the issue by the North American Commission for Environmental Cooperation, the environmental body created by NAFTA. The request was granted, despite immediate industry efforts to malign Chapela and Quist's research. The commission formed an expert panel to carry out the investigation. This was no slapdash inquiry. Headed by noted Mexican scientist José Sarukhán, the research involved some eighteen authors contributing ten chapters covering the evidence of gene flow, the risks to human health and the environment, the implications for biodiversity, and frameworks for assessing risks and benefits. Each chapter was peer-reviewed by an additional set of experts, and the public was invited to review drafts and submit comments. The result was the most cutting-edge scientific assessment ever carried out into transgenic gene flow and its implications.[6]

I was in Oaxaca City in 2004 for the commission's presentation of its draft report. The luxurious Victoria Hotel barely contained the crowd of nearly 400, a mix of government officials, researchers, environmentalists, and, most notably, indigenous maize farmers from the surrounding area. Many farmers spoke movingly of their reverence for maize and its importance to their cultures. Some held disfigured ears of maize that they said came from the transgenic contamination. They stressed that they considered the contamination an invasion, that they had not been consulted or informed it was taking place, and that they had no interest in exploring the possible benefits of GM maize in their fields.

The commission's report was more sober, but no less clear. It confirmed the gene flow found by Chapela and Quist, and it identified potential threats to both maize biodiversity and wild biodiversity, stressing that the U.S. GM experience, with little native maize diversity to protect, was a poor guide for mega-diverse Mexico. Similarly, the chapter on human health impacts confirmed that to date there had been few negative impacts from consuming existing GM crops, but Mexico had particular reasons for precaution because Mexicans directly consume so much maize. All the safety evidence came from the United States, where consumers, the unwitting (and unconsenting) guinea pigs in the industry's unlabeled GM human feeding trials, eat a lot of GM food—in more processed foods than we would like to believe—but almost none directly, as ears, kernels, or meal.

Almost no country in the world gets a larger share of its calories and protein from maize. Tortillas, tamales, and other maize-based foods provide an estimated 53 percent of the calories and a substantial share of the protein for the average Mexican.[7] Commission researchers recognized that we really don't know what the health impacts might be with such high consumption levels. Less known still are the potential health effects of GM maize on vulnerable populations—pregnant women, babies, and young children.

Citing these uncertainties and Mexico's particular vulnerability, the commission's scientists recommended precaution in Mexico's interactions with GM maize. They even recommended the suspension of Mexico's importation of unlabeled maize from the United States unless it was milled into cornmeal immediately upon entering the country, to prevent farmers from unknowingly planting it. Mexico's National Commission for the Knowledge and Use of Biodiversity (CONABIO), the National Institute of Ecology (INE), and the Bureau of Biodiversity, Genetic Resources, and Protected Areas of the Secretariat of Environment and Natural Resources submitted a joint statement generally supporting the report's characterization of the science literature and the scientists' call for precaution.[8]

The commission's own Joint Public Advisory Committee, which involves civil society representatives from the three NAFTA countries, went further in a letter to the U.S., Canadian, and Mexican environment officials. "Minimally, a moratorium on imports of transgenic corn to Mexico should be put in place until the risks to human health, cultural integrity of maize producers in Mexico and the environment generally are better understood and appropriate long-term decisions can be made."[9]

The biotech industry, of course, went ballistic, calling for "greater scientific objectivity" and asserting, with no new evidence, that GM maize "does not represent a threat to landrace maize breeds."[10] All three governments, most notably Mexico's, toed the agribusiness line, rejecting the report's recommendations. No restrictions on imports. No precautionary policies. The U.S. government insisted on having its objections published as an appendix in the final commission report, accusing the commission of failing to adequately include input from "key stakeholders." We all knew whom they were talking about: biotechnology firms. (Biotech would similarly prompt the U.S. government to pull its support from the 2009 International Assessment for Agricultural Knowledge, Science, Technology, and Development, a comprehensive interagency report that proved too critical of biotech solutions for world agriculture.[11]) The summary report was published, but the full set of studies never was, though they remain publicly available thanks to the commission's strong transparency provisions.[12]

The Mexican government barely waited for the critical report to be published before contradicting its recommendations. In 2005, Mexico lifted its seven-year-old moratorium on planting and pushed through a biosafety law—dubbed "the Monsanto Law" by critics—that allowed the experimental and commercial planting of

GM crops, including maize.[13] The Mexican government had dis-
banded its Biosafety Commission years earlier. The law stipulated
that GM maize could be planted, but not in any area of Mexico
considered a "center of origin." That vague recognition of the need
for special protection of native maize would help in the later legal
challenge.

The Answer Is Blowing in the Wind

Dr. José Sarukhán, chair of that esteemed commission, received
me in his office in Mexico City's Tlalpan district. He now headed a
more permanent commission, Mexico's national biodiversity commission, CONABIO, an agency within the country's environment
ministry. On the issue of GM maize, he was getting no more respect than he had a decade earlier, even though he was now within
the government. He seemed tired but determined.

"We should avoid gene flow when the impacts remain uncertain,"
he told me. Sarukhán had initially offered conditional support for
the GM maize trials, because they were confined to the less bio-
diverse northern part of the country. His agency's 2006 map had,
in effect, defined what parts of Mexico should be considered "centers of origin," with significant populations of native maize, and
which shouldn't. The map actually ignored existing expertise on
maize diversity, which documented plenty of native maize in northern Mexico. CONABIO's 2006 map, which was used in the 2012
government document to define the areas protected as "centers of
origin and genetic diversification," in effect declared sections of
northern Mexico, including most irrigated areas of the industrial
maize state of Sinaloa, open for GM business.[14]

When I saw Sarukhán in 2014, he had changed his mind, and
he told me why. His agency had commissioned a new survey, col-
lecting samples (called "accessions") for the nation's gene bank. It
showed a much different picture. "We had 7,000 accessions in our
gene banks" before the new survey, which was published in 2011.
"We ended with 23,000." More than three times the number of

distinct varieties, thanks to the more extensive survey. He said researchers may have identified six new landraces and several places where *teosinte*, the mother of modern maize, was still growing. Most important for the GM maize lawsuit, researchers found a far greater diversity of native maize in the north, in the areas where the government had approved GM planting. In Sinaloa, home to Monsanto's GM trials, the known number of distinct native varieties increased 253 percent.[15] Sarukhán said they had submitted a new map, to update the legal definition of "center of origin." It showed that 90 percent of Mexico's agricultural land contains native maize species worthy of protection from GM maize. To date, the government—his bosses—had not accepted it.

Sarukhán said he now believes the government should cancel all GM maize plantings, even on the remaining 10 percent of farmland. "I don't believe this country has the capacity—or the will—to regulate transgenic maize," he told me. Small amounts of GM cotton, a non-food crop, had been given planting permits several years earlier, yet now researchers had found transgenes in cotton's wild relatives, far from the designated zone for planting. "If the government can't regulate something as simple as cotton, how is it going to regulate something as large and promiscuous as maize?"

Francisca Acevedo, CONABIO scientist, gave me a beautiful poster showing the newly expanded number of Mexican landraces. The diversity jumps off the page. Sizes vary from long and fat to short and squat. Kernel patterns are equally varied. And the colors boggle the mind: every shade of yellow-orange, some pure white, pinks and reds, and purples so dark they almost look black. Why, I asked her, are the companies so interested in getting into Mexico, given the widespread opposition and the obvious reasons for precaution?

"It's like getting to the moon and planting a flag," she said after a thoughtful pause. "If you can do it in the center of origin for maize in Mexico, you can do anything."

"The entire country is a center of origin," said Antonio Serratos when I met him later. He should know. He participated in the new survey of maize biodiversity, and he had published a study intended to define "center of origin" based on existing research.[16] "You can't just isolate the communities where you find native maize." His own study for the CONABIO project, which found native maize within the confines of Mexico's sprawling capital city, had surprised him in two ways. "First, that we found so much diversity. In an area so small, so urban, it was so unlikely," he said, and encouraging. "The other surprise was finding transgenics." Researchers found transgenic traits in 70 percent of the samples from the area of Xochimilco and 49 percent of those from nearby Tlalpan.[17] Other studies have found the presence of transgenes in native maize in nearly half of Mexico's states.

Serratos offered a particularly educated perspective. He has a PhD in biotechnology from Mexico's most important biotech research center. "I was fascinated by the science, which was new in 1985." He started out working to develop transgenic maize varieties. "I began to have doubts when I saw mutations, unexpected changes, in my own research." He served on the biosecurity commission that drafted the 1998 law, which included the moratorium on GM maize, and he was a researcher on the NAFTA study of GM contamination. He clearly felt now that the government had failed to heed its clear warnings. I told him I was surprised in my research that so few people seemed to even know about the NAFTA study.

"It is Orwellian that this history is unknown." He shook his head. "It's as if the biotechnology debate just began. Only the present matters, there is no past. History does not matter. This is not just a disagreement between Monsanto and a few environmentalists."

I told him I'd heard Monsanto say that in its experimental fields they had reduced gene flow to just 0.5 percent of nearby plants, a level they deemed acceptable. Serratos nearly choked on his taco. "Maize pollen has been known to travel as far as one kilometer." He took a deep breath and explained the science of gene flow to this nonscientist.

An acre of maize will have about 15,000 plants. One-half a percent of that is 75 plants. Each plant has about 200 grains on one ear of maize, with each grain pollinated separately through the plant's silk threads. If 75 plants get some level of contamination, that can mean up to 15,000 grains. And if any of those grains are later planted as seed, they will produce pollen, even if they don't produce usable ears of maize. That pollen will travel with the wind, easily pollinating maize within 100 meters, further spreading the transgenes.

And wind-borne gene flow isn't even the most pervasive source of contamination, he told me. Seeds travel far and wide—in farmers' pockets and in transport across Mexico. Small-scale farmers are relentless experimenters, trying every seed they get their hands on to see if it produces something valuable. That's how maize has evolved into the wide and useful range of varieties we see today. That is also how imported GM maize traveled to Oaxaca, got planted by an unwitting farmer, and spread transgenes to native plants.

"If the seeds of maize are sold or exchanged, the contamination will grow exponentially," he warned. "That is the point of no return." He feared that the levels of contamination Mexico was already seeing in its native maize, even without commercial GM production in the fields, were proof that the country had already waited too long.

"We are working in evolutionary time," Serratos warned. "In Mexican fields, transgenic native maize is being created."

"It is inevitable," said Antonio Turrent, former director of INIFAP, Mexico's agricultural research institute. An Iowa-trained maize breeder and soil scientist, Turrent is president of Mexico's Association of Socially Committed Scientists (UCCS by its Spanish acronym), and he is one of the plaintiffs in the class action suit. Biotechnology advocates downplay concerns about gene flow. They argue that the "introgression" of transgenes doesn't confer an evolutionary advantage on the plants, so farmers will not select such maize for seed and replant. Not so fast, says Turrent. "The Bt transgene might prove effective in controlling a pest it was never even tested for." In that case, an unsuspecting farmer might select the successful seed and unknowingly propagate an entirely new crossbred maize, one of Serratos's transgenic native varieties. "This could happen in any part of Mexico," warned Turrent, inadvertently undermining the integrity of native maize varieties.

"You don't know it," explained Serratos, "but you're adapting a native plant to an Iowa GMO. It's a blind selection. Like a genetic disease transmitted only by the mother, like hemophilia."

High Risks, Few Rewards

It was easy to understand why small-scale farmers growing native maize varieties would oppose the entrance of GM crops. They had nothing to gain and quite a bit to lose. But what about larger-scale commercial farmers, like those in the northern state of Sinaloa? No matter what the seed companies say about helping poor farmers and feeding the world, their market is industrial-scale farms producing commercial crops. To listen to the companies, such farmers in Mexico are clamoring for access to the same advanced technologies as their competitors to the north.

From what I could tell, they are not, and the reason is simple. Existing GM maize varieties deal with two problems most Mexican farmers don't have, at least not in the same way farmers do in Iowa. Bt maize is engineered to have an insecticide in the maize plant itself to repel the European corn borer. Herbicide-tolerant maize, such as Monsanto's Roundup Ready variety, fights a broad range of weeds by allowing frequent broadcast spraying of Roundup. According to a recent academic study by Michelle Chauvet and Elena Lazos, Sinaloa's farmers would see limited savings, if any, due to reduced insecticide applications, thanks to Bt seeds. They just don't have the same corn borer problems, since the main growing season, under irrigation, is during the cooler fall–winter months. And they wouldn't save much on herbicides or farm labor from the reduced weeding afforded by Roundup Ready maize, because farm labor is inexpensive and the weed problems in northern Mexico's fall–winter season are not as severe as in Iowa. They spend very little now on weed and pest control, so Monsanto is offering something they don't really need. And the increased cost of GM seeds would be significantly higher, more than offsetting any savings.[18]

Victor Suárez, head of Mexico's largest independent association of basic grains farmers, which goes by the Spanish acronym ANEC, said that one Sinaloa farmer told him he wasn't opposed to GM crops in principle, he just didn't see any use for the ones on the market now. He already gets high yields, without GM maize, and his costs are lower. Suárez also told me that they don't want to jeopardize sales to markets that demand non-GM maize. He said China had just been on the market, specifying that they wouldn't buy GM. Why would farmers limit the potential demand for their products?

What about Suárez's own farmers, mostly midsize commercial growers with 10–100 acres of land? He sent me out to see for myself. Olga Alcaráz Andrades, the dynamic woman who leads one of the association's most successful cooperatives in Guayangareo, west of the city near Morelia, was openly dismissive of GM crops. She said the biggest problem her farmers face is high input costs and monopoly control of markets by multinational firms. Why, she asked, would we want to increase our dependence? Instead, farmers are breeding their own hybrid maize varieties, with help from the national research station. They now sell high-quality seeds to local farmers for 30 percent of the cost. She showed me their composting operation, which was giving farmers some respite from high fertilizer prices. Nearby farmers in Irapuato were doing the same for sorghum, after realizing that 95 percent of the seeds on the local market were from the transnational firms. The national research station found in its gene banks a highly productive variety that the companies hadn't wanted to produce because they didn't own the seed. Farmers grew it out themselves and they now offer high-quality sorghum seed at a 70 percent savings.

I asked Alcaráz if she thought her farmers would benefit from a drought-tolerant GM seed if one came on the market. She looked exasperated. "Sure, if it's also flood-tolerant, heat-tolerant, and cold-tolerant." That range of extreme weather was how their climate was changing. Working with ecological scientists, they were adapting without GM, thank you. ANEC's lead agricultural engineer, Juan José Valdespino, wasn't as gracious. "I wish we could genetically modify their brains so they could see other alternatives."

Maize Is Different

And consumers? Was René Sánchez Galindo right when he told me that even the judge eats tacos and knows maize is different? Cristina Barros, a Mexico City food writer, explained why UNESCO had recently recognized the country's maize-centered cuisine as a protected Patrimony of Humanity. "I don't think there is any crop in the world that has as deep a connection to its culture, starting with our myth of origin." According to Mayan lore, god created humans from maize, a mythology Mexicans embrace when they say they are *hombres de maíz*, people of maize. "No other crop has generated as many different dishes, not rice, not wheat," said Barros. "Maize is exceptional in every sense." She told me the government had not even supported the application to UNESCO, which she worked on. "They knew it would impede the entry of GM maize."

I met Marcela Bris at her restaurant, El Cardenal, which had grown from a popular little downtown lunch spot to become the Hilton Hotel's main dining room. El Cardenal had a reputation for its authentic Mexican dishes using traditional local ingredients. "We are in danger of losing our maize," she said, which is why she and other chefs are so actively supporting the anti-GM cause. They had recently published a letter demanding that the government stop supporting the biotech companies.[19]

We talked over lunch, which she ordered to impress, as if I were a restaurant reviewer instead of a wonky researcher. I complimented her on her tortilla soup, with its rich tomato broth filled

Hundreds of thousands of farmers flood the streets of Mexico City in January 2008 to protest anti-farmer government policies. *Enrique Pérez S/ANEC*

with avocado, mild Mexican cheese, dried ancho chile strips, cream, raw onions, fried corn tortilla strips, and a healthy squirt of lime. What makes Mexican cuisine so distinctive, she said, is "avocado, chile, lime, and maize. Above all maize."

A fresh basket of warm tortillas from a native maize variety arrived at the table, on cue. "Do you know that tortillas have a left and a right side?" she asked. The right side, she showed me, is the second side that cooks when the raw *masa* pancake is turned into a tortilla. As the first side cooks, the other side puffs with warm air, so when it's flipped the right side ends up with a slightly crispier center. "That is the side you put the filling on," Marcela said as she spooned *mixiote* from an earthen bowl, explaining that the native dish was made with beans, onions, and *escamoles*—ant egg sacs the size and texture of Israeli couscous—all gently seasoned and sautéed. I did the same, on the crispier right side of a tortilla. The taste was sweet, delicate, nuanced.

In the United States, GM crops are approved quickly because, the industry argues, they are "substantially equivalent" to non-GM varieties. That doesn't get very far in Mexico. Bris visibly stiffened at the concept. "Transgenic maize is just a commodity," she said. "I can't make a good *pozole* from a commodity. Or a good tortilla. It is substantially *different*, not substantially equivalent! Besides, if it's not different why can Monsanto patent it?"

Bris said she was glad the class action suit focused on the threat to native maize and not concerns about human health. "I see the ownership of patents over seeds as more horrific than the issue of health." She was right. Not only would farmers not be allowed to replant GM maize, any presence of transgenes in their own crops would subject them to legal action for patent infringement. Monsanto had certainly demonstrated its willingness to unleash its fierce legal department on unsuspecting farmers, even those who had not intentionally infringed on the company's patents.[20]

Monsanto's "2020 Vision": Market Dominance

I had, of course, asked to meet with Monsanto officials, to get their perspective. I expected a polite "no" or maybe a short meeting with a foot soldier in the company's public relations army. After all, I'd written critical pieces about the technology and the company. So I was a little surprised to find myself in a conference room in Monsanto Mexico's high-rise office in the Santa Fe business district for what would turn into a five-hour interview with six company officials.

I introduced myself, told them what I was researching, and said I would be particularly interested in their responses to the criticisms I'd heard thus far. After all, farmers, researchers, chefs, and even government officials had basically told me that gene flow from GM to native maize was a real danger, that farmers didn't need or want it, and that consumers didn't either. They listened politely and launched into a detailed sales pitch, starting with a slick PowerPoint titled "Vision 2020" on the beneficent nature of their work. In that genetically modified vision, transgenic maize is key to feeding Mexico and the world. In Mexico, it would help double Mexican maize production, reduce persistent rural poverty among the country's small-scale maize farmers, restore the country's self-sufficiency in its key food staple, and reduce the negative environmental impacts of maize farming. It would feed a growing population, estimated to reach 150 million by 2050, and combat climate change, projected to reduce the country's agricultural productivity by 26 percent by 2080. Monsanto, they told me, was all about "improving the quality of life for farmers." It was, they told me, about achieving "food sovereignty" for Mexico.

I nearly fell off my chair. This was more than a vision; this was a hallucination. Food sovereignty? That is the most radical of agriculture policy fireworks. The term was coined by La Via Campesina, the international peasant movement, and one of its targets was multinational agribusiness firms like Monsanto, which are seen as imposing their technologies on the world. The right to save seeds is at the heart of food sovereignty. I don't think I'd ever heard a more breathtaking, tone-deaf attempt at co-optation. I fastened my seat belt and reminded myself to take very, very good notes.

Dr. Juan Manuel Oyervides, a crop breeder and former colleague of Antonio Turrent's at the national research station, presented a long-view perspective on yield gains in Mexican maize. He chose to highlight his speculative estimate that the government's delay in allowing GM maize had resulted in a "lost decade" of productivity stagnation since 2000, sacrificing 12 percent of potential yield improvements worth $9.3 billion. If GM maize is approved, he projected a doubling of yield gains over current projections by 2030.

"Lost decade?" I asked him to go back to that historical slide. Doesn't your graph show that the fastest yield growth in maize had come since 2000 using conventional hybrid seeds and native maize varieties? It sure didn't look like yields were stagnating, just the opposite. And doesn't your data on Sinaloa, the heart of industrial maize production, show that yields are already comparable to those in the United States even without GM maize? Oyervides directed my attention back to the supposed 12 percent reduction from the denial of GM permits and the spectacular growth Mexico could see from widespread adoption.

That growth, of course, is a complete fantasy. A 2016 National Academy of Sciences report found "there was little evidence" that introduction of genetically modified crops in the United States has led to yield gains beyond those seen in conventional crops.[21] The main benefit, when there was one, came in the reduced need for labor. Since Mexico's rural poverty problem has everything to do with the lack of jobs, it was hard to see how labor-saving technology would be a boon to the rural poor.

Oyervides's projection was also just plain insulting. Here Monsanto was calculating the gains from wholesale adoption of GM maize throughout Mexico. But the law prohibits the use of GM seeds in the areas of Mexico considered centers of origin. Clearly the company had its transgenic sights set on more than yellow maize in Sinaloa in northern Mexico, even though that's what the majority of their suspended permits allowed. Just as the north was considered safer for environmental reasons, yellow maize was seen as less objectionable because the product was not directly consumed by humans. Most U.S. maize exports to Mexico are yellow maize, and they are used for livestock and in a lot of processed foods. Mexicans have grown accustomed to yellow GM maize, via imports, but they don't have to eat it, at least not directly. (Like us, they eat more than they know in their growing diet of imported and processed foods, which have given Mexico the unenviable distinction of toppling the United States from the number-one position in childhood obesity.[22]) There had been a big backlash when Mexicans discovered that the two tortilla conglomerates in the country were adulterating their tortillas, traditionally made with the kind of white maize grown in Sinaloa, with cheaper imported yellow maize. The practice was supposed to have stopped. Everyone knows that Mexicans don't want anyone to mess with their tortillas.

I asked my Monsanto hosts whether their goal was to open only yellow maize markets in Mexico to transgenics. You already have the Mexican market for yellow maize seeds, right? Some 95 percent of U.S. maize is GM, and that is where nearly all of Mexico's yellow maize comes from. Your seed market won't get bigger because some of the seeds get planted in Mexico, right?

The response was surprisingly frank, a less clouded 2020 vision. "In order for the penetration of biotechnology crops to be successful, it will have to be for both white and yellow corn," said Jaime Mijares Noriega, the company's Latin America director for corporate affairs. "If it was only yellow, we would not be investing."

I was shocked. Why would company officials, in the middle of a lawsuit, state so openly that their goal is to put transgenic maize into Mexican tortillas? Did they have GM white maize ready for Mexico? "We are prepared for both white and yellow." He said he thought as much as half of current hybrid white maize could be converted to GM varieties. Their sights were clearly set on Mexico's tortillas, and on maize land that could extend well into the areas deemed to be "centers of origin" for maize.

What about their field trials, now suspended by the class action suit? Oscar Heredia, head of regulatory agronomy, gave me the rose-colored version of the results: a 10 percent yield gain over hybrid maize seeds, 13 percent in Sinaloa. That is a very small gain for a technology that will be much more expensive. He touted the great benefits of improved insect and weed control, but noted that production costs were 13–24 percent higher.

So why, exactly, did they think anyone would buy their controversial seeds? Monsanto's own data show that Sinaloa's farmers, using nontransgenic varieties, already get yields higher than those on the company's carefully controlled experimental fields. Even if they got approval to plant, wouldn't the company have a tough sell in Sinaloa? They nodded: it might take time to win over Mexico's farmers.

Won't it also close off markets in countries that do not want GM maize? I asked. "The loss of export markets is a red herring for

Mexico," said Philip Eppard, regional representative for regulatory affairs and the only other U.S. native in the room. "Mexico is not exporting." That would be news to farm groups trying to increase non-GM maize exports to bolster sagging prices.

Heredia went back to the field trials. He wanted me to understand how safe GM maize was. One of the things they were testing was gene flow, with different buffer zones to reduce cross-pollination. He proudly announced that at 25 meters gene flow was detected in just 0.5 percent or fewer of plants. I asked if the company's goal was to achieve zero percent gene flow. He said that would be unrealistic. Indeed it would, which is why people like Antonio Serratos are concerned.

"We are very sensitive to Mexico being a center of origin, to the cultural significance of maize," said Mijares, sensing my concern but then showing complete disregard for it. He noted that most gene flow comes from transported maize. "If there is pollen flow to native maize, what happens? There are very few pure landraces in Mexico today. Many have already gotten genes from hybrids. And the native seeds are preserved in gene banks."

And how did they expect to control GM gene flow if transgenic maize was more widely planted? "We can't really ensure how grains are transported and where they end up," Heredia said. "It's almost impossible to control," said another colleague, as if to hammer home Dr. Sarukhán's rationale for opposing GM permits.

Were Monsanto officials really telling me that gene flow is inevitable and it doesn't matter anyway because contamination from the company's imported transgenic maize had already polluted the native gene pool? I was shocked. Not that they thought such things; their actions spoke louder than their "2020 Vision" presentations. I was shocked they would state them, and so dismissively. I guess my outrage didn't register on my face, and certainly not in their minds. So the conversation continued.

I was surprised they had barely invoked the threats of climate change in their 2020 vision. In Africa, that was the cudgel being used to beat governments into opening their regulatory doors to

GM crops. How will you feed your teeming hordes without our drought-tolerant maize, with our magic "cold gene" that confers some resistance to water stress? It doesn't, at least not very much and not in the kinds of droughts I'd seen in Southern Africa. I told my Monsanto hosts what farm leader Olga Alcaráz had said when I asked her about drought-tolerant GM maize: Sure, if it's also resistant to floods and heat and cold. One of the intrepid plant breeders was quick to respond. "They're going to need our stacked traits," he said with a straight face. He said future seeds might have as many as twenty different transgenic traits "stacked" within the genome.

This was genetically modified thinking at its worst, the reductionist "monoculture of the mind" Vandana Shiva had so brilliantly called out.[23] I thought of what Cecilia Conde, at Mexico's environment ministry, had said when I asked her if GM maize was a solution to climate change, which was projected to cut the country's maize production by up to 20 percent.[24] "It is a very inflexible response in the face of an uncertain future."

The Monsanto meeting had gone on for five hours. I was exhausted and hungry. I was relieved they did not invite me to lunch. I was starting to feel like a corn borer in a field of Bt corn; I wouldn't have touched anything they served.

"Our Problems Are Not Solved with One Gene"

Victor Suárez did offer me lunch. He could tell I was a little battered from my Monsanto meeting. He ordered me a shot of smooth tequila and a warm bowl of my favorite comfort food, tortilla soup for the soul. I was comforted, and I told him about that last response about the stacked traits to deal with climate change. He's been at this a long time, he's seen and heard it all. But that one surprised even Suárez.

"We need complex solutions to complex problems," he said. "Transgenics are simplistic. Our problems are not solved with one gene."

His jaw dropped when I told him Monsanto said it was promoting "food sovereignty." Monsanto Mexico was everything he and the other advocates of food sovereignty were committed to stopping. Monsanto *is* the threat to food sovereignty, using its political and economic power to lobby the Mexican government for regulations that could permanently limit, via contamination of native maize varieties, the ability of Mexico's people to determine how they want to meet their future food needs.

Suárez's organization was all about food sovereignty, and it didn't just involve growing more maize by applying more inputs. He called their new program "Peasant Agriculture with Integrated Knowledge Systems."[25] It was another case in which the Spanish, "conocimientos integrales," was far more eloquent than the English, "We need to bring scientific expertise together with farmer expertise," explained Suárez, with those two knowledge systems enhanced by recent scientific advances in understanding the soil and plant microbiomes. Suárez was excited, describing the recent discovery of 2,000 new families of microorganisms. "It's like discovering the Americas, or a new planet." And the implications are profound. "It allows us to analyze the metabolism of the plant and the soil."

"This is not about the defense of traditional agriculture. We are not idealizing smallholders, we are promoting technological progress," Suárez told me. "The strategy is to bring the innovation straight into the producers' organization, so the innovation comes from the producers." He clarified that much of the farmer work I'd seen in Guayangareo and Irapuato was driven precisely by this vision of food sovereignty, of freeing farmers from their dependence on transnational firms. They were producing their own seeds, generating their own compost, even producing their own microbial soil applications. In Guayangareo they were culturing their own Bt, the same bacterium from which Monsanto had derived the gene for its Bt corn and cotton. Bt, which has been used for a long time, has a host of valuable properties for soil enrichment, beyond pest resistance.[26] "Industrial agriculture's strategy is to kill pests. We seek to understand them and help the plant respond."

"I'm not an ecologist," Suárez told me defiantly, indicating he was tired of taking U.S. environmentalists around ANEC's farms only to hear them criticize the farmers for still using some chemical fertilizer. "My focus is making the peasant farmer viable. I don't come to it through agro-ecology. I come through survival, lowering costs, increasing independence. We got to this program through economic necessity." And for ANEC's producers—small- to mid-scale farmers, many of them heavily dependent on chemical inputs to grow hybrid white maize and other crops, often in monoculture, for commercial sale—that necessity has everything to do with the kinds of pressures George Naylor faces in Iowa. The new solution is not a pure agro-ecology but a transition, reducing costs by reducing the need for commercial inputs, mainly by using agro-ecological science to improve the quality of farmers' soil.

Juan José Valdespino, ANEC's soil-meister, was as passionate about the potential of emerging soil science as he was about the dead end of current technologies. "Who controls agriculture? The seed companies, the chemical companies. We need to break that paradigm," he told me as we headed out to the experimental field station in Villa Diego. "There is no one magic solution. It is not a seed. It is not a fertilizer. It is an entire system that needs to be managed, beginning with the soil. We are not just changing the input recipe, we are changing the understanding of what agriculture is. People don't understand that it isn't just about chemicals."

We met Leobardo Contreras, the manager of the station, in the field. The two of them showed us the difference between a healthy soil and one lacking organic matter. Valdespino pointed to some soil rich in organic matter but without the microbial diversity to effectively metabolize nutrients for the barley they were growing there. That's where the new soil science comes in, he said, with precision microbial applications to regenerate a living soil. Valdespino said when he got there the soil was fairly rich in organic matter thanks to Contreras, but it was lacking soil microbes.

Contreras was a believer. "He achieved in sixty days what I haven't been able to do in seventeen years here." He said the soil became soft and rich. Barley yields jumped from 4 tons per hectare to 6.5 tons. More important to the farmer, earnings went up even more dramatically, doubling with the reduced cost of inputs. That's on ex-perimental fields. What about among ANEC farmers? According to one study of early adopters, maize production increased 30 percent, costs went down 30 percent, and profits increased 60 percent. For sorghum, similar gains in production and reductions in cost took producers from bare subsistence to healthy profitability.[27]

One Jalisco maize farmer explained to me how that worked. With the help of ANEC's extension agents he had reduced input costs by two-thirds and, despite a slight drop in productivity at first, he experienced a significant increase in profitability. Slightly lower yields but much lower costs. What practices was he introduc-ing? Some associated with agro-ecology, such as compost instead of fertilizer, and microbial applications to release soil fertility. And some that are not part of the agro-ecology package, such as hybrid maize seeds that his cooperative could produce for one-third the cost of the varieties sold by multinational firms. He said his fer-tilizer applications had been reduced from two to one per season, and pesticide use had declined as well. Soil quality was slowly im-proving, and he expected further reductions in chemical use. Did he expect he would reduce it to zero? No. Did he care? Not much.

Suárez doesn't care much either. He cares about food sover-eignty. "Our goal is the small producer, not the northern consumer who wants organic food even if it's made by transnational compa-nies," he told me, taking a slap at those U.S. environmentalists. "That agenda is completely controlled by transnationals. We can learn from the new science and leave farmers in control."

After Monsanto, Suárez's optimism was welcome, bringing my own depleted reserves back to life. "This is a living agriculture grow-ing new solutions to our problems. The extreme idea of capitalism is to turn agriculture into an industry. They either turn it into an extractive industry, like a mine, or they turn it into an industrial process. But they don't make it a better system, a better *culture*.

"Native seeds are living things. They need protection," he went on. "But to survive they need investment in their improvement and devel-opment, which is investment in the farm communities themselves."

Achieving Mexico's Maize Potential

That's what ANEC has been doing for years. With small funding for a pilot program to raise maize yields among small- and medium-scale producers, they trained and deployed extension agents to work with ANEC farmers to close the so-called yield gap, the difference between current and attainable yields using readily available technologies. Studies have shown that the yield gap among Mexico's industrial-scale farmers is very low, around 10 percent, but among smaller scale farmers without irrigation yield gaps are estimated at 43 percent. Most of the country's small- to medium-scale maize farmers are operating at less than 50 percent of potential.[28]

In just a few years, ANEC got dramatic results, raising yields 55 to 70 percent in one project carried out in several states. The project did not presume the introduction of new seeds. No transgenic fantasy projections here, just basic soil analysis, improved use of fertilizers and other inputs, and the incorporation of more sustainable soil management. They saw positive results among producers on both high-quality and more marginal lands and with those using hybrid seeds as well as those relying on native maize varieties.[29]

Inspired in part by this impressive pilot project, Antonio Turrent, Elise Garvey, and I had previously published a report demonstrating that Mexico could indeed regain its self-sufficiency in maize production, without transgenic seeds or the hallucinations they seem to induce. We examined the potential productivity gains in Mexico's diverse maize-producing sectors—irrigated and rain-fed, industrial-scale and small-scale, using hybrid seeds and native varieties, with strong and weak access to natural resources. We estimated that within 10–15 years Mexico could increase annual production on current lands from 23 to 33 million tons. That would eliminate the need for imports from the United States, which currently cover the country's annual shortfall of about 10 million tons, the imports costing more than $4 billion in 2008. Additional public investment in irrigation and infrastructure projects in the southern part of the country, where water is plentiful and rural poverty is the most prevalent, could allow producers to grow another 24 million tons per year. This would be more than enough to meet Mexico's growing demand for maize, estimated to reach 39 million tons per year by 2025. Mexico could even become a maize exporter.[30]

This is exactly the kind of pro-poor investment in small-scale farming that international agencies advocated in the wake of the food crisis. Public investment should go where the yield gaps are the greatest, among small- to medium-scale farmers. This is also where private investment is scarce and where market failures are prevalent.[31]

In Tlaxcala, just east of Mexico City, they aren't waiting for public investment to protect their native seeds or improve their productivity. The state government passed its own law declaring Tlaxcala a GM-free zone. Pánfido Hernández Ortíz, of the Vicente Guerrero Integrated Rural Development Project, had no doubts about what food sovereignty meant to Tlaxcala. "We have a simple message: Mexico is not appropriate for GM maize." He said they were following a basic "food first" strategy. "If we can ensure the provision of maize and beans, we can deal with other problems."

The cooperative, which is part of ANEC, is doing its part by maintaining a seed bank of native maize varieties and promoting their use, along with the adoption of sustainable farming methods. They use the same kind of tried-and-tested farmer-to-farmer training I'd seen in Malawi, and the cooperative now has some 5,000 producers using native seeds and making that transition to agro-ecological methods. They showed me the elaborate earthen seed bank, which stood in the back of their small headquarters. I climbed the ladder to look down at a neatly labeled set of maize collections.

Emiliano Juárez Franco took me out to his farm. He has about 5 acres and uses a variety of maize seeds, native and hybrid, and *acriollado* varieties developed locally as farmers experimented with cross-breeding native seeds with hybrids. He grows them in rotation with beans and squash in the classic *milpa*, the "three sisters" intercropping method, developed by the Mesoamerican cultures that predated the Maya, to regenerate the soil without having to leave it fallow while providing a diverse diet. His fields, which sit on a gentle slope, are terraced to prevent erosion and retain water. Many farms are terraced, and he told me it was because the community had restored the tradition of *mano vuelta* work exchange, in which everyone pitches in on a particularly labor-intensive job knowing their turn will come. Think barn-raising, with everybody pitching in to help their neighbors.

I asked Juárez how long he had been farming this way. He smiled, "Since our ancestors." He said he'd been working with the cooperative to improve his farming for many years. And why not? Even with the intercropping, which uses maize land for beans and squash too, Juárez said his maize harvests have quadrupled with the agro-ecology methods. He now grows enough to last the whole year—it used to run out after ten months—and he still has 40 percent of the harvest to sell for cash, giving his family of eight the money it needs for other expenses. Costs are way down too, with most seeds saved year-to-year, and with fertilizer applications cut from two applications to one. Push-pull pest control methods have reduced the need for pesticides.

This was closing the yield gap, the key to restoring food self-sufficiency in Mexico. As the co-op leaders stressed, this was about food sovereignty, protecting their agriculture and food systems with a moratorium on GM seeds while they reduced dependence on purchased inputs through their journey toward agro-ecology. Whether they reached that destination or not.

Food Sovereignty in Puebla

They'd pretty well reached the destination in Cuetzalán, a collection of remote villages in the northeastern corner of the state of Puebla, east of Mexico City. There, a remarkable union of cooperatives called Tosepan Titataniske had drawn on the communities' indigenous Nahuatl traditions and used their remoteness to carve out not just an area free of transgenics but a territory free of megaprojects. It hadn't come easy.

When the environment ministry announced the large "Cloud Forest" ecotourism project for the area in the late 1990s, the community mobilized. They had already seen the negative impacts of such projects. Mines were contaminating rivers. Hydroelectric projects, taking advantage of the abundant rains in the mountainous area, were destroying the local environment. There were ninety-eight land concessions for such projects in the area.

Tosepan Titataniske, which means "together we shall overcome" in the local Nahuatl language, organized, taking advantage of a national law that allows communities to zone for different land uses. With a series of technical studies and community consultations that involved up to 5,000 people, they approved their "Ecological Land-Use Zoning for the Sierra Norte of Puebla." The plan identified areas approved for conservation, restoration, sustainable use, and protection (including the main watersheds). Mining and most other megaprojects were defined as categorically incompatible with all four zones.

Getting the plan enforced was another matter, as the companies pushed back. Tosepan created its own Territorial Defense Committee to monitor company activities and filed a class action suit to have its zoning plan recognized and enforced. They won their case in March 2015, but enforcement is still a problem. Still, Tosepan leader Enrique Fernández told us that they had successfully stopped four hydroelectric projects and a Walmart through a mixture of legal action, lobbying, and direct action to stop the bulldozers and backhoes.[32]

Stopping Walmart and the national electric company got my attention. Was this another little David taking on a different set of Goliaths? Little wasn't the word that came to mind as I learned more about Tosepan. The organization, which started in 1977, now has 410 cooperatives involving more than 30,000 families in 25 municipalities (similar to U.S. counties) across the remote region. Leonardo Durán Olguín, the young multilingual local who briefed our small group on the organization, said the goal of the group was *yeknemilis* in Nahuatl, *buenvivir* in Spanish, and of course we don't really have a good phrase for such a lovely concept in English. Good living? No matter, they showed us what they meant.

Their schools, which were in session, were a good place to start. Tosepan runs its own autonomous school system recognized by the government under a program for remote communities. They get no funds from the government, just some books. It's supported like many other cooperatives in the community, with donations and a lot of volunteer labor. Their teachers, however, are trained on the Montessori model as bilingual Spanish-Nahuatl instructors. Indeed, in one fourth-grade class the teacher went back and forth between the two languages seamlessly. The goal is to have all children functionally bilingual by sixth grade. She said that younger children come in with stronger Nahuatl (or Tutunaku, the other indigenous language in the region) than Spanish. They want children to be able to function in the larger Spanish-speaking society, assigning books and book reports in Spanish. ("In a country where our president does not read books," one teacher told us, "we want children who read." Amen, I thought in 2015, and I didn't even know what was coming back home.) They keep older children from losing their local language by involving them in cultural projects, including their own weekly radio show in Nahuatl, called *Vida Digna* in Spanish. (Again, our English isn't up to the elegance: Dignified Life?) It includes high-schoolers interviewing their grandmothers or older community leaders in their native language.

These were impressive kids, particularly the girls, so poised and articulate as they toured us around the school, showed us their school newspaper, explained how they make biological fertilizers as part of their practical work curriculum. No wonder. Their regular school day involves only two and a half hours of academic instruction. The rest is spent on farmwork, physical education, and arts and local crafts, with an hour for recess and lunch. The food is donated by community members and prepared by a student-staffed cafeteria. Everybody's involved in community projects. The eco-lodge we stayed in, made entirely with bamboo from a Tosepan project that makes furniture and building materials, is run by a youth cooperative. Other students staff the community store, selling eggs and other farm produce. It is just part of the culture, with all community members participating in *tequio*, or community labor.

Economic projects center mainly on coffee, which grows on

beautiful shaded hillsides that contain 150 different plant species. Their cooperative control of the process has boosted farmer income from coffee 200 percent. Cooperatives also have a successful organic bee/honey operation and the bamboo workshop producing furniture for the local market. We visited the large processing plant in town where they produce high-quality organic pepper for export to the Middle East and Europe. And of course they grow maize, usually intercropped with beans, squash, chiles, and other edible plants. Leonardo said the community is largely self-sufficient in basic foods.[33]

It was easy to romanticize Tosepan as being "off the grid," but as Leonardo made clear they know that with megaprojects threatening them they need to engage with the larger national and international economy. They just need to do so strategically, not letting the market decide their collective futures. Certainly Monsanto was not going to decide what they grow or eat in Tosepan.

Biodiversity as a Right

I was back in Mexico City in September 2015, participating in ANEC's international agro-ecology conference. The title of the conference left no doubts about its agenda: "Food and Nutritional Sovereignty and Security: With Peasants and Agro-Ecology, Without Transgenics, Monopolies, or Free Trade Agreements." Victor Suárez was at his fiery best, taking advantage of the ceremonial presence of new agriculture minister José Eduardo Calzada Rovirosa to decry "the tyranny of the market," demand that the government "resist pressures from monopolies like Monsanto," and "stop treating peasants like poor people, instead of producers." In front of 200 people, with TV cameras rolling, Suárez even demanded a meeting and presented the captive minister with ANEC's demands. It was an offer he couldn't refuse.

Meanwhile, those seed monopolies weren't taking no for an answer on their GM maize. The judge who had ruled on the injunction had unexpectedly retired six months earlier than expected. His replacement had immediately declared the injunction invalid.

Monsanto celebrated with a blizzard of triumphalist propaganda, declaring the issue settled, just in time for the Sinaloa cropping season. The class action plaintiffs made sure the issue was anything but settled. David & Co. LLC filed an appeal within hours, keeping the precautionary injunction in place until the appeal could be heard.

Adelita San Vicente, lead plaintiff for the class action, reminded people at the conference that we were approaching the second anniversary of the precautionary injunction against GM maize. She lauded the national campaign "Sin Maíz No Hay País" (Without Corn There Is No Country) and its determined campaign to "save the country by saving the countryside." When I spoke to her at lunch, she was worried—about the case and about contamination levels, which the environment ministry had confirmed, right in the bull's-eye inside the center of origin, in southwestern Mexico.

Before I returned home I made another stop at the Church of San Judas Tadeo. When I'd first investigated this case a year and a half earlier, I'd said a prayer for what seemed like a difficult case, if not a lost cause. But I wasn't a true believer. Now I was a little bit more of a believer. The injunction had withstood repeated challenges, more than the nonbeliever in me would have predicted. At the church, the priest was blessing the desperate. I lit my candle and said my prayer.

Nearly three years later, as this book goes to press, I'm even more of a believer. The injunction remains in place, headed to the Supreme Court, while lower courts consider the central claim of the class action that GM maize poses uncontrolled risks to Mexico's maize diversity. Decisions are not expected before 2019. Monsanto and the other seed Goliaths will have lost a remarkable five planting seasons to the legal action, creating a huge sunk cost on their investment. They'd suffered other defeats as well. In November 2017, a judge revoked the company's permit to plant GM soybeans in seven states after a different set of plaintiffs had filed suit over the contamination of their organic beehives and honey with transgenic pollen from nearby soybean fields.[34] And on July 1, 2018, the Gene Giants may have suffered their most decisive defeat with the landslide victory of presidential candidate Andrés Manuel López Obrador and his Morena movement in national elections. López Obrador has been outspoken in his opposition to GM maize and his support for native maize producers. When he takes office December 1, he could withdraw government support for the companies' GM permits. As this book goes to press, the legal case goes on and the injunction remains in effect.

For Adelita San Vicente, the injunction's success was no miracle. "The collective's action was the product of many years of organization and struggle by the Mexican people. No country in the world has mobilized as much resistance as Mexico to the planting of transgenic maize."

Meanwhile, the companies were trying to bypass the courts altogether, with the U.S. government proposing in NAFTA negotiations that the three countries agree to accept one another's food and crop safety assessments, overriding Mexican law and undercutting its judicial system. More worrisome still, GM maize contamination had spread to the most popular of Mexico's foods, including its precious tortillas. A 2017 study had found that 90 percent of store-bought tortillas revealed the presence of transgenes. A shocking 82 percent of maize-based foods also showed some level of contamination. Many also contained traces of glyphosate, the herbicide in Monsanto's Roundup. No one could say whether the pollution came from illegally planted GM maize or from food companies adulterating prepared foods with cheaper imported U.S. maize.[35] Did that prove those cynical Monsanto forces of darkness right, that the damage has already been done, that resistance is futile?

Adelita San Vicente couldn't have been clearer. She cited Judge Walter Arrellano Hobelsberger's January 2014 decision upholding the injunction: "The use and enjoyment of biodiversity is the right of present and future generations." "We will defend our seeds and our sovereignty," said San Vicente, "not just in the courts but in the fields, in the streets, and in our collective demands for government policies that respect our rights."

Part III

Trading Away the Right to Food

THE GREATEST THREAT TO Mexican maize diversity isn't genetically modified maize, it's free trade, facilitated by the North American Free Trade Agreement (NAFTA), which eliminated trade barriers among Canada, Mexico, and the United States. Since NAFTA took effect in 1994, goods and capital have flowed relatively freely across borders. Iowa's cheap, plentiful corn has poured into Mexico, driving down the prices farmers can get for their own crops, putting some out of business. When they go, so do their native seeds, and genetic erosion slowly builds.

Trade and investment agreements such as NAFTA are among the main vehicles through which multinational corporations have expanded their reach and power in the age of globalization. The United States alone has fourteen trade agreements with some twenty countries.[1] Bilateral investment agreements are even more common. These are written to ensure the rights of foreign investors in overseas markets, protecting them from government actions that favor domestic firms. These can be as extreme as expropriation, but they can be as straightforward as revoking a building permit for public health reasons. Most controversial, they often grant foreign investors the right to sue the host government for actions that reduce the expected profits from their investments, a right not enjoyed by domestic firms. The United States has negotiated a remarkable forty-seven investment agreements with foreign governments.[2]

At the global level, the World Trade Organization (WTO) includes 164 countries under a 1995 agreement. It promotes the lowering of trade barriers and disciplines member governments for taking extreme protectionist measures, with an agreed process for settling disputes. At best, it offers a needed set of rules for global trade. Not surprisingly, though, those rules heavily favor the dominant rich-country exporters where most of the multinational firms are based. Some of those rules make it easier for global agribusiness firms and rich-country exporters to sell the surplus farm goods generated by all their investment in agricultural technologies.

The unfairness of the agreement has provoked a backlash, particularly with the emergence of large developing countries such as China, Brazil, South Africa, and India. Citizens around the world have also objected, as they have seen wages and farm prices fall with unchecked global competition. In 2001, WTO members agreed in Doha, Qatar, far from the protests that had derailed earlier attempts, to a new round of negotiations designed to rebalance the agreement, formally recognizing the need to give developing countries "special and differentiated treatment" as they liberalize their economies. The Doha Development Round was born. It has largely stalled since, as rich countries like the United States lose interest in giving up their global economic advantages.

Only 23 percent of the food consumed in the world is traded across national borders, yet global trade exerts enormous control over local market conditions.[3] That's how U.S. overproduction of corn can depress prices all over the world when we export our surpluses. It is also how U.S. ethanol expansion can drive prices to damaging highs, not just for corn in the United States but for a wide variety of crops all over the world. What happens in the United States does not stay in the United States. It ripples outward, backed by policies and regulations that favor global agribusiness firms. Those ripples can build to tsunamis in globalized markets, as we saw with the 2007–2008 food crisis.

Global trade is an important arena in which the battle for the future of food is being waged between family farmers trying to defend farms, seeds, and livelihoods and agribusiness firms trying to expand their markets. Here I examine two emblematic battles: the plight and resistance of Mexican farmers to U.S. "agricultural dumping" under NAFTA; and the defense by India's right-to-food movement of its hard-won National Food Security Act—the most ambitious anti-hunger program in history—against charges by the United States in the WTO that India is providing an unfair subsidy to farmers.

8

NAFTA's Assault on Mexico's Family Farmers

It seemed to me the biggest threat to maize diversity in Mexico came not from potential GM planting in northern Mexico but from free trade. After all, widespread contamination was already happening in Mexico, even without approval for commercial planting. Researchers had found traces in the vast majority of maize-based foods. Perhaps more worrisome, a recent study by the environment ministry revealed ninety-six cases of GM contamination of native maize varieties in six states in southern Mexico, far from the GM maize trials. That didn't come from widespread planting, it came from free trade. GM maize has flowed freely into Mexico—as grain not as seed—since NAFTA opened the door and the Mexican government swung it wide open for the transgenic visitors from the north. As the environment ministry study showed, some native maize is already contaminated, and not just in the relatively industrialized agriculture of the north. In the true geographical center of origin of the crop.

But GM contamination itself may not even be the biggest threat to native maize from NAFTA. The flood of imported maize has made life precarious for the poor producers most likely to be cultivating native varieties. NAFTA has driven prices down dramatically, not just for maize but for a variety of crops small-scale farmers depend on. Those economic pressures have made farming untenable, driving farmers from their land. More maize varieties may well be lost to extinction than to contamination, if the communities that grow them abandon their traditions and their farms. In Mexico, most everyone seemed to understand that the legal case is one important battle in the larger war to preserve and strengthen peasant maize production in Mexico. A new expanse of GM maize in northern Mexico wouldn't be the end of that war, just some lost territory—literally. The real assault was NAFTA, along with the neoliberal economic policies adopted by the Mexican government of which NAFTA was an integral part.

In 2018, thanks to changes in leadership in the United States and in Mexico, the anti-NAFTA movement had opened a new front in that larger war. U.S. president Donald Trump vowed to "make America great again" by renegotiating NAFTA, stating that Mexico was stealing U.S. jobs. That played about as badly as you would expect in Mexico. Trump piñatas appeared in street vendors' stalls, and center-left presidential candidate Andrés Manuel López Obrador rode the nationalist wave, winning a landslide victory in Mexico's July 1, 2018, election. López Obrador has been a NAFTA critic since the agreement was first adopted, and his previous two presidential campaigns (which he almost won) featured an anti-NAFTA message and strong support for measures to protect and support small-scale farmers. In his current campaign, he pledged to oppose the approval of GM maize and he endorsed the pro-farmer Plan de Ayala reform proposal.[1] His first public statements on NAFTA have been conciliatory, promising to cooperate with the outgoing government to continue negotiations toward a new agreement. The farmers who mobilized to support him clearly hope he will defend them from underpriced U.S. exports.

Mexico had once proudly been the poster child for free trade, promising that it would modernize Mexican agriculture and bring the country into the first world. Now that child, obese on his imported U.S. diet, offers a warning that the promises of free trade are exaggerated while the threats—to farmers, food security, public health, and the environment—are very real.

NAFTA: A Trail of False Promises

With even the U.S. president now calling NAFTA a disaster, it is hard to remember the trade agreement's original promise. Mexico would enter the "first world" of developed countries on the crest of rising trade and foreign investment. Its dynamic manufacturing sector would create so many jobs it would absorb millions of peasant farmers freed from their unproductive toil in the fields. Mexico would import cheap corn, driving down food prices, and export electronics and strawberries. The Mexican government promised that NAFTA would solve the migration problem, allowing Mexico to "export goods, not people."[2]

For the Mexican elite seeking to break with the country's nationalist economic policies, hitching the country's economic wagon to the United States made perfect sense. NAFTA was really the first such free trade agreement, and it was expansive. It not only reduced tariffs—the taxes countries place on imports to earn revenue and protect domestic producers from competition—it liberalized the flow of capital. Like many developing countries, Mexico restricted foreign investment with a variety of measures, such as limiting foreign ownership to less than 50 percent of any enterprise and approving such investments only if certain "performance requirements" were met, such as buying from local vendors or training Mexicans for technical positions. NAFTA broke down those barriers so the investment could flow freely. With tariffs and other trade restrictions reduced or eliminated, trade would be the engine of Mexico's growth, driven by demand from the massive U.S. consumer market and easy access along the 2,000-mile border the two countries share. Foreign investment from the United States, particularly in the country's manufacturing sector, would turbocharge economic growth. No longer would U.S. industrialists be limited to the free trade zone along the border, where *maquiladora* light assembly plants had operated for years.

For agriculture, the promise was modernization. Mexico already had industrialized, commercial farmers. The Mexican government's plan, clearly articulated at the time, was to reduce the agricultural population to less than 10 percent of the workforce by making traditional producers compete with U.S. farmers, who got triple the yields.[3] Protections for domestic producers would be phased out, as would a variety of government institutions that supported the sector with everything from crop research to extension services, price supports, and marketing services. Mexico would import cheaper crops from the United States, making food cheaper for consumers, and the country would become the chosen export platform for winter fruits and vegetables into a U.S. market hungry for year-round fresh produce.

Mexican president Carlos Salinas de Gortari led the reform movement, which encountered mass opposition from a wary public. The electorate was so mistrustful, in fact, that even in the "perfect dictatorship" that was Mexican democracy, with the one dominant Institutional Revolutionary Party (PRI by its Spanish acronym), Salinas had to resort to massive electoral fraud to win the 1988 election that opened the door to NAFTA. Cuauhtémoc Cárdenas, running on a nationalist platform, was winning in the early count before the electoral machinery mysteriously went down, only to restart with Salinas making a suspicious comeback.[4]

The die was cast for NAFTA negotiations, largely with U.S. president George H. W. Bush and Canadian prime minister Brian Mulroney. They were confronted by a well-organized tri-national opposition from labor, farmer, environmental, and consumer organizations. For Mexico, maize was by far the most important crop included in NAFTA; it covered 60 percent of the country's agricultural land. In terms of employment, maize was by far the single most important commodity in the economy, providing livelihoods for more than 3 million producers, some 8 percent of Mexico's population at the time and 40 percent of those working in the agricultural sector. Maize almost was not included in NAFTA; U.S. negotiators did not think the Mexican government would end protection for such a sensitive crop.[5] Salinas did, to intense protest in Mexico. He promised large-scale investments in irrigation for farmers and negotiated a fifteen-year phaseout of tariff protection to manage the transition.[6] He would renege on both promises.

NAFTA took effect at midnight on January 1, 1994, and the agreement got no honeymoon period in Mexico. Within hours, the Zapatista Army of National Liberation launched armed attacks in southern Mexico, declaring NAFTA "a death sentence for all of the Indigenous ethnicities in Mexico."[7]

On its own narrow terms—increasing trade and investment— NAFTA succeeded. By 2007, Mexican exports had quadrupled, with the growth predominantly in manufacturing, where productivity increased about 80 percent in Mexico's domestic manufacturing sector as Mexican firms were forced to compete with foreign firms. Agricultural exports doubled. Foreign direct investment, overwhelmingly from the United States, tripled.[8] Mission accomplished? Not so fast.

All that trade and investment didn't translate into either rapid

A farmer in Xalapa, Veracruz, waits for a *coyote* to take him north. NAFTA caused a surge in migration as farmers lost their livelihoods to cheap imports.
© *David Bacon dbacon@igc.org*

economic growth or an employment boom. Overall, there was a small rise in manufacturing jobs as multinational firms, especially in the auto sector, relocated to Mexico. But a countryside inundated with cheap U.S. maize and other basic foods expelled three *campesinos* for every new factory job. The only significant growth was in services, where most new jobs were in the informal sector—street vendors, junk collectors, and off-the-books workers. Fifteen years into NAFTA, it was telling that the share of the working population in that shadow economy had grown, from an already-embarrassing 52 percent to 57 percent after NAFTA.[9] Needless to say, Mexico did not stop exporting people. In fact, the migration rate surged to some 500,000 per year. The one market NAFTA hadn't freed was labor; the agreement legalized the free flow of capital and goods but not people. Desperate Mexicans brought that market into equilibrium themselves, braving increasingly strict U.S. immigration enforcement to go where the North American jobs were—the United States.[10]

Dumping, Displacement, and Dependency

Many of those migrants were coming from the post-NAFTA disaster that was rural Mexico. The country's 3 million maize farmers were under assault. Their government had eliminated key agencies that supported small-scale producers, such as CONASUPO, which bought and marketed basic grains at supported prices. In its modernization push, the government had also forced through a modification of the Mexican constitution, written in the wake of the Mexican Revolution in the early twentieth century, which recognized communal rural property, as *ejidos* or as communal lands in indigenous areas. The constitutional reform created a path to privatization, which many feared would result in the dispossession of poor farmers. And then there were NAFTA's reduced tariffs. To deepen the assault, the government had unilaterally decided to forgo the transition periods for most agricultural tariffs, which would have phased them out over 5–15 years to allow a more orderly adjustment of these sensitive markets. From day one of NAFTA, Mexico opened its doors and maize farmers got no transitional tariff protection.[11]

U.S. goods certainly poured through those open doors. By 2007, U.S. exports to Mexico of wheat, cotton, and rice had all increased more than 500 percent over pre-NAFTA levels. Meat exports jumped as well, with beef up 278 percent, poultry 363 percent, and pork a remarkable 707 percent. Soybean exports went up 159 percent. Maize exports increased more than 400 percent.[12]

Worse still for Mexican farmers, those imports entered at dumping-level prices, below what it cost to produce them. In part, that was because the U.S. Congress added insult to NAFTA's injury with its 1996 farm bill. The Orwellian "Freedom to Farm Act" eliminated all vestiges of supply management, which had been the cornerstone of U.S. agricultural policies since Henry A. Wallace introduced them during the Great Depression. Their demise meant that the U.S. government no longer used a mix of price supports, reserves, and land set-asides to manage the precarious balance between supply and demand, which without government intervention often saw supplies outstrip demand and prices fall to unsustainable levels. Surprise: the reforms created an immediate crisis when prices plummeted. Millions of acres of land that had been held out of agriculture came back into production. Land planted to eight major U.S. crops increased 6 percent and crop prices fell, prompting a farm crisis that threatened to provoke a run on rural banks. The government stepped in with a series of emergency payments to farmers, which evolved into the mix of farm subsidies we see to this day. Farm program costs increased from their pre-1996 levels of around $10 billion per year to around $20 billion per year.

So Mexican farmers weren't just facing an import flood of competitively priced farm products, they were being asked to compete with dumped goods. I had estimated the so-called dumping margins between 1997—after full NAFTA liberalization and the U.S.

farm bill—and 2005, the year before the speculative run-up in commodity prices began. For five key crops, the U.S. exports were sold at between 12 and 38 percent below their average costs of production. Corn was exported to Mexico in those nine years at 19 percent below what it cost to produce.

This helped push down producer prices in Mexico. Adjusted for inflation, producer prices fell between 51 and 67 percent from their pre-NAFTA levels. Corn prices plummeted 66 percent. But if the United States exports yellow corn, for animal feed and industrial uses, and Mexico grows white corn for tortillas and other foods, why would cheap U.S. corn drive down Mexican prices? The markets have been closely connected for a long time, with one price quoted on the Chicago Mercantile Exchange and often with a price premium in Mexico for white corn. After the integration that came with NAFTA, those markets became more closely intertwined, and prices converged downward with U.S. corn prices.[13]

Mexican farmers in a few short years had seen their government abandon the family farm sector and then open the gates not just to cheaper industrial U.S. maize but to below-cost grain. I estimated that Mexican farmers in those nine years would have earned $6.6 billion more from the sales of their maize if prices had just been at cost, without the dumping. But at least the tortillas were cheap, right? Wrong, as the magic of the imperfect market once again confounded free trade's true believers. Despite the drop in maize prices, tortilla prices ten years into NAFTA were about one-third higher, adjusting for inflation.[14] The two companies that dominated the tortilla market didn't pass on the price reductions, and the Mexican government's elimination of subsidies undercut the consumer benefits of cheaper maize.

The impact on rural Mexico was devastating. Production of soybeans, wheat, cotton, and rice all fell with the import surge. Maize production, remarkably, increased 50 percent, which analysts have attributed partly to Mexico's own farm subsidy program, which favored maize over other crops. But for poor farmers who received a small share of those subsidies, the increase in maize production represented a "retreat to subsistence," the long-observed tendency of poor farmers to increase production of basic food crops in an economic crisis. If you can't make money selling them, you'll at least have something to eat.

And this was a certifiable rural crisis. Rural poverty went up to 55 percent, with 25 percent in extreme poverty.[15] Not surprisingly, many left agriculture to look for work. According to the 2007 agriculture census, an estimated 2.3 million people had left agriculture since 1993, more than one-quarter of the farming population.[16] The displacement was actually far worse than that. Another 3 million had left their households as internal migrants, seeking wage income as seasonal laborers in the booming tomato and strawberry fields. The fruit and vegetable export operations, mostly large commercial farms operated by multinational firms like Driscoll strawberries, had expanded dramatically under NAFTA. In 2017, $5.5 billion worth of fresh vegetables and $6.0 billion in fresh fruit were shipped to a seemingly insatiable U.S. market.[17] But that didn't do anything for Mexican farmers. The good news was that those farmers hadn't given up their farms, despite the constitutional reform intended to make them to do just that. The common household survival strategy involved sending young and able-bodied family members off to earn money they could send back home. They picked strawberries for Driscoll, harvested tomatoes in Sonora state, or went to the cities to join the informal workforce. Many rural migrants, of course, simply headed north to the United States, where the North American jobs were.

By the mid-2000s, many rural villages looked hollowed out, with grandparents raising their grandchildren after all the working-age family members had migrated. It was an extreme version of what I'd seen in Iowa, with its depopulated rural communities. This was far more devastating for families, with parents separated from children. For those who migrated to the United States, the wage remittances they sent home became a lifeline sustaining rural communities, and almost defining a new rural economic order. You could tell who had family members in the United States by which household had the new roof, the cement floor, the car. Remittances from the United States to Mexico topped $20 billion, making it ironically one of the largest sources of U.S. dollars, even greater than U.S. foreign direct investment.[18] Mexican migrants were sending as much capital to Mexico as all those coveted foreign investors. Strict U.S. immigration policies didn't really slow the northward migration, they just inadvertently increased the number of permanent undocumented residents as migrants chose to stay rather than risk the return to Mexico.

NAFTA not only devastated rural Mexico, it undermined the larger society. Mexico may have been exporting more fruits and vegetables to the United States, but its imports of basic grains and meats left the country dangerously dependent. Mexico had been relatively self-sufficient in maize before NAFTA, importing in lean years. By 2007, the country was importing one-third of its maize. Import dependency increased for other crops as well, most notably from 18 percent to 57 percent for wheat, the very crop Norman Borlaug had bred in Mexico for the first green revolution. Overall, Mexico is now estimated to be importing a disturbingly high 46 percent of its basic grains, most from the United States.[19] That import dependency made Mexico particularly vulnerable when maize and other commodity prices spiked in the United States in 2007–2008. The country's agricultural trade deficit with the United States went negative as the gamble on cheap food went sour. The rising cost of maize imports alone accounted for Mexico's entire $2.5 billion agricultural trade deficit in 2011.[20]

And that imported food, with the shift to U.S.-style diets, is making a lot of people sick. As a revealing *New York Times* feature showed, NAFTA has indeed exported obesity to Mexico.[21] Part of the problem is the prepared foods Mexico imports, many of which are processed and high in sugar, salt, and fat. Soda is a big winner under NAFTA. Some of the problems come with the crops, as cheap maize and soybeans provide cheap feed for the growing consumption of meat and dairy products. And part of the NAFTA effect comes through U.S. multinational retailers like Walmart, which coax Mexicans to give up their tortillas, beans, and tamales for cheap processed foods like pizza slices. Altogether, the diet changes have given Mexico the dubious distinction of having the highest child obesity rate in the world, surpassing the previous title-holder, its NAFTA partner to the north.

"Assume We Have Employment"

One version of an old joke features a shipwrecked economist on a deserted island who, when asked by his fellow survivors what expertise he can offer on how they can be rescued, replies, "Assume we have a boat." Economists, particularly those of the neoliberal persuasion, have a well-deserved reputation for making their theories work only by making unrealistic assumptions about how the real world operates.

I was reminded of the joke at Mexico's National Autonomous University during a 2010 conference on Mexican farm policies in the wake of NAFTA. A World Bank economist had just spoken during the seminar, and I realized the blind assumption that allowed him to defend the shipwreck that is NAFTA was: "Assume we have employment."[22]

The economist delivered a barely modified version of the World Bank's long-standing diagnostic on small-scale agriculture, apparently oblivious to Mexican reality. Small landholdings make inefficient use of land, he explained, and the food crops smallholders grow can be produced much more efficiently by industrialized farmers in Mexico and the United States. NAFTA gives Mexico tariff-free access to those goods, so Mexico's 2 million small-scale maize farmers should enjoy the cheaper tortillas and seek more productive activities, taking advantage of the country's comparative advantages by growing high-value crops or moving out of agriculture into low-wage manufacturing. Mexico's agricultural policies should be geared not toward increasing smallholder food productivity but toward providing the social safety net that can help them make that transition while improving infrastructure and public services in rural areas.

Moving out of agriculture? Into what? "Assume we have employment" can be the only answer. Because just as shipwrecked survivors can't sail home on an economist's theoretical boat, Mexico's
small-scale farmers needed real jobs, not assumed jobs, if they were
to give up their lands and their homes. They were looking out at the
post-NAFTA economic landscape, and it was bleak. The country's
comparative advantage seemed to be in informal work, the range
of illegal activities from street vending to drug trafficking, from
illegal migration to the human smuggling networks that took migrants across the U.S. border. After all, one booming industry after
NAFTA was the *coyote* business: the shady operators who charge
fees to take migrants to *el norte* had raised the price of the trip
from $500 to $4,000 since the NAFTA migration boom.[23] Supply
and demand at work in the one area not liberalized by NAFTA,
labor.

Poor farmers with a little land sent their able-bodied relatives
where the work was and actually increased their maize production. Irrational? Hardly. Small-scale farmers are at least smarter
than World Bank economists. They know that growing maize, with
limited technology and low yields, is inefficient only if they have a
more productive use for their land or their labor. The land is often
the only asset the family has, and most smallholder land is unsuit-
able for strawberries or high-value crops. As for their labor, they
send family members as seasonal or permanent migrants and use
the remittances to keep farming back home. Are their low maize
yields proof of inefficiency? Or do they show that smallholders are
maximizing their available labor and resources?

The World Bank economist didn't fare well, not with farm movement leader Victor Suárez on his panel. Since NAFTA, Suárez
railed, we've had a flood of dumped maize and other products from
the United States, a financial crisis and recession, a rise in migration, a food crisis that caused tortilla riots, and all the World Bank
can say is that our farmers are unproductive and should get out
of farming. Our farmers have increased their productivity, despite
all the disadvantages, Suárez shouted, despite being written off

by the World Bank and the Mexican government, despite Mexico channeling its own farm subsidies to the biggest industrial farmers. Imagine what we could do if the government valued our work, he concluded, pointing to the wide range of rejected policy proposals his organization and others had made in recent years.[24]

I'd read an even more succinct response to such neoliberal orthodoxy from a Mexican farmer: "We've been producing corn in Mexico for 8,000 years. If we don't have a comparative advantage in corn, where do we have a comparative advantage?"[25]

Maize Diversity and the Globalization of Market Failure

The answer, unfortunately, is that native varieties are not the kind of maize that global markets value, which is why many farmers are more concerned about globalization than GM maize as a threat to Mexico's maize diversity. Global markets value bulk, uniform commodities that can be traded and used as raw materials for everything from animal feed to high-fructose corn syrup. Or even commodities such as hybrid white maize that can feed Mexico's industrialized tortilla-makers. The U.S. corn belt and Mexico's Sinaloa state have those comparative advantages, not the small-scale and indigenous farmers who still grow native varieties of maize, in the process serving as unpaid stewards of the crop's diversity.

Why? Because markets fail to value that diversity while at the same time placing no price on the so-called negative externalities associated with industrialized maize farming. The water pollution in Iowa's farm production is paid for by taxpayers to fund the Des Moines Water Works, but the price of U.S. maize does not reflect any such environmental costs. Soil erosion has no immediate cost, nor do greenhouse gas emissions from factory farms and over-fertilized fields. As a result, U.S. maize goes out into the world doubly underpriced. First, it is overproduced and subsidized, leading to dumping at below the financial costs of production. Second, it fails to reflect the environmental costs of production. If it did, U.S. maize would lose some of its competitive market advantage over Mexico's native maize, which the market undervalues by failing to put a price on the maintenance of agricultural diversity.

Globalization under a free trade agreement such as NAFTA brings underpriced U.S. maize into direct competition with undervalued native maize in Mexico, and the environmental damage is worse than the sum of its parts. Pollution-intensive U.S. maize displaces more sustainably produced Mexican maize, undermining the long-term value of Mexico's maize diversity.

Economist James Boyce has called such phenomena the "globalization of market failure," as economic integration links imperfect markets in environmentally destructive ways. Market failures—when a market fails to operate competitively and fails to price all costs and benefits—are recognized by even the most orthodox economists. Boyce carried out field studies of traditional jute production in Bangladesh, which was being displaced by imported synthetic fibers, and traditional maize production in Mexico. In both cases, the market prices for modern, northern products fail to incorporate significant negative environmental externalities. Meanwhile, traditional producers go uncompensated for the positive environmental externalities associated with traditional production. The study showed that nearly the entire price advantage enjoyed by synthetics over jute in Bangladesh—about 35 percent—would be eliminated if environmental externalities were factored into prices.[26]

It is well known that global economic integration increases pressure on agricultural biodiversity. Market integration promotes specialization and an exclusive focus on high-yield varieties, as national markets become dominated by low-priced imports from the agricultural surpluses of the largest global producers. This leads to the loss of local varieties as well as minor crops. Globalization also replaces local cultural traditions with "modern" preferences; wheat bread—or pizza—supplants the market for tortillas in Mexico. Livelihood pressures lead to the need for off-farm employment to supplement incomes. This results in declining attention to traditional farming, and often to wholesale migration and the abandonment of farming altogether.[27]

Genetic erosion, in fact, is built into the current system of economic incentives. Modern agriculture depends on traditional agriculture for genes but returns nothing to it, resulting in the erosion of the source on which it depends for raw material. Modern crop varieties are bred from gene banks filled with native seeds, public goods easily appropriated for private gain.[28] Environmental economists have attempted to quantify the value contributed to modern agriculture by the genetic stocks maintained by traditional farmers. One study estimated that genetic improvements to U.S. crops from existing diversity—the seed diversity created and maintained by farmers over generations—increased the value of harvests by an average of $1 billion per year from the 1930s.[29] In effect, indigenous Mayan farmers have contributed to Iowa's maize productivity by creating the raw material for plant breeding. Now, Iowa's high productivity directly threatens the ability of those indigenous farmers to maintain their native varieties.[30]

Niche markets, such as for certified organic products that earn a price premium for the producer, are one market-based way to recognize such value. Unfortunately, the scale of crop diversity—and its erosion—are so vast that no niche market large enough to address the problem is likely to emerge for native maize. In any case, agro-ecologist Miguel Altieri and others have argued for a more expansive understanding of crop diversity, taking an approach that emphasizes the preservation not only of distinct crop varieties but of the ecosystems and human cultures that developed and maintain them.[31] The crops, they argue, cannot be isolated from the cultures of local people or their viability as producers.

The Assault on Indigenous Producers

I saw how far-reaching NAFTA's effects were in Soteapan, a small municipality on the slopes of the Santa Marta volcano in Mexico's southeastern state of Veracruz. Colleagues from El Colegio de Mexico (ColMex) took me there to better understand the connections among trade, poverty, and the environment. Under the direction of Alejandro Nadal, they had been studying the Popoluca indigenous farmers in Soteapan—from small-scale commercial producers in the lowlands to subsistence producers in the highlands—to assess the impacts of NAFTA and liberalization on cropping patterns and environmental management. They wanted to compare current practices to those before NAFTA, and to the cropping practices documented in great detail in a 1960 anthropological survey.[32]

These are poor indigenous farmers, the kind you can find across southern Mexico. The vast majority lived in crowded homes with dirt floors and no indoor plumbing. Education levels were low. In 2000, more than 90 percent of households were in extreme poverty. The fall in maize prices had cut into producers' incomes, and related changes had compounded the problem. Prices for other important crops in the area had also fallen. Coffee prices declined 66 percent while prices for common beans, another Mexican staple, fell 41 percent. This left producers with few alternatives if they wanted to shift crops to avoid the NAFTA maize crisis.

The other dramatic impact on local producers came from the restructuring of local and regional markets with the expansion of Maseca, the multinational Mexican firm that controls a large share of the domestic market for maize flour. Through its national network of suppliers and its access to inexpensive imports, Maseca can provide year-round supplies of flour, *masa* (dough for tortillas), and tortillas, something local millers cannot match. As one tortilla-seller in town told me, he wanted to keep milling maize for local farmers, but that would have left him with tortillas only in the months after the local harvest. Because Maseca used its market power to insist on year-round contracts with its distributors, he had to stock the company's tortillas even when local maize was available to mill. The competition drove prices down to the point that it was not economical for him to buy local maize and sell local tortillas. Of the three main tortilla-makers in town, none was making and selling local maize tortillas. According to my colleagues, the demand for maize in the region surrounding Soteapan increased 59 percent from 1990 to 2004, but Soteapan producers' share of that market dropped by 40 percent, to just 6 percent. This had a particularly harsh impact on commercial producers in the lowlands who were sending a majority of their maize to market. Local millers were continuing to go under, unable to compete with Maseca.

The income impacts were dramatic. Between 1993 and 2005, commercial producers saw their incomes, adjusted for inflation, decline by more than 40 percent. Subsistence producers saw their real incomes fall by half.

How did such brutal income losses affect maize diversity and the environment? Since that 1960 survey there had been significant declines in the traditional *milpa* system of maize intercropped with beans, squash, and other crops. If the observations from Soteapan are accurate, the *milpa* will be a thing of the past unless present trends are reversed, and with the *milpa* will go some of Mexico's rich store of agricultural biodiversity.

One source of pressure on the traditional *milpa* comes from diversification, as producers seek crops that can bring more income than maize. They had tried coffee, papaya, and even African palm. They also were using more of their land as pasture for livestock. Since 1993, non-commercial Soteapan producers had reduced the share of their land devoted to maize from 40 percent to 30 percent. In the lowlands, commercial producers had responded to the crisis by expanding maize with the intensive cultivation of hybrid maize varieties, abandoning intercropping altogether. Highland producers had also begun to grow hybrid maize on their traditional plots. The reason, in large part, was a shortage of labor, particularly at key harvest times, another indirect effect of NAFTA.

In 1993, few Soteapan households reported any significant migration, either seasonal within Mexico or permanent to the United States. By 2005, more than 20 percent of middle-income households reported at least one family member migrating temporarily, many to the tomato harvest in Sonora state. Among some of the middle-income producers, one-fifth of households reported permanent migration by at least one family member to the United States. Because the seasonal migration comes at the time of the most intensive need for local labor, the *milpa's* labor-intensive cultivation process is undermined.

Many farmer strategies were designed to reduce the labor investment in the family plot. Livestock is less labor intensive than the *milpa*, and so is palm and fruit cultivation. Unfortunately, so too is more intensive cultivation of monoculture maize from hybrids using rising levels of agro-chemicals. That shift increases production costs and leaves households with a greater need for cash to buy the inputs, forcing them to take on more off-farm employment, adding to their harvest-time labor shortage.

The impact on agricultural biodiversity was dramatic. Survey data from the region showed that whereas the typical producer in 1960 used as many as 12 difference native varieties of maize in the *milpa*, now even traditional producers were growing only 3, with another 2 *mestizo* varieties (hybrids crossed with local varieties), and with 8 different hybrid varieties. The biodiversity decline is even more dramatic for the *milpa* as a whole. In 1960, researchers found as many as 32 different plants in a seven-and-a-half-acre plot; now the most researchers could find was 8.

My ColMex colleagues summarized this sad transformation: "Where the *milpa* survives, it has been significantly altered and the number of species greatly reduced, with the result that agrochemical inputs become a necessity and the old methods of pest and weed control based on agro-biodiversity are no longer functional."

"The entire social structure that has supported corn production in Mexico is imperiled and may be gradually collapsing in front of our eyes," said ColMex economist Alejandro Nadal. The process is insidious. Native varieties of maize fall into disuse on one farm, or maybe many farms, or maybe all of them. A variety that is no longer planted stops evolving with its local environment, as seed selection, the annual interaction between the farmer and the environment, ceases. This is the threat posed by NAFTA's assault on the rural poor in Mexico.

Hogging the Gains from Trade

Just up the Veracruz coast, farmers have lived their own NAFTA nightmare, and not just on the Mexican side of the border. The Perote Valley is now home to some of Mexico's largest hog slaughterhouses, which expanded with all the perks that came with the trade agreement. U.S.-based Smithfield Foods, then the largest pork producer in the world, took control in 1999 of Granjas Carroll, a large industrial hog operation that had expanded operations in the valley in 1993. Between them, they turned the local economy into a living laboratory for all that is wrong with NAFTA, and with the agriculture, labor, immigration, and environmental policies that benefit agribusiness on both sides of the border.

The first blow to the local economy came with new industrial-scale hog operations. Local farmer David Ceja grew up on a farm with pigs, chickens, and cows, which were the family's savings banks when it needed cash. "Sometimes the price of a pig was enough

David Ceja left the Perote Valley in Veracruz, migrating to work at Smithfield's Tar Heel slaughterhouse, where he helped win a union drive at the plant.
© David Bacon dbacon@igc.org

to buy what we needed," he told *Nation* reporter David Bacon, "but then it wasn't. Farm prices were always going down."[33] They couldn't get a decent price for their pigs, as Granjas Carroll undersold local producers. Part of that came from local production and part came from imports, which multinationals like Smithfield now exported to Mexico tariff-free.

U.S. pork exports grew a destabilizing 700 percent after NAFTA, and hog producer prices in Mexico fell by more than half.[34] "We lost 4,000 pig farms," Alejandro Ramírez, of the Mexican Confederation of Pork Producers, told *The Nation*. He estimated that Mexico lost 20,000 direct jobs in the industry and as many as 120,000 when you count indirect jobs lost in related industries.[35]

Wouldn't those new industrial hog operations increase the local demand for maize and soybeans, the two main ingredients in feed mixtures? Not under NAFTA. The Perote Valley sits just over the mountains from Veracruz, one of Mexico's most important Gulf ports. Container ships laden with U.S. maize and soybeans, now tariff-free under NAFTA, provided the new factory farms with all the feed they needed, and at a discount thanks to U.S. dumping. And Smithfield was dumping pork on Mexico thanks to below-cost feed at hog operations like its giant Tar Heel plant in North Carolina. Smithfield was getting a 26 percent discount on feed, its most important operating cost, saving the company nearly $284 million a year.[36] So Ceja's family couldn't get a decent price for their pigs, and they couldn't sell its maize at a profit either, despite the rise in local demand.

But things got still worse in the Perote Valley for farm families. NAFTA didn't liberalize only goods trade but also investment, and Smithfield came into Mexico hard through its joint venture with Granjas Carroll. The company expanded its hog farms to become Mexico's biggest supplier, with at least 25 percent of the domestic market. From the Perote Valley alone they were raising nearly 1 million pigs a year in some eighty complexes scattered around the area.[37] With the economic devastation of NAFTA, the area was desperate for employment, but these were highly automated operations so the job creation was limited. The new factory farms created an estimated 1,200 jobs; NAFTA had probably displaced far more than that.

But weren't they good jobs? NAFTA proponents had promised that foreign investment would at least bring better jobs, a so-called harmonization upward toward U.S. wage and labor standards rather than a "race to the bottom," as critics warned. The critics were proven right. David Torres worked for eight years in one of the Perote plants, and he told *The Nation* that the pay was low for 50–60 hour workweeks. Worse still, he was employed as a contractor, not an employee hired directly by Granjas Carroll or Smithfield. "Since we work for a contractor, we're not entitled to profit-sharing or company benefits," said Torres.

Smithfield's foreign investments made particular sense because back home state governments were finally cracking down on the environmental damage caused by factory farms. A Virginia judge had fined Smithfield $12.6 million in 1997 for dumping hog manure into a tributary to the Chesapeake Bay. The same year, North Carolina, long the regulation-free home for industrial animal facilities, enacted a moratorium on new open-air manure lagoons and placed limits on further expansion at the Tar Heel plant, the largest hog-processing facility in the world. Mexico had no such enforceable limits, and neither did Veracruz. As the hog farms expanded, so did the complaints about water pollution and air quality. NAFTA's environmental side agreement was no match for Smithfield. Despite regulations calling on the companies to cover their manure lagoons and seal them to prevent leaks, there was little enforcement. Local wells were reported contaminated, and the stench of manure made communities nearly unlivable. "The company can do here what it can't do at home," said Carolina Ramírez, of the Veracruz Human Rights Commission.

By 2005, the community had had enough. After petitioning the government to stop licensing new hog operations, they took matters into their own hands: 1,000 residents confronted a construction crew preparing to install another hog shed and manure pond. The uproar would eventually force the company to suspend temporarily the construction of new hog operations in the Perote Valley. But the gods were by no means done with Perote: it was time for a plague. In 2009, a five-year-old boy in nearby La Gloria was diagnosed with the first case of swine flu, the beginning of the A(H1N1) virus outbreak that would kill forty-five people in Mexico. Everyone agreed the virus came from pigs and most agreed that it had probably spread to humans when a plant worker had inadvertently brought it home on his shoes or clothing. But Smithfield and Granjas Carroll quickly denied it came from their plants, and no clear link was proven. According to one local, "no one believed it."[38]

So the communities were becoming dangerous and unlivable, the jobs certainly weren't good ones, and making a living from farming had grown more difficult with NAFTA's dumped imports. What was a young worker to do? Smithfield had an answer for that, too. The company's Tar Heel plant in North Carolina, beset by unionization efforts among its largely African American workforce, started hiring workers from Veracruz. That's where David Ceja ended up, paying $1,200 to a *coyote* to smuggle him across the border. When he got to Smithfield's plant he said he was surprised to see many of the kids he'd played with at home. "I'd see many of them working in the plant."[39]

"The company thought the undocumented would work cheap, work hard, and they wouldn't complain," said Keith Ludlum, a white worker at the plant, which employed 5,000. And their fear could be exploited to undermine unionization efforts by the United Food and Commercial Workers (UFCW), which had come close to winning union votes in Tar Heel in 1994 and 1997. They hadn't because U.S. labor law was (and still is) so toothless that the company could engage in what the National Labor Relations Board would call "egregious and pervasive unfair labor practices," including the firing and intimidation of pro-union workers, yet still keep out the union. With its growing Mexican workforce, which it knew was undocumented, Smithfield could pit the U.S.-born workers against the immigrants, making the cynical claim that the immigrants were taking Americans' jobs.

That's where U.S. immigration policy comes in. Smithfield had little trouble getting undocumented workers from Veracruz to North Carolina. It was even easier to get them out. All it took was an anonymous call to Immigration and Customs Enforcement (ICE). The company made sure that periodic raids reminded Mexican workers how vulnerable they were if they caused any trouble.

Remarkably, they caused trouble anyway. With the plant's workforce a majority Latino, the union sent in a new set of organizers who could work with the immigrants, teach them English, and remind them of their rights in the workplace. Short wildcat stoppages started taking place in 2003. As on any fast-moving assembly line, any small group of workers could shut down the whole line. David Ceja was part of a stoppage in 2004. The immigrant workers were gaining confidence and the union was gaining strength. The Tar Heel plant practically shut down on May 1, 2006, when workers joined nationwide immigrant rights protests, leaving work to march in nearby Wilmington, North Carolina.

Later that year, the company announced it would fire undocumented workers for using false Social Security numbers, claiming it was just obeying U.S. immigration laws. A work stoppage slowed the company action, and even inspired African American workers to demand a paid holiday for Martin Luther King Day. When the company refused, they too shut down the line. Eventually, though, ICE came through the plant and the communities, arresting or driving away some 1,500 immigrant workers.[40]

In December 2008, on the heels of Barack Obama's historic victory in the U.S. presidential election, the remaining Latino, African American, and white workers at the Tar Heel plant finally forced and won a union vote, ending one of the longest organizing campaigns in U.S. labor history.[41] That remarkable victory came in spite of, not because of, U.S. agriculture, trade, immigration, and labor policies since NAFTA, which had pushed cheap commodities south and driven people north. On both sides of the U.S.-Mexican border, transnational livestock firms like Smithfield had taken advantage of such policies. They had gotten cheap feed for their animals, a favorable investment climate in Mexico, tariff-free exports to Mexico of finished pork products, and tariff-free imports of feed for operations there. And they had benefited from a growing supply of low-wage labor on both sides of the border.

In migration policy, people speak of "push factors" that compel people to migrate, and "pull factors" that attract migrants. Under NAFTA, Smithfield provided both, pushing people out of the Perote Valley and pulling them to the United States as undocumented low-wage workers. As UCLA professor Gaspar Rivera-Salgado, who founded and led a bi-national organization of indigenous people from Mexico's Oaxaca state, some living in Mexico and some in the United States, told *The Nation*, "We need development that makes migration a choice rather than a necessity—the right to not migrate."[42]

Giving Away Everything of Value

I was pleasantly surprised to be invited by the Consejo Nacional Agropecuario to speak on a keynote panel at their 2013 annual forum in Aguascalientes, Mexico.[43] Surprised because the CNA is the country's largest agribusiness association, bringing together large farmers and agribusiness firms—domestic and foreign—to promote their policy agendas. Needless to say, my trail of publications clashed with CNA positions on almost every issue, from factory farms to GMOs, from NAFTA to Mexican farm policy. The theme for this year's CNA gathering was "New Perspectives on the Challenge of Feeding the World." I'd written a lot on the subject, so I understood how they found me. It was harder to understand how Mexico, which was importing almost half its food, would be worried about feeding the world. It wasn't doing so well feeding its own people.

I'd been arguing for Mexico to reconsider its agriculture and trade policies for years, and it was not too late to do so. The country still counted on more than 3 million small- and medium-scale farmers to produce a significant share of its white maize. The government hadn't invested in the sector for two decades, leaving *campesinos* to fend for themselves in the face of NAFTA's deluge of imports. Mexico's rain-fed maize producers were producing at less than half their potential. Most had still not given up, despite low crop prices, a lack of credit, and monopoly grain buyers. Small investments in basic extension services, coupled with appropriate technology, could yield large benefits. My own research had shown that Mexico could produce the 10 million tons of maize it now imports just by investing in current farmers on existing land. With more substantial investments in irrigation, particularly in the water-rich southern part of the country, home to the poorest smallholders, Mexico could become a net exporter of maize.[44]

If I had any expectations of openness to new thinking, they were dampened by my chat with the U.S. Embassy's agricultural attaché at a lush pre-conference cocktail reception, held at the elegant Posada Museum. I said something about Mexico's agricultural trade deficit, which had hit $4.6 billion in 2008, and he immediately took offense. "This year," he proclaimed, "Mexico may actually run a surplus."

I knew better; I'd seen this statistical sleight-of-hand many times. "Do you mean the 'agri-food' trade balance?" I asked. He nodded. "The one that has beer as one of Mexico's biggest agricultural exports?" He nodded again, and not sheepishly. Beer has undoubtedly been a NAFTA success story for Mexico, at least in terms of export volumes. Mexican brands like Corona, Modelo, Tecate, and Dos Equis had captured an impressive share of the U.S. market. At the time, Mexican exports had risen to an impressive $1.8 billion since NAFTA, and by 2017 they would reach $3.3 billion.[45] "Beer is a product of agriculture," he said, with conviction.

I took a sip of my margarita. "Don't you think including beer distorts how Mexican agriculture is really doing under NAFTA?" I asked. In agricultural goods, the country was importing much more than it was exporting. Not at all, he replied, the beer sector is a perfect example of the kind of integration NAFTA can achieve in agriculture. "Look, Mexico's even importing the barley malt from us to make its beer!" he added.

"So Mexico's agricultural contribution to its beer exports is . . . what?" I asked. Nervous laughter. You could make a case for tequila, which at least used local agave plants. But beer? Mexico had seen no increase in domestic barley production since NAFTA, which mystified me until I looked to see that U.S. malt exports had grown some 650 percent by 2008, with Mexico relying on the United States for nearly all of its barley and 80 percent of its malt for its supposed agricultural success story.[46]

Here was a case where NAFTA has gotten the United States to open its market to something of value that Mexico could export, and Mexico couldn't even capture the value from it. The industry's growth benefits U.S. barley growers, U.S. malt-makers, and the multinational beer companies that own the Mexican brands. Mexico mostly doesn't even import the barley and make the malt themselves. So the country is basically a *maquiladora* for beer bottling. I guess Mexico contributes the water, which it doesn't have enough of. In fact, in early 2018 residents in the Mexican state of Baja California were actively protesting the giveaway of scarce water to Constellation Brands, which was constructing a massive brewery in Mexicali to produce an astonishing 4 million bottles a day of Corona, Modelo, and Pacífico for the nearby U.S. market. "We're already having water shortages," said protester Ana López. "Now imagine when the plant starts working."[47]

This was Mexico under NAFTA in a nutshell. Giving away everything of value, then deluding itself that its farm sector is doing fine because its Corona beer, bottled from U.S.-grown ingredients, is a big hit in the States. Now that the country's two biggest beer companies are owned by foreign conglomerates, even the profits don't stay in Mexico.[48]

The next day, I found myself on a large stage in a converted train station in front of the largest crowd I'd ever spoken to, easily 3,000 people. Huge video screens were everywhere. I mostly stuck to the global situation, showing how the food crisis had indeed changed the import-export equation for developing countries. Mexico's deepening dependence, once promoted as a cheap-food policy, was now just the opposite. What are needed now, I argued, are policies that reduce import dependence by investing in small- and medium-scale farmers using agricultural practices less dependent on imported chemical inputs.

I was provocative, but the panel's moderator was moderate. In a question-answer session, he asked me if open markets weren't the best policy for agricultural development. "Everyone likes to point out that China and Brazil are development success stories from the last twenty years," I said. "Neither country signs free trade agreements with the U.S. That's because they don't want to commit to across-the-board liberalization. But they aren't closed economies, not at all. They've just chosen to open their markets strategically, something the Mexican government has not done."

I let that one sink in. "Korea, in its bilateral trade agreement with the United States, did not include rice. Why? It's the staple food for the Korean people, important for the country's food independence, and it provides employment in rural Korea." Everyone knew what was coming next. "Why would Mexico liberalize maize trade with the United States? It's not about being open or closed, it's about being strategic."

Making Rural Mexico Great Again

What is particularly striking about NAFTA is that Mexico did poorly under even the most optimal conditions for such a trade agreement. No other country will ever have the advantages Mexico had: access to the largest consumer economy in the world, a country with which it shared a 2,000-mile border and a network of trading relationships; privileged access, because the United States hadn't yet struck preferential deals with other countries, and China hadn't yet entered the World Trade Organization; and access during what turned out to be the longest economic expansion in U.S. history, with strong foreign investment by multinational firms.

If your free trade model can't generate growth and jobs under those kinds of conditions, it's time to consider a new model.

With the election July 1, 2018, of center-left presidential candidate Andrés Manuel López Obrador, Mexico may well be ready to do just that.

Mexican farmer organizations understand that defending native maize, not just from GM contamination but from disuse, is part and parcel of rescuing and revitalizing rural communities. In 2012, they drafted their Plan de Ayala Siglo XXI, a twenty-first-century manifesto and program for rural Mexico based on Mexican revolutionary Emiliano Zapata's original Plan de Ayala from 1911. With more than 100 organizations signing on, the program was the basis for a campaign to put someone in Mexico's White House who would take on the continent's powerful agribusiness interests and make rural Mexico great again. They found their candidate in Andrés Manuel López Obrador, who formally endorsed the plan in his 2012 presidential run. He later endorsed the Campesino Movement's detailed program in April 2018 in his successful run for the presidency.[49]

That program explicitly calls for "food sovereignty" and commits to promoting Mexico's self-sufficiency in key food crops by 2024, not just maize but beans, wheat, and other products. It explicitly does away with policies that write off poor producers as worthy only of welfare, treating all small- and medium-scale farmers as potentially productive. The plan commits to a transition toward agro-ecology, bars transgenic crops, and creates a National System for the Protection and Improvement of Mesoamerican Agro-biodiversity, with a special program, "Native Maize-Tortilla 2050," to promote the cultivation and consumption of native maize. This is just the sort of directed action that can revalue indigenous cultures and practices as a point of national pride while actively supporting the production of native maize, be it in the traditional *milpa* or in monoculture. The plan addresses chronic market failures in the Mexican countryside, with credit programs, crop insurance, and protection from anticompetitive practices by agribusiness buyers and sellers, targeting support to producers farming fewer than 50 acres. Plan de Ayala also calls for "a State strategy to guarantee the right to not migrate . . . and defense and support for the labor and human rights of rural migrants in the United States and Canada."

Not surprisingly, the Plan de Ayala Siglo XXI demands a very different renegotiation of NAFTA than López Obrador's predecessor, Enrique Peña Nieto, was carrying out. Peña Nieto was giving away the store to U.S. agribusiness, especially to the biotech firms, agreeing to a "Mutual Recognition Agreement" that would force each of the three NAFTA countries to respect the safety assessments of the other countries.[50] NAFTA would then give Monsanto what the courts, following Mexican environmental laws, would not: the right to plant GM maize in Mexico. Other agreed provisions, proposed by U.S. negotiators, would bar Mexico from putting labels on unhealthy foods, preventing a key measure to address Mexico's growing obesity epidemic.[51]

The Campesino Movement's proposal called for a wholesale renegotiation of the agricultural chapter of NAFTA, removing maize and other key crops from the liberalization regime. Protective tariffs would be negotiated, and prices would be supported with good old-fashioned supply-management policies featuring floor prices, government purchases, grain reserves, and marketing support. None of these would be easy to get approved, and they would be even harder to carry out. López Obrador said during the campaign that he did not want to tear up NAFTA, but he might need to if he wants to make such sweeping pro-farmer reforms.

The Plan de Ayala Siglo XXI may be a wish list for rural regeneration, but in July, the movement got its first wish: a president with a radically different agenda for rural Mexico and an explicit commitment to the farm movement's goals. He has already announced a new Office of Food Self-Sufficiency within the agriculture ministry. But one of the farm movement's goals is to get a better deal for Mexico in a new NAFTA or to withdraw from the agreement,

a demand captured in the slogan: "New NAFTA or No NAFTA."
López Obrador seems unlikely to challenge powerful business interests by withdrawing from NAFTA. Without greater freedom to
protect priority crops, it is hard to see how he can free Mexican
farmers from the unfair competition posed by dumped U.S. farm
goods.

9

Trading in Hypocrisy: India vs. World Trade Organization

I took the train from New Delhi to Gwalior, in the Indian state of Madhya Pradesh. It didn't take long to be reminded that despite its rapid economic growth India is still an overwhelmingly poor and agricultural country. The train crept south through the kinds of slums that so often seem to find railroad tracks. One-room homes, made of mud, brick, or just cardboard, extended as far as the eye could see, tin roofs glistening in the morning sun. Soon, neatly delimited fields carpeted the landscape. These were not the depopulated expanses of the U.S. Midwest. These were small- to medium-sized plots busy with activity—farm families getting in the sorghum harvest, small tractors plying the land for the next crop. Nearly half of Indians still make their living from agriculture, and 85 percent of those work plots smaller than 5 acres.[1]

As I drove with my hosts from Gwalior to Shivpuri, seemingly far from the reaches of global trade, it was easy to see the desperate poverty that still plagues the country. This was the "other India," far from the skyscrapers of New Delhi and Mumbai, where the majority of Indians coax a living from the soil and where hunger is a pervasive fact of rural life.

This was the region where starvation deaths in 2001–2002 had shocked the nation, and pushed the country's Supreme Court to intervene and insist that the government do more to ensure poor citizens' right to food. A decade later, in response to continuing citizen demands, the government passed the most ambitious food security initiative in the world. The National Food Security Act (NFSA) of 2013 legislated a wide range of nutrition and health measures, including the expanded government purchase of basic food crops from Indian farmers for distribution at nominal prices to India's poor. The goal was to provide basic food rations to more than 800 million people, a remarkable two-thirds of the population.

More remarkable still, this humanitarian program had recently run afoul of trade rules at the World Trade Organization (WTO), where the U.S. government had accused India of unfairly subsidizing its farmers by paying a purchase price higher than market prices. I'd seen this conflict play out at the WTO's 2013 summit in Bali, Indonesia. I'd written then about the hypocrisy of my own government, notorious for its high farm subsidies and cheap exports, accusing the country with the most poor people on earth

WTO protesters in the streets of Buenos Aires, where U.S. representatives continued to threaten India's National Food Security Act (December 2017). *Timothy A. Wise*

of unfairly paying a higher price to its poorest farmers. I'd come to India in 2015 to see this controversial food security program for myself, and I was in the very region where civil society groups had filed the lawsuit that prompted India's Supreme Court to act.

As it turned out, I visited these villages in November just after the soybean harvest had come in. Even though drought had cut into crop production, food was available even in the most under-developed areas. Three months earlier I would have seen the hungry season, that paradoxical period when the fields are green with early growth but last year's stores have long run out. Farmers desperately await the new harvest. In regions as poor as Shivpuri, there is a different name for that season.

"We call it the season of death," said Sachin Jain, of Vikas San-vad, a member organization of the Right to Food Network in the state capital of Bhopal.

"The Season of Death"

In 2001 and 2002, after consecutive years of drought, twenty-six people had starved to death in Rajasthan, across the state border from Shivpuri. Most were children or elders, and they died in spite of government safety-net programs that were supposed to prevent such calamities. Most galling, they died of hunger in a year in which storehouses had plenty of grain even after a weak monsoon. This was just the sort of paradox that Indian economist Amartya Sen had documented on his way to a Nobel Prize in Economics: famine is not mainly the product of food shortages.[2]

The Rajasthan tragedy highlighted the poor performance of India's social protection system. Frustrated after years of government unresponsiveness to complaints, the People's Union for Civil Liberties (PUCL) of Rajasthan filed a petition to the Indian Supreme Court, arguing that government negligence violated Indians' "right to food," which they argued was implicit in the "right to life" guaranteed in Article 21 of the Indian Constitution. The case targeted the government of India, the Food Corporation of India (FCI, the agency responsible for food distributions), and six state governments regarding their inadequate drought response. Later, the case would grow to encompass the larger issue of chronic hunger.[3] It would mobilize India's nationwide Right to Food Network and lead to the reform or creation of a range of new anti-hunger programs.

The initial petition to the Supreme Court focused on two areas of alleged government negligence: the deterioration of the public distribution system (PDS) and the weak performance of the Integrated Child Development Services (ICDS), the government program designed to protect young children.[4] The PDS had been in existence since World War II, when it began as a rationing measure. By the 1970s, it had evolved into a universal scheme for the distribution of subsidized food before succumbing to the economic fashion of the 1990s to target benefits only to those below a low poverty line. The system functioned badly and failed to reach many of the poor, such as those in Rajasthan.[5] As for the ICDS, the Supreme Court charged the nationwide agency with failing to fulfill its core mission: the protection of young children through nutrition, health, and other wellness programs.

The Supreme Court not only took the case, it ruled expansively that the constitution guarantees Indians' right to food and that government has an obligation to promote the realization of that right. It ordered a host of investments and improvements in public programs, and not just in the states named in the case.

The court ordered immediate improvements in the PDS and mandated universal coverage, nationwide, for the ICDS, making it the largest child nutrition program in the world. As of March 2015, 13.4 million ICDS centers—known as Anganwadi Centres (AWCs)—covered an astonishing 102 million beneficiaries under the supplementary nutrition program.[6] Arguing that a child's health and nutrition cannot be addressed separately from those of the mother, the court ordered coverage for pregnant women, lactating mothers, and adolescent girls.[7]

The court augmented those two programs, mandating the

so-called Mid-day Meals (MDMS) program under which state governments have to provide nutritious hot meals in all government-supported primary schools.[8] Not only did the meals encourage school attendance and pupil learning among the 120 million children, they immediately boosted school enrollment for girls and reduced caste-based discrimination. The program was quickly recognized as a cost-effective way to reduce poverty.[9]

The court order also mandated food-for-work programs, which in 2005 became the National Rural Employment Guarantee Act (NREGA). Taking on board economist Jean Dreze's impassioned reminder that "economic democracy" is enshrined in the Indian constitution, the initial 2001 petition had argued that "assured employment at a living wage is the best protection against hunger."[10] A controversial and sweeping public works project, NREGA stipulates that "anyone who is willing to do unskilled manual labor at the statutory minimum wage is entitled to being employed on public works within 15 days (subject to a limit of '100 days per household per year'), or failing that, to an unemployment allowance."[11] The program at its peak offered paid work to some 75 million people, a key cash supplement to the food-based anti-hunger programs.[12]

A court order is one thing, but implementation is another, particularly in a country as large, diverse, and unevenly administered as India. The same flaws in public administration that led to the Rajasthan starvation deaths remained obstacles to the court-ordered measures. The Supreme Court was clear and uncompromising in its ruling: state governments would have to start or improve the mandated programs, and they would have to find the money to do so, with assistance from the national government for some portion of some of the programs.

Madhya Pradesh did not shine in the early implementation. In 2006, after repeated reports of malnutrition-related deaths in the Sheopur District just west of Shivpuri, a Joint Commission of Enquiry found widespread flaws in many of the region's food-related programs.[13]

As Sachin Jain told me in his Bhopal office, "If Madhya Pradesh were a country it would be one of the poorest on earth." The statistics back that up. According to the 2015–2016 *National Health and Family Survey (NHFS-4)*, the state had the highest infant mortality rate in India, with 51 deaths per 1,000 live births. The state ranked first in child mortality and second in anemia for children under five.[14] Nearly 52 percent of children under five were stunted, with 32 percent severely so. Forty-one percent were underweight, with 16.5 percent qualified as severely underweight, a measure based on weight in relation to age. Seventeen percent were "wasted," based on weight in relation to height.[15] As one of India's most populous states, with 73 million people, the human costs of food insecurity, even in just this one state, boggled the mind. In 2005, an estimated 160,000 children died before their fifth birthday, a child death rate of 94 per 1,000 live births. By 2015, when I visited, the state's death rate for children under five had improved considerably, but it was still 65 per 1,000 live births.[16]

The tribal regions fare much worse. Madhya Pradesh is often referred to as the "tribal state of India," with more than one-fifth of the state's people coming from one of forty-three so-called Scheduled Tribes, the official designation. Nearly three-quarters of tribal children in Madhya Pradesh are underweight (74.1 percent), with 42 percent severely underweight. Almost three-quarters are stunted (73.4 percent), more than half (53.6 percent) severely stunted.[17]

The Sahariya, who live on either side of Madhya Pradesh's border with Rajasthan, are one of three tribal groups considered especially vulnerable; in fact, they have the formal designation as a "Particularly Vulnerable Tribal Group."[18] They are concentrated in the Sheopur, Shivpuri, and Guna Districts of Madhya Pradesh, in addition to communities across the state border into Rajasthan.[19]

Ending Desperate Food Poverty

Sunil, one of my hosts, met me at the Gwalior train station and led me to an old SUV, essential for navigating the rugged dirt roads that connect the region's small villages. He told me he worked on child nutrition for Parhit, their community organization. The name is Hindi meaning "for the welfare of others," and its social welfare mission was typical of many of the members of the Right to Food Network. Sunil introduced me to Manoj Bhaduria, Parhit's coordinator for food security, and to Rahul, our driver, and we set off for Shivpuri.

As we drove southwest on a highway under construction, the farms seemed to shrink in size, tractors became less common than draft animals, and the land itself grew dustier, less obviously fertile. Some surely was not, as it was uncultivated, a rarity in such a densely populated country. Sunil and Manoj briefed me about the region and the importance of the NFSA. They explained that the NFSA increased the basic ration from 20 to 35 kilos per month of cereals for a family and expanded eligibility so the majority of rural Indians could qualify. Beyond the basic grains—rice and wheat—the NFSA entitled recipients to distributions of sugar, salt, and kerosene for cooking. All were distributed by the public distribution system (PDS) through a network of thousands of village-level ration shops, public distribution centers. Recipients pay very low, subsidized prices; a kilo of rice that might cost 20 rupees in the market costs just one rupee in the ration shop—about one penny per pound instead of ten. A ration card was issued to qualified residents, and the card would be stamped and registered to show compliance, a system soon to be replaced with more corruption-proof fingerprint-based biometric systems for identifying beneficiaries and documenting distributions.

Manoj confirmed the main complaints I'd heard about the NFSA. The rations still are not large enough; the Right to Food Network had fought for 50 kilos per family. He said basic needs are for 10 to 15 kilos per month per person, and households average seven people. So this was by no means a living ration, just a supplement. Younger individuals and couples living on their own get only 5 kilos per person, including for their young children. This is also seen as inadequate, even if it is better than before. Equally important, the range of goods covered does not guarantee a balanced diet, particularly since it lacks the main local sources of protein (lentils or pulses) and fat (cooking oil). Manoj said they are still advocating to get these included in the program, along with native local grains like millet. Some states included these, but not Madhya Pradesh.

Are people happy with how the program is running? Yes and no, he said, though he indicated that things were definitely improving. Ration shops are not open every day, and in some communities they are open only a few days a month and not on a reliable schedule. People can miss their allotments. Supplies can also run out, something Manoj said was getting better with the expansion of the procurement program so objectionable to the WTO. The government was buying more from local farmers and expanding and improving the distribution network to get the crops to the villages. There were fewer seasons when key supplies weren't available.

Our first stop was Upsil, a small collection of stone homes near the town of Pohri, to visit a ration shop. The village itself was obviously poor, with cloth sheets covering thatched roofs over one-room structures made of loose stone. Some had electricity, none running water. Cooking seemed to happen on open fires outside the front doors of the homes.

Given the village's underdevelopment, the ration shop was pretty much what I expected. We were welcomed by a weathered old man wearing a scarf. He opened the padlocked door to a dark, one-room enclosure with a dirt floor. In the back corner stood sacks of foodstuffs and some metal barrels, presumably of kerosene. He and Ajay, the local administrator, proudly showed me each of the rations, dropping samples of rice, wheat, and sugar into my outstretched hand. They seemed to assume that I was a foreign expert who might be grading the quality of their crops, one of many charitable interpretations of my presence. (Some were not so charitable, at least to me. When I got my amateur translator to actually translate what a village elder was saying when he introduced me to a small group, it turned out I was being introduced as being "from the World Trade Organization.")

Outside the ration shop, a group of men and boys gathered to speak to me, herded there by the Parhit community organizer. One showed me his ration booklet, which showed his household information and his entitlement, 35 kilos per month. Such papers may soon be a thing of the past, even in this remote rural area. Biometric identification is coming even to rural India, in part to cut down on "leakage" in which people come to collect another's rations. The men there told me that wasn't such a problem in their village. There had been one case of a local official getting hold of thirty-five cards and reselling the allotments, but they said he had been caught and fined, and he paid back all of what he stole.

The men echoed the complaints I'd been told about—too-small rations, no lentils or cooking oil, difficulty getting new couples enrolled with sufficient rations for their young families. But they all nodded that the program was better than it was, that supplies were reliable. None of the farmers said they were selling to the government under the crop procurement program, but this area scarcely produces any surplus to sell. These were forest peoples resettled on bad agricultural lands, and they were struggling just to grow enough for subsistence.

It was easy to see the importance of the expanded NFSA as a vital welfare program, and I could sense people's confidence that it was improving its delivery of vital foods. I was told that most children attend school, and most benefit from the hot midday meal offered there as a result of the Supreme Court ruling. Some also benefit from the National Rural Employment Guarantee Agency (NREGA), the public works program, but this entitlement seemed to be lagging behind the NFSA in its delivery.[20]

When we pulled into the village of Benskedi, local organizers led us to a small gathering of men in a dirt field outside some small buildings. A heated argument between two middle-aged men was under way, with a village elder trying to mediate. Twenty others looked on. I was told this was the equivalent of the local village court. No one explained what the dispute was about, and the men were asked to step aside for a few minutes. Through my translator, I heard much the same story of progress, but not enough of it.

Soon, ten women and some girls joined the group. I'd begun to wonder if I was going to end up speaking only to men about a program largely managed, at the household level, by women. One of the NFSA's striking features is its insistence that the ration card be in the name of the oldest woman in the household. This was an intentional effort to put food in the hands of the person most responsible for feeding each family, and in a society as sexist as rural India, it was radical to give women control. So I wanted to hear from the women.

In the Benskedi town square, the women sat together off to one side, their colorful saris fully covering their heads and faces. None spoke until I spoke to them directly, and then they replied reluctantly, quietly. I have no idea who they thought I was, but I imagined they saw me as someone who could respond to their complaints.

"It is good for the children," said one woman through her fabric, "but we need more, and we need better-quality grains." Others nodded. They needed lentils, oil, and why not milk, ghee (the clarified butter central to Indian cooking)? And the quality was sometimes poor, with the ration shop getting only rain-damaged grains to distribute. One offered that her family's health was improving, and she pushed forward a sweet, dusty seven-year-old girl. Do you go to school? I asked. She nodded, looking at the ground. Another woman pushed her child forward. Do you get a good meal at school? "Yes, we get good food," she said in a small but confident voice. "Dal, sweet rice, poori, chapathi." The mothers nodded that the school meals were a godsend, and a useful incentive to send the children to school.

I asked if children all went to school, and the mothers said they did, at least through ninth grade. Those schools are in the villages or nearby. What happens after that? I asked. A young woman stepped forward, pushed by no one. Her face was not covered, and her bright eyes met mine. She said her name was Kavita. She explained that she was fifteen years old and was not now in classes.

The school was three kilometers away, and it wasn't safe for her to make the trip. Girls are often victims of violence by men, and her family thought it was too dangerous to send her.

"I hope you will go back to school, Kavita," I said. "You seem very smart." She smiled but didn't look away. "What do you want to study?"

"I want to be a doctor. I want to help my community."

Emboldened by Kavita, her friend Krishna spoke up. Krishna said she was still in school, living in the hostel the government offers for students who don't live nearby. Krishna told me she wanted to be a teacher, so she could teach here in her village.

Krishna and Kavita walked with us to the ration shop. I asked them what their favorite subjects were in school. "English," both replied, giggling. Until then we had spoken only through my translator. I said in English that I was sorry that I hadn't known that, we could have spoken in English. More giggles, then Kavita fixed me with that clear-eyed look. "I want to speak English," she said in clear English. "You will," I said, "and you will be a very good doctor in your village."

After one last visit with a group of women and girls in Bineka, perhaps the least-developed of the villages I visited, I told Manoj that the children looked poor, but they did not look sickly. Manoj nodded: The NFSA had indeed made precisely that contribution, moving many from desperate food poverty to "mere poverty," not a small step in this tribal region in one of India's poorest states. This was not, he stressed, a substitute for more significant economic development. This last group of eighty-five families, for example, had no reliable access to water; they depend on a tube well controlled by another village. This was indeed "the other India" far from New Delhi and its double-digit economic growth.

Investing in Mothers and Children

The next day at Vikas Sanvad's modest Bhopal headquarters, Sachin Jain offered me tea and a seat on some pillows on the floor lining the walls in what appeared to be the group's casual meeting space. A thin, middle-aged man with a gentle manner, Sachin asked me what I had seen in Shivpuri. He knows the region well, having worked for years to fight for policies to deal with extreme hunger in the state.

While things have slowly improved with the court order, which his group was actively involved in monitoring and implementing, he told me that these communities still live very much on the edge of starvation. Nineteen people in the region died in 2011 from malnutrition. Six died just two months before my visit, during that dreaded "season of death."

"The worst time is right after the monsoon, mid-June to mid-September," he sighed. This year the monsoons had been bad. Crops were poor, pushing many over that edge. Not only is there too little food, Sachin explained, farmers can't earn enough from their crops to pay off the debts they've incurred for seeds, fertilizers, and other inputs. "We've had 700 farmer suicides in the state so far this year." He confirmed that farmers often kill themselves by ingesting the very agricultural chemicals they have gone into debt to buy.

He was oddly pleased to hear the complaints I reported from the villages. His group, like most of the Right to Food Network, is critical of how slowly and unevenly the government has implemented the NFSA. But he sees the progress it represents, and Madhya Pradesh has seen faster results than most. He told me government spending on programs for children under six years old had increased twentyfold in the last decade, in part thanks to the Right to Food Network's tireless effort to raise awareness and outrage over the issue of child malnutrition. He said the child death rate had been cut almost in half in ten years.[21]

I told Sachin I had found few farmers who were benefiting from the procurement program. He said I'd visited one of the least productive areas of the state, where lands are poor, productivity is low, and farmers generate little surplus for the government to buy. The rural employment program, he explained, was critical because for people who didn't have crops to sell, particularly landless laborers and subsistence farmers, it gave them a source of cash income.

Sachin confirmed that government procurement in the early part of the NFSA was disproportionately from larger-scale farmers in a few states. But he said expanded procurement under the NFSA was changing that, and Madhya Pradesh was one of the leaders in making that change.

"You will see one of the reasons why," Sachin said as he motioned for me to follow him to the taxi waiting for us outside his office. He'd arranged a meeting with Dr. Manohar Agnani, state commissioner for Food, Civil Supplies, and Consumer Protection, the agency in charge of the public distribution system. "He is our food commissioner," Sachin told me on the short ride to the complex of state offices in downtown Bhopal. "He has heard our voices."

Feeding the Hungry Majority

Dr. Agnani was waiting for us in his large, uncluttered office. He presented as every bit the Indian civil servant, in the best sense of the term: trim, well-dressed but casual, with a graying moustache. I thanked him for meeting me on short notice; Sachin told me he had come in from holiday for the meeting.[22]

As we awaited our tea, Dr. Agnani explained that his background is in public health, not agriculture, and that his job since 2013 has been to run the public distribution system. "I started when the NFSA came in," he said with evident pride, "so I have been involved from day one."

His pride came from presiding over what many regarded as one of India's best-performing states in terms of NFSA implementation, and one of the most in need of the program. Dr. Agnani told me that the state was well on its way to meeting the NFSA's ambitious goal of reaching 75 percent of rural households and 50 percent of urban households with its food distributions.

"The food security act has given us the confidence to move forward," Agnani said. Under his direction the PDS now reaches some 53,000 villages in the state through 23,000 village councils. The NFSA mandates that ration shops be administered by NGOs, cooperatives, or so-called self-help organizations (often women's

groups), and Agnani says his goal is to have at least 30 percent of
the ration shops run by women's self-help organizations.

I told him I'd been in Shivpuri. He knew the region well, having
served there as a district administrator. People there were benefiting from state efforts to expand the number of beneficiaries beyond
those considered to be below India's poverty line. That measure, he
said, left out a lot of hungry people. Nationally, some 40 percent
of Indians are considered below the official poverty line, but under
the NFSA 67 percent will qualify for food distributions.

In Madhya Pradesh, they expanded the rolls by including entire groups based on occupation or condition. The state identified
thirty-four different categories of beneficiaries, from tribal groups
to landless laborers, rickshaw drivers to farmers hit by drought.
This brought into the PDS system groups of people, such as migrants, who before might have lacked the formal documents to
demonstrate incomes below the poverty line.

Agnani told me that they've been so successful that they expect
soon to exceed their PDS quota—and budget. Madhya Pradesh,
with its high poverty levels and strong program inclusion, expects
to enroll 75 percent of the state population, not just 67 percent,
more than 60 million people. For reference, that is more beneficiaries than the United States has in its entire SNAP program. Agnani
says they will eventually reach 80 percent of rural and 63 percent
of urban households.

I brought up the U.S. food assistance program, and economists'
frequent criticism that India's program is inefficient and prone to
"leakage" and corruption. "Why not just give the poor cash for food
instead of creating this complex government procurement and distribution system?"

He scoffed. "We can transfer funds electronically, that is not a
problem," he explained. Indeed, cell-phone banking reaches many
of India's most remote regions. "But India is not a just society. We
have discrimination based on gender and caste. In a society like
India's, cash transfers don't make sense." Many male heads of
household would use cash distributions for things other than food,

and for themselves rather than their families, and men would more readily control the income. "I don't believe in efficiency at the cost of effectiveness and gender equity," he went on.

I was not sure I could remember hearing a male public official bring up gender equity without even being asked. When I did ask, he was even more adamant. "Make your society gender-sensitive, gender-neutral, and many of your problems will go away," he said. Sachin later told me Agnani had started his own foundation to support women and girls, and in Shivpuri he had used his power as district administrator to wipe out five gangs that were terrorizing girls. Girls, I imagined, such as Kavita in Benskedi, too afraid to walk the three kilometers to school.

Agnani was special, as Sachin had told me.

"Much More Than a Welfare Program"

"The NFSA is much more than a welfare program," Agnani stressed to me. "It starts with farmers and procurement. We then get food grains to people who most need them. Will cash transfers do that? I don't think so. Cereals are not available in many areas, they are exported and sold in foreign markets." In other words, the goods go where the money is, responding not to need but to "effective demand."

"Public procurement gets food to poor people," Agnani went on. "Of this I am convinced."

He attributed their success in the state to "good supply chain management," a phrase he seemed pleased to borrow from the private sector. This included a coordinated system of procurement from farmers, decentralized warehousing, distribution to the network of ration shops, and ultimately food distributions to that large beneficiary population.

I'd seen the latter parts of that system in the villages, but not the procurement. As an agricultural development specialist, that was my strongest interest. It was also the part of the NFSA that my government was objecting to at the WTO, the payment of subsidized prices to Indian farmers.

Dr. Agnani leaned forward, knowing that such complaints relate to government inefficiency. "Our system is very decentralized, with 3,000 collection centers in the state mostly managed by cooperative societies. The government is buying about 40 percent of the state's wheat, and even sending it to other states. And farmers are now paid within 7–10 days."

But aren't the larger farmers and the middlemen the ones who benefit from the minimum support price? I asked. I'd heard stories of local traders buying up farmers' crops at lower prices and reselling to the government at the support price.

"We are buying from the smaller farmers," Agnani said. He explained that in Madhya Pradesh they have reduced this sort of leakage by registering all farmers who want to sell to the government in one computerized system just recently finalized. One of the conditions is that you can't be a large-scale farmer. Another is that you can't be a trader. Still another is that you can't be from another state. Agnani thought this would reduce leakage to less than 10 percent, and he said the coming use of biometric identification for both farmers and beneficiaries would reduce losses to near zero.

I was impressed. He didn't deny any of the problems. Apparently, he just fixed them, with "good supply chain management." I brought up the WTO complaints and asked how high the support prices were. Procurement programs only work if farmers will sell to the government, so the government generally has to offer an attractive price. Agnani picked up the phone and asked his assistant to bring the latest data on market and support prices.

"I usually see market prices higher than the government support prices," he said as we waited, but it varies depending on the local area and the season. His assistant brought him current information, and sure enough the support prices were comparable to market prices for wheat and rice.

Why do farmers sell to the government? I asked. And how does the government end up procuring 40 percent of the state's wheat without offering a higher price?

He explained that for farmers the main benefits of the NFSA go well beyond the price. As important as the price level was the fact that the price was guaranteed. Farmers know going into planting season that they can count on at least that minimum price even if the market is weak at harvest time. Better still, farmers are not locked into a contract to sell to the government, so if prices are higher at harvest time farmers can sell on the open market. Agnani said another attraction is that the government will relax quality standards somewhat in bad years like this one, so farmers can get the support price at a time when traders would be bidding down their prices due to lower-quality grains.

Agnani picked up speed. He clearly wanted me to understand the rural development piece of the NFSA puzzle. "The collection system eliminates the problem for many farmers of needing to arrange and pay for transportation," he explained. That is often a huge challenge for farmers, which makes them dependent on local traders. Now, said Agnani, the government determines a local collection center and the dates for collection. That makes it easier for farmers to cooperate in pooling their production for the government buyer rather than competing with one another for the best deal from a trader.

One of the most important benefits of the program, Agnani concluded, was that it stabilized prices. With the state government procuring 40 percent of the state's wheat, the support price creates a price floor for the market where there was none before. Middlemen can't pay low at harvest time when the crop is plentiful, and they can't sell high later when people are hungry. Such practices are commonplace in rural areas, and not just in India. Agnani attributed the relative price stability in rice and wheat, even in bad crop years such as this one, in part to government procurement, and he contrasted the current market for lentils, which were seeing price increases that made this Indian staple more expensive than chicken. India was importing 25 percent of its lentils and other pulses.

Agnani favored adding pulses to the PDS system, which would make a lot of sense for food security purposes because it adds needed protein, and it would also create a stable market to stimulate domestic production. Economists have long observed that decent and stable prices promote investments in farms, where highly volatile prices leave farmers unsure whether to risk buying that tractor. It would also equalize the subsidies for the different staple crops; one of the reasons lentil production is down may well be that guaranteed prices for wheat and rice make them a safer bet for farmers.

Agnani seemed particularly proud of the role the NFSA plays in stopping exploitative traders from taking advantage of poor farmers. He said that the program's prompt payment for crops is now forcing speculators notorious for withholding promised payments to pay, in effect making them compete not just on price but on service to the farmers.

I told him that his list of benefits to farmers beyond the price sounded like a point-by-point response to what economists call market failures, cases in which markets fail to respond efficiently to supply and demand, prices fail to reflect costs, and market "imperfections" allow unscrupulous—or just intelligent—economic actors to take advantage of others. The lack of competition locally leaves farmers and rural consumers at the mercy of traders, who can exploit those market failures for their own gain while worsening the lives and livelihoods of farmers and the rural poor alike.

Dr. Agnani smiled at my reference to market failures. "Yes," he said confidently, "we are eliminating the information asymmetries." Nobel Prize–winning economist Joseph Stiglitz couldn't have said it better. With the NFSA, Agnani told me, the government was making rural markets work, not distorting them. At least in Madhya Pradesh, government involvement was less a market distortion than it was a market correction. And the winners seemed to be farmers and consumers, the losers the traders who could no longer exploit their advantages for personal gain.

Everywhere I'd gone in India, I'd asked people what they thought of the U.S. WTO complaint about the NFSA. Agnani, who has since moved on to a job with the national health ministry, was understated. "I only hope we can continue this program." He clearly couldn't imagine any other outcome.

Back at the Vikas Samvad office, Sachin Jain's strident response was more typical. "The WTO is intervening in the internal affairs of the country. The WTO is above our democracy when it comes to India's food security," he said, clearly exasperated that this distant trade body would bother itself with such a local matter. "We can't forget that farmers are committing suicide. The NFSA is key to preventing that."

National Progress on the Right to Food

I returned to New Delhi convinced that the program may have flaws, but it was the most ambitious initiative in the world today to address chronic hunger and malnutrition in the country that by far has the most people in need. And it was a domestic matter that should not be subject to challenge by the world's richest country on the basis of the selective application of outdated WTO methods for estimating farm subsidies.

Dipa Sinha is one of the dynamic "co-convenors" of the Right to Food Network, the massive decentralized nationwide network of community organizations working to fight chronic hunger. Dipa had gotten involved after several years of working on programs for children under six. In the small, bustling office charged by the Supreme Court to monitor, implement, and litigate the right to food case and hundreds of related cases, Dipa sounded hopeful. She had been with the court commissioner's office for the last five years, and they were starting to see the kind of progress I witnessed in Madhya Pradesh.

The NFSA is broad in scope, mandating the near universalization of some of the court-ordered programs, not just the PDS but the whole gamut of health and nutrition programs. Dipa said India was close to meeting national targets for PDS food distributions, despite some lagging regions. Urban distributions have progressed more slowly than those in rural areas. But expanded grains distributions are now on target in 28 of the country's 29 states, she said.

Dipa addressed some of the criticisms leveled at the NFSA. She thought it nonsense that the various NFSA programs fail to improve nutrition, as some have charged. The Mid-day Meals program is widely seen as a success, with relatively low costs, and the ICDS is as well, with its combination of health and nutrition monitoring. The PDS programs give less nutritional bang for the buck, but they too have been shown to have measurable poverty and food security impacts.[23] She said the Right to Food Network had been campaigning from the beginning to get pulses included in PDS rations, which would provide urgently needed protein and reduce some of the distorted incentives to farmers to grow only rice and wheat.[24]

Dipa said the expansion of the program was reducing corruption and "leakage" of rations to non-beneficiaries, a chronic problem. The data are hard to pin down, but some have claimed that as much as 40 percent of PDS distributions end up in the wrong hands. Dipa says those reports are outdated and exaggerated, and the states that are actively implementing the NFSA have brought leakage down from around 30 percent in 2004 to about 10 percent now. "I expect it will fall further," she said.[25]

Many have criticized the high cost of the NFSA, citing recent cost increases. There is no doubt the budget outlay is significant, estimated at 1.45 percent of GDP in 2014.[26] Other researchers have pointed out that a temporary increase in costs was associated with the post-NFSA expansion of procurement, but the government is now procuring all it needs. Costs are expected to stabilize and even fall if supplies increase and prices fall with the NFSA stimulus.[27]

Critical to keeping costs down is managing food reserves well, and that has certainly been a problem for the Indian government, and others using food reserves. Procure too much and storage costs mount as grain rots in the silos. The NFSA's decentralized procurement and distribution system is expected to help, forcing the government to develop local and regional storage facilities and giving the government a ready outlet for procured crops with expanded PDS distributions. But when I was there in 2015, I was told that government silos held 25 percent more than was budgeted.[28]

Preventing the accumulation of unaffordable surpluses is also key to avoiding the dumping of grain on domestic and international markets. Again, the NFSA's expanded distribution should reduce that problem.

Dipa expressed dismay but not surprise that the procurement side of the NFSA—buying from farmers at subsidized prices—is moving more slowly. It was not part of the court order, so the expansion effort is more recent. Until recently, procurement had been from areas with existing storage facilities and decent roads, so it had tended to favor larger-scale farmers. That was changing, she said, and the government had an economic incentive to make it happen. With the mandate to supply 535,000 ration shops all over the country with procured grains, and with storage costs high, the government needs a large and decentralized supply network linked to the distribution system if it is going to meet NFSA targets.[29]

But as I saw in Shivpuri, the poorest of the rural poor don't benefit directly from the procurement program because they either have no land or are too poor to produce a surplus the government could buy. Dipa stressed that the rural jobs program, NREGA, was key to reducing poverty and hunger in those populations, and she was troubled the Modi government was cutting it back.

Dipa seemed hopeful that the NFSA could fulfill its mandate, and she attested to concrete improvements since the passage of the sweeping law.

WTO: The Land of Hypocrisy

Biraj Patnaik, Dipa's colleague in the Supreme Court commissioner's office, was eager to hear about my travels through Madhya Pradesh and my thoughts on the WTO issue. I'd met Biraj two years earlier in Bali, at the 2013 WTO ministerial conference where the NFSA controversy erupted. He was there with Anuradha Talwar, one of the leaders of the Right to Food Network, to defend India's newly minted NFSA against the U.S. threats. Anuradha was formidable, a sturdy, charismatic, veteran activist from West Bengal, clear-eyed and calm in a way that let one know she had seen a lot of struggle. Biraj, an activist in his own right, had become the principal adviser to the Supreme Court commissioner charged with monitoring the right to food case. Biraj might have been forty at the time, but his energy made him seem younger.

When I first spoke with them in Bali, they told me they still couldn't quite believe they were at a meeting of the World Trade Organization. Weren't they anti-hunger activists in a million-person network that had won a major victory in their long battle to address the worst concentration of hunger on the planet? Shouldn't they be organizing Indians to demand the full implementation of this ambitious government program? Shouldn't international development organizations be applauding and supporting such a sweeping anti-hunger effort, which recognized the internationally agreed principle on the human right to food? What did international trade have to do with any of that? And why was the global body charged with negotiating and enforcing the system of rules that govern trade even involved?

"Why are we here?" Biraj asked plaintively. Of course, he knew very well why they were there; he and Anuradha were by then passionate and articulate defenders of the NFSA, and they had learned to speak WTO.

In multiple forums and in interviews with the media, they patiently explained that the NFSA did, in fact, provide a kind of subsidy to farmers, by paying farmers a price slightly above prevailing market levels so the government could take those staple foods and sell them at subsidized prices to the poor. That consumer subsidy—selling below market prices—was not considered an agricultural subsidy, and it was protected from WTO disciplines in the so-called Green Box. That's where the U.S. food stamp program resides. It is considered not to distort trade, so it is allowed.

Paying subsidized prices to farmers, though, is a different matter. I must have heard Biraj explain twenty times to clueless journalists why India was actually not in violation of anything and wasn't distorting international trade in any meaningful way. First, he said, the NFSA purchases domestic grains for a domestic food security program, and WTO rules make an allowance for exactly such programs. In any case, Biraj would go on, the Indian government does not export the grains it purchases; if they have undistributed surpluses they are sold competitively on domestic markets, though some may end up being exported. But they are almost always sold at prices higher than the government procurement price.

The high subsidy U.S. negotiators were alleging was also a fiction, an accounting trick really. India's actual subsidies—the portion of the support price above market prices—was far lower than the WTO alleged. The WTO makes it seem large by comparing the support price not to current market prices but to a so-called reference price, a market price from thirty years ago. Thirty years of inflation makes that old price ridiculously low, so it makes India's apparent subsidy ridiculously—and misleadingly—high. As Biraj patiently explained, India's 13,600-rupee-per-ton support price for paddy rice that year was only 100 rupees higher than market prices, but it was 2,280 rupees higher than the 1980s reference price.

It was a cynical accounting trick designed to put India on the defensive. I had estimated that if the United States had to report its own subsidies based on the same archaic reference prices, our $5 billion in corn subsidies the previous year would appear to be a subsidy of $30 billion. India was being scapegoated for its NFSA, and several other countries were running similar, if smaller, public stockholding programs; they were also vulnerable to this manufactured violation.[30]

The more I heard Biraj and Anuradha have to argue such an obvious point, the more incensed I became. This wasn't just any government trying to shut down India's food security program, it was *my* government. And it was doing so claiming unfair farm subsidies to some of the world's poorest farmers while it subsidized some of the richest farmers on earth.

The hypocrisy was infuriating, on so many levels. First, India's program was almost exactly what the U.S. government had done coming out of the Great Depression, and for many of the same reasons—low crop prices, poor farmers, hungry consumers, limited government budgets. You can look it up: the New Deal's Federal Surplus Relief Corporation.[31] And it worked, raising prices for farmers and feeding the poor.

Second, U.S. support prices for its own farmers have provided much more support than India's over the last twenty years, with subsidy payments reaching $20 billion in some years. And unlike India, the United States exports most of the crops—corn, soybeans, wheat, rice, cotton. And those low-priced exports have undermined developing country farmers in devastating ways, as they did in Mexico under NAFTA.[32]

Third, the United States spends about $75 billion per year for its Supplemental Nutrition Assistance Program (SNAP), the main domestic food aid program that reaches 47 million people. India's program was much cheaper, provided less than one-quarter of the benefits, and reached ten times the number of beneficiaries—475 million—who were some of the world's poorest people.[33]

In Bali, the U.S. government refused to back down, but India held firm, thanks in part to the immense popularity of the NFSA across India. The conflict nearly derailed a meager set of agreements of greater interest to U.S. multinational firms. In the end, the U.S. conceded a "peace clause" granting India and other countries with similar programs five years in which no formal disputes could be filed against them and during which the WTO would negotiate a "permanent solution" to the issue. India left Bali with its peace clause and went back to implementing its ambitious food security program.

Biraj and Anuradha went home more exhausted than elated. "The agreement on the table today is going to make it even more difficult to achieve food security for our people," Anuradha told me with a sigh. "And it was hard enough already."

U.S. vs. Them: Undermining Development

By the next WTO summit, in December 2015 in Nairobi, Kenya, there had been little progress on the promised "permanent solution" on what was now referred to as the "public stockholding" issue, in reference to the program's food reserves. I arrived in Nairobi more enthusiastic about India's National Food Security Act than ever, after my eye-opening trip to India the previous month. The U.S. charge that it involved massive trade-distorting subsidies to Indian farmers seemed even more cynical than it had two years earlier. After all, the U.S. Congress had just passed the 2014 Farm Bill, which thumbed its nose at WTO disciplines with much larger subsidies to much wealthier farmers for a wide range of crops, many of which were exported, distorting trade in overseas markets. Would the U.S. negotiator refuse to concede an exemption from outdated WTO rules for food security programs such as India's?

In a word: yes. And he did so with a straight face and a scowl. U.S. trade representative Michael Froman not only refused to negotiate on the public stockholding issue, he rejected negotiations on any of the outstanding agriculture issues—relief from U.S. agricultural subsidies, special relief for Africa's cotton farmers from continued U.S. subsidies, the right to use emergency tariffs to counteract surges in agricultural imports that could damage domestic markets. No, said U.S. negotiators and a few allies, mostly from developed countries. Instead we should declare the Doha Development Round over—even though none of its development objectives had been achieved—to focus on "new issues" of greater interest to rich countries: protection for foreign investors, disciplines on government procurement programs that favored domestic firms, and other rich-country issues.

Froman fanned the flames in a pre-summit op-ed in the influential *Financial Times*. He said the time had come to abandon Doha, with its ambitious development goals; it had "failed to achieve anything." And he called on WTO negotiators "to move beyond the cynical repetition of positions designed to produce deadlock."

Negotiators in Nairobi were shocked that Mr. Froman would throw down the gauntlet so baldly. Here was President Barack Obama's trade representative, whose intransigence on so many of the issues central to the agreed Doha Development Agenda was largely responsible for the WTO's failure "to achieve anything," denouncing other countries for not being constructive.

Yet Mr. Froman came to Nairobi refusing to even discuss such massive distortions to international markets, which undermine the efforts of developing-country farmers to feed themselves and their communities. And he came offering no concessions on India's far less trade-distorting NFSA, with its far lower support prices and its urgent dual mission to support hungry farmers and feed hungry consumers. He offered no willingness even to calculate India's subsidies in a commonsense manner instead of the ridiculous WTO methods that used old market prices.

Mr. Froman got most of what he wanted in Nairobi: a weak acknowledgment of "outstanding Doha issues," an opening to introduce "new issues" of concern to rich countries, and an ineffectual set of agreements that didn't even look good on paper. A handpicked group of five—U.S., EU, China, Brazil, and India—agreed on the lame final declaration, with the Indian negotiator later forced to explain back home why she caved in to U.S. pressure.[34]

When the WTO reconvened in Buenos Aires, Argentina, two years later, U.S. negotiators were even more intransigent. The new administration of President Donald Trump added disdain for multilateralism to his predecessor's unbridled promotion of U.S. exporters. The summit represented the formal deadline for negotiating a "permanent solution" on the public stockholding issue, but there was no such deal, just tacit agreement to allow the peace clause to continue into the indefinite future.

WTO press officer Keith Rockwell could only smile smugly as he reported the trade body's failure to deliver. He was enthusiastic, however, about what may have been the summit's most telling, if dubious, breakthrough. For the first time ever, the WTO Business Forum had convened as part of the meeting. In a photo-op ceremony, representatives from the International Chamber of Commerce posed with WTO Director General Roberto Azevedo as they presented their "recommendations," a predictable set of measures to make the world safe for investors and exporters, not farmers.

Multinational firms already had undue influence over such trade negotiations. Now that role would be formal. "From the standpoint of host hospitality," PR flak Rockwell said later, "I can say that this ministerial has been a success." Certainly the International Chamber of Commerce would agree.

Members of global civil society groups had a different opinion. Protests filled the streets of Buenos Aires outside the barricades that protected negotiators and their business allies from reality. Familiar placards—"WTO out of Agriculture!" "WTO Kills Farmers!"—mixed with demands to reject a brutal series of austerity measures from the government of Argentine president Mauricio Macri. Tear gas filled the downtown air, but the winds blew the acrid clouds away from the WTO summit. Negotiators never got that faint whiff of danger that might have made them think twice about their decisions.

On the Wrong Side of History

India's NFSA is still in operation, but it remains under threat at the WTO. The conservative government of Narendra Modi seems prepared to cave in to international pressure. The government ended the long-running right-to-food court order, making enforcement in India's more recalcitrant states more difficult. And Modi is allowing states to experiment with welfare programs that substitute cash benefits for food distributions, a move that complies with WTO dictates but eliminates the support prices that now help sustain some 10 percent of the country's farmers. The program's intended 8 million beneficiary farmers are four times the number of farms in the entire United States.

A broad-based social movement had tirelessly protested and lobbied to get the Indian government to make good on its constitutional promise of the right to life and the implied right to food. The government had approved an imperfect but ambitious initiative to address the country's chronic hunger issues, and it wasn't just welfare; with the support prices and procurement from farmers it was a rural development program. That was more than citizens in most other hungry countries had been able to win in their own struggles. With crop prices low and cheap U.S. exports again undermining developing country farmers, such programs represent a critical way for governments to protect their food producers. As I'd seen in Malawi, Zambia, Mexico, and other countries, agricultural investment dries to a trickle when prices make it scarcely profitable to expand production. Why grow more if you can't sell it for a profit?

India's NFSA is a noble experiment in the national recognition of the right to food. The country is filled with even more noble experiments of sustainable food production not beholden to agribusiness prescriptions: cooperatives of organic producers, self-help groups of formerly hungry people growing and marketing nutritious foods for their families and the larger community. Aren't those the sorts of initiatives the U.S. government should be supporting?

At the least, the U.S. government should stop threatening to undermine the world's largest democracy in its effort to make the right to food a reality in the world's hungriest country.

10

Conclusion: The Battle for the Future of Food

Fortunately, in the battle for the future of food I found plenty of hope and inspiration. Much of it comes from the array of initiatives and movements broadly associated with the right-to-food movement. At a crucial time in history, when food price increases seemed to highlight all the glaring contradictions in our corporate-dominated food systems, here was a refreshing new narrative that started with the hungry, focused on rights, not yields, and openly advocated for the elimination of the many obstacles to achieving those rights. In India, such a movement had won recognition of those rights by the Supreme Court and succeeded in passing the National Food Security Act. Mexico had also reformed its constitution to recognize the right to food, and Malawi had a right-to-food bill on its legislative agenda.

In 2004, the 187 Member States of the General Council of the UN Food and Agricultural Organization adopted the "Voluntary Guidelines to Support the Progressive Realization of the Right to Adequate Food in the Context of National Food Security," an extension of the 1976 International Covenant on Economic, Social, and Cultural Rights. The guidelines mandate not only governments' obligation to *fulfill* the right to adequate food, through provision and facilitation of food delivery, but also the obligations to *respect* and *protect* the right to food. These require the government to refrain from actions that impede people's access to food (respect) and to protect their rights by preventing actions by non-state actors that undermine that access.[1]

Olivier De Schutter was named the UN Special Rapporteur on the Right to Food in 2008 just as the food crisis was breaking. Under his leadership, the right to food took hold as a framework for responding to the crisis, not with welfare but with structural reform. His six-year tenure, which ended in 2014, established the urgent need to bring climate-resilient, ecological agricultural development to small-scale farmers, particularly women. De Schutter explicitly challenged the dominant agribusiness-friendly responses of donor governments, philanthropists, and multinational firms, identifying some of their initiatives as incompatible with the right to food.

This was just the kind of fresh approach we needed in the new crisis, and it was one of the things that inspired me to write this book. The right to food offered a radically different answer to the question: How can poor countries grow more of their own food? Poor farmers were, in this view, victims of a violation of their economic and social rights. They were also the agents of change who could claim those rights, eating today and confronting the obstacles that were keeping them from eating tomorrow. After all, a high-level interagency report on the future of agricultural development had concluded that business-as-usual was no longer an option.[2] The emerging consensus called for governments to invest in these food producers and to do so sustainably.

That consensus was actually not new at all, less a road not taken than one overgrown with neglect. This was simply a rediscovery of basic development theory, practiced successfully in recent years by China, Vietnam, Brazil, and a diverse range of countries that, in their own very different ways, recognized that in poor agricultural countries development starts with food producers. These countries not only ignited long periods of dynamic economic growth, they dramatically reduced hunger.[3]

Agribusiness glanced at that road less traveled and quickly plowed it under, planting it in high-yield seeds drenched in synthetic fertilizer. In my research, I had a hard time finding any evidence of government action to follow that new consensus on sustainable smallholder farming. On the contrary, most governments have eschewed sensible, low-cost, pro-poor initiatives in favor of expensive programs that channeled scarce public funds into corporate-dominated value chains. Corporations captured most of the value. Drought-tolerant replantable seeds? No thanks, try our hybrid or GMO varieties that you have to buy every year. Soil-building, home-grown compost? No thanks, buy some more synthetic fertilizer. Intercropping a variety of food crops, to diversify nutrient-poor diets, rebuild soils, and reduce dependence on synthetic fertilizers? Nope, keep those monocultures, and buy more, not less, of our chemical inputs.

The pro-corporate agenda also blinded policy-makers to two measures that have proven key to other countries' successes, redistributing land among small-scale farmers and giving them decent prices for the surpluses they grow. Neither issue was on anyone's agenda in Southern Africa. Much of Malawi's best land was devoted to colonial-era tea and tobacco plantations. Mozambique seemed intent on giving its best irrigated land to foreign companies, not poor farmers. Zambia's food producers were farming ever-smaller plots as urban elites and foreign investors captured vast swaths of prime land. Industrial meat production was consuming rising shares of maize, soybeans, and other crops, driving unsustainable resource use in the countryside.

Those farmers who have enough land to grow surplus crops to sell often can't get a decent price for their crops. As I'd seen in India, the procurement program in the National Food Security Act can stabilize markets for farmers, reducing the speculative role of middlemen and giving farmers confidence that if they invest in their farms they will be wealthier when they sell the surplus. In 2017, Malawi's farmers saw the good news of strong rains and a great harvest undone by terrible prices from the global grain glut and its own mismanaged harvest-time surpluses, which punished farmers for their productivity.

It's not easy to end hunger, but we know what works.[4] China's economic takeoff began with rural development. Key to that was raising farm prices for small-scale farmers who had enough land and support to grow a surplus. We saw it in the United States, when supply-management policies kept supply and demand in balance so farmers and consumers would see stable and decent prices. We've forgotten those days, at great cost to farmers and consumers, at great profit for agribusiness.

No Sign of a Green Revolution in Africa

It would be one thing if the promotion of industrial agriculture actually led African countries toward prosperity and food security. The Alliance for a Green Revolution for Africa, the standard-bearer of this agribusiness-led development crusade, has been a bust. I'd seen its failures in Malawi, Zambia, and Mozambique. Those weren't anomalies. When I looked at the data, there was little evidence that, after ten years of AGRA, any sort of green revolution had come to Africa.

Even on its own flawed terms, AGRA was failing in its thirteen chosen countries. With the clearly stated goals of doubling productivity and incomes for 30 million African farm households by 2020, there was little sign the well-funded initiative would come close to meeting either of those objectives. Between 2006 and 2014, more than halfway into the AGRA initiative, yields had increased slowly—38 percent for maize, 22 percent for rice, 23 percent for wheat, and just 9 percent for cassava, all priority crops. Production had grown more quickly, not mainly from productivity gains but from bringing new land into crop production, as I'd seen in Zambia. Still, overall cereal production increased only 33 percent over the eight-year period.[5]

Maize has been an obsessive priority for AGRA, yet Nigeria and Kenya, two of AGRA's top five maize producers, saw declining yields, while a third, Tanzania, saw annual yield growth of just 1 percent. Three of AGRA's four "breadbasket" countries, Tanzania, Mozambique, and Ghana, had annual yield growth rates below 2 percent despite receiving larger amounts of AGRA funding and support relative to other countries.

What limited gains African countries achieved were due more to input subsidy programs than AGRA. The subsidies got farmers to use more fertilizer; use increased by 39 percent on average across AGRA countries. But average application rates of 20 kilos per hectare remain far below the target of 50 kilos per hectare.[6] Even then, the subsidies produced weak productivity gains, which often were not sustained over time as yields from monoculture farming on depleted soils stagnated.

The subsidies drove land into favored crops such as maize, pulling land out of other more sustainable and nutritious food crops. Traditional drought-tolerant crops such as millet and sorghum saw declining or stagnant production, with negligible yield increases over the period. This reduced diet diversity in addition to undermining crop diversity and climate resilience.

While hunger and malnutrition had declined across AGRA countries, Global Hunger Index scores remained in the "serious" to "alarming" category for 12 of the 13 AGRA countries. In 6 AGRA countries, half or more of the rural population lives below the national poverty line. Poverty affects between 22 percent and 78 percent of the rural populations in AGRA countries.[7] As I saw in Zambia, increasing maize production had almost no effect on the country's alarming rural poverty.

A recent article in the journal *Food Policy* surveyed the evidence from seven countries with input subsidy programs and found little evidence of sustained—or sustainable—success. "The empirical record is increasingly clear that improved seed and fertilizer are not sufficient to achieve profitable, productive, and sustainable farming systems in most parts of Africa," wrote the authors in the conclusion.[8]

In the field, I kept looking for signs of success. But even the apparent successes, like Malawi and Zambia, illustrated the deep flaws in the green-revolution approach. The closest I got to green-revolution success was in Southern Malawi when I met with the One Acre Fund. The initiative, which is getting decent results with its promotion of a very traditional green-revolution package of hybrid maize seeds and synthetic fertilizer, has gotten a lot of attention and funding, in part thanks to favorable coverage from Roger Thurow and other journalists.[9] I could see what they found positive. The program works with very small-scale farmers, some 10,000 in Southern Malawi. It focuses on food crops; in Malawi that was maize. One Acre provides not only credit but crop insurance, rarities in the region. Perhaps most important, the program invests heavily in training a large team of local extension workers who work closely with farmers to ensure optimal planting density, ridge-planting, weed management, pest management, fertilizer application, and harvesting and storage.

Chris Suzdak, the young U.S. economics major who managed the One Acre program there, explained that it was very much a business model. Those extension workers were "sales staff," who go village to village to promote different "product offerings." These are variations on the basic starter pack of maize seeds and fertilizer, the usual green-revolution package. That, of course, is the central contradiction in the program. Fertilizers are inorganic, purchased on the market, the seeds are mainly maize and they are all commercial varieties. I asked Suzdak if One Acre was promoting any open-pollinated varieties (OPVs) that farmers did not have to purchase every year. He said no, noting that they want to work closely with government and Malawi's government is heavily promoting hybrids. He then added, a little sheepishly, that the organization's business model is based on continuous sales of its products. An OPV would reduce the demand for seeds.

That admission, of course, leaves One Acre alongside Monsanto, Seed Co, and the other seed companies as self-interested parties in the seed choices offered to farmers. Not surprisingly, the program seems to do little for long-term soil health. It really wasn't much on Suzdak's radar, though he was interested. In Southern Malawi, they don't promote intercropping, though they don't discourage it. They do not encourage composted manure, through the addition of goats or other small livestock. They don't teach no-till agriculture or how to leave residues in the fields to improve the organic content of the soil. Most farmers still burn off their crop residues. Almost nothing One Acre was doing addressed long-term soil fertility.

One Acre Fund seemed to be getting productivity and income gains for the farmers they worked with. After my time in Southern Africa, I had a hard time calling that success. Their labor-intensive way of propagating green-revolution technologies, without investing in long-term soil health, would just put Malawi and the rest of Africa on the well-worn technology treadmill that mines nutrients from the soil and lines the pockets of the seed, fertilizer, and chemical companies without addressing the underlying soil issues that are the continent's biggest challenges, especially under the pressures from climate change. They aren't even promoting the kind of "integrated soil fertility management"—with compost, crop residues, and other soil-building supplements to inorganic fertilizer—advocated on paper by AGRA.

Malawi's seed and soil specialist, Elizabeth Sibale, was aghast when I told her of the program's inattention to the soil. "If you don't do anything about the soil, performance will decline," she said, confirming the problem of the yield plateau. "Manure should be required, even with the use of inorganic fertilizer. Fertilizer should just top things up after adding manure and organic matter. It's not because of poverty that you use manure; it is basic soil biology."

Eating Tomorrow

If anyone at the World Food Prize ceremonies in October 2017 back in Iowa was paying attention, reality was waving its arms in warning about this unsustainable model of agricultural development. Days before, Reuters had reported that the continued development of high-yield agriculture had generated a "global grain glut" that had driven crop prices so low farmers weren't sure they could afford those technologies.[10] Meanwhile, the FAO had announced that the number of people suffering chronic hunger had increased 5 percent the previous year.[11] Hunger amid plenty. No one at the annual agribusiness celebration was paying attention. With the usual pomp and circumstance the World Food Prize Selection Committee awarded the 2017 prize to former AGRA director Akinwumi Adesina, oblivious to the program's failures. Meanwhile, the nitrates flowed freely down the Des Moines River, again threatening to shut down the city's water supply. The dead zone in the Gulf of Mexico hit a new record, growing to the size of New Jersey.

We will never restore balance in our agricultural ecosystems if we can't restore a reasonable balance between family farmers and agribusiness. Right now, agribusiness is calling all the shots, from Iowa to India, Mexico to Mozambique. That leaves us wedded to policies and practices that have failed to feed the hungry while undermining the resource base that can feed us all in a climate-constrained tomorrow. And it leaves us blind to the solutions all around us.

Helping poor food producers grow more food is a "win-win" solution. Allowing them to eat today, from a rich diversity of intercropped foods, is the very thing that can help them—and all of us—eat tomorrow from their restored, resilient soil. In the process, we directly address the needs of the largest group of hungry people in the world: small-scale farmers and their families. Such a "zero hunger" approach isn't charity, it is a long-term investment in the productivity of many countries' largest group of working people.

In that sense, the investment pays multiple dividends, not just the avoidance of lost lives—and for economists lost productivity— from malnourished children whose stunting in their first 1,000 days handicaps them for a lifetime.[12] The investment also revitalizes rural communities, as farm families grow a surplus they can sell and then better their lives by spending that money in their local economies. On eggs or some other food item they can't produce themselves, putting money in the pockets of those who can. On improving their houses, stimulating the local market for cement to replace a dirt floor, roofing materials to replace tin or straw, a toilet to replace an unsanitary open-air latrine.

With more money in farmers' pockets, they'd see implement dealers selling farm machinery, maybe a bank, a hardware store, maybe even a club to respond to demand for nightlife from a youth population that no longer has to migrate to escape poverty and boredom, and to earn money they can send home. Picture those rural Iowan communities of old, wistfully recalled by George Naylor and Patti Edmundson. Why not? That's what the early stages of agricultural development look like. If agribusiness no longer gets to call all the shots, the later stages don't have to look like the Iowa of today.

Former UN Special Rapporteur on the Right to Food Olivier De Schutter and his new institute, the International Panel of Experts on Sustainable Food Systems, argue persuasively for a decisive shift away from the agribusiness model. In their report, "From Uniformity to Diversity," they show that sustainable agricultural practices can grow all the food we need to feed a growing population.[13] The FAO recently added its institutional weight to that conclusion after convening its second conference on "Scaling Up Agro-ecology."[14] Evidence suggests that in Africa, a shift to farming practices based on diversity, mixed farming, and participatory plant breeding doubled food production in between three and ten years.[15] In doing so, farmers can meet the challenges posed by a changing climate while reducing agriculture's contributions to climate change, and they can do so more equitably than does our current corporate food system.

De Schutter and his colleagues are painstakingly clear that the central obstacle to changing course is the overwhelming economic and political power of agribusiness. Even before the recent wave of mergers—Bayer-Monsanto, ChemChina-Syngenta, Dow-DuPont— three seed companies controlled 50 percent of the commercial market. Seven multinational fertilizer companies accounted for nearly all sales, while five companies captured two-thirds of the agro-chemical market. Just four firms had 90 percent of global grain trade.[16] The top five global meat and dairy conglomerates threaten to undermine any meaningful commitment to address climate change; according to a recent report just those five firms are responsible for more greenhouse gas emissions than Exxon-Mobil, Shell, or BP.[17]

Economic power conveys political influence. Agribusiness spent $133 million lobbying U.S. Congress in 2015, more even than the defense industry.[18] In the battle for the future of food, they are the main obstacle to change, and recapturing our democracies from corporate influence is a crucial step in surmounting that obstacle.

The good news is that in the battle for the future of food, farmer resistance is strong, and so are their alternatives, many advanced under the banner of "food sovereignty." In Malawi, farmers and their allies resist the imposition of a seed policy drafted by Monsanto and pursue an independent path using their own improved maize seeds in soils growing more fertile with their agro-ecological practices. In Mozambique, farming communities defend their hard-won land rights from land grabs while promoting climate-resilient farms. Zambians fight for a just national land policy that recognizes women's rights to secure village land and demands limits on corrupt land deals that give the best lands to foreigners and the rich. In India, the right-to-food movement defends its National Food Security Act against hypocritical trade complaints from the United States, pushing for grassroots rural development in the world's hungriest country. In Mexico, farmers and their allies sustain a multiyear resistance to the forced adoption of genetically modified maize, promote a transition to agro-ecology, and elect a president who might just reverse the trade and agricultural policies that have undermined small-scale farmers. And even in Iowa, residents demand clean water from more sustainable farming practices, livable communities not polluted by factory farms, and checks on the control agribusiness exerts over government policies in the state.

All are striving for the same thing: the right of everyone to eat safe and healthy food today while ensuring that we steward our natural wealth so we can all eat tomorrow.

Acknowledgments

Throughout this book, I sing often of the unsung heroes, the many farmers and farm movement leaders who generously shared their time, homes, farms, and food with me. They are feeding the hungry world, and they are the inspiration for my work. Their wisdom and resilience have changed my understanding of the world, and even how I garden in my own backyard *machamba*.

This book took shape under the warm embrace of the Open Society Foundation, which awarded me the fellowship that launched my research. The foundation, and especially the Open Society Initiative of Southern Africa, provided encouragement and collaboration, and the Human Rights Initiative supported my continued work on the issues raised in the book. I am particularly grateful to Stephen Hubbell, Louise Olivier, Masego Madzwamuse, and Mohamed Sultan. The foundation's in-country partners provide much of the wisdom and inspiration in the book, including Zambia Land Alliance, Malawi Farmer-to-Farmer Agroecology project, Farm Radio Malawi, Justiça Ambiental Mozambique, and ADE-CRU Mozambique.

The academic research that informs this work was incubated at Tufts University's Global Development and Environment Institute, directed by Neva Goodwin. It was completed under the encouraging gaze of the Small Planet Institute, which welcomed my

Land and Food Rights Program. Director Frances Moore Lappé generously helped shape my approach to the book and brilliantly thought of its title. Additional financial support for research and writing came from American Jewish World Service. As I published stories along the journey, *Global Post* and *Food Tank* were supportive and enthusiastic outlets. The New Press has been enthusiastic and skillful, with Marc Favreau's clear and gentle editorial pen steering me straight. Many great characters and stories fell to the cutting-room floor. I can't blame Marc for that, and I apologize to those who offered me their time and wisdom but don't see themselves in the book.

This book draws on the brilliant contributions of many research assistants I've had the pleasure to work with. That includes Rachel Gilbert, Rebecca Lucas, Ashley Higgs Hammell, and Laura Brisbane, who helped directly with the book, but also those who worked with me at Tufts's Global Development and Environment Institute on the research that would inform this project: Regina Flores, Elanor Starmer, Elise Garvey, Betsy Rakola, Alicia Harvie, Emily Cole, Muriel Calo. That research also benefited from collaborations with writers far more knowledgeable than I on many of these topics: Sophia Murphy, Antonio Turrent, Alejandro Nadal, Hilda Salazar, Kevin Gallagher, Jomo Kwame Sundaram, Biraj Patnaik, Marie Clarke, and her colleagues at ActionAid USA. In-country collaboration and assistance has been critical as well, especially from Euclides Gonçalves and Mariana Santarelli in Mozambique, Billy Mayaya, Mangani Katundu, and Stacia Nordin in Malawi, Nsama Nsemiwe in Zambia, Biraj Patnaik in India, Adelita San Vicente and Victor Suárez in Mexico, and Rachel Garst in Iowa.

I sought and received invaluable reviews of chapter drafts from more colleagues than I can mention here. Many offered the time and patience to educate me on the complex science and history behind the wide-ranging issues and places in this book, hopefully saving the reader (and me) from basic factual inaccuracies. Special thanks to Ricardo Salvador, Matt Liebman, Alan Guebert, Antonio Turrent, Adelita San Vicente, Antonio Serratos, Cristina

Barros, Sachin Jain, Sachin Kumar, Blessings Chinsinga, Ephraim Chirwa, Nicholas Sitko, Peter Riggs, and Jennifer Clapp, among many others for sharing their particular expertise with me. Jack Spence, Katherine Yih, and Steve Wasserman were generous readers throughout the journey. Adam Eichen was a skilled and enthusiastic proofreader.

Special thanks, too, to Action Aid USA, David Bacon, Enrique Perez at ANEC, and Justiça Ambiental Mozambique for permission to use their beautiful photos.

Special gratitude, of course, to my beloved Claire, who always believed I had this in me and put up with the obsessive behavior such an endeavor requires. So did my own next generation, who make the future more hopeful: Eve, Diego, and Jackson, who composed the fight song that kept me going down the stretch. Finally, to my late mother, Barbara Wise, a gifted writer who never got the chance to write her own book. She would have been thrilled with mine, red pen at the ready to correct those pesky stylistic errors.

Notes

1. Introduction

1. Author's calculations from "Food Dollar Application," Database, United States Department of Agriculture, Economic Research Service, March 14, 2018.

2. For my analysis of the food price crisis, see Timothy A. Wise and Sophia Murphy, "Resolving the Food Crisis: Assessing Global Policy Reforms Since 2007," *Global Development and Environment Institute and Institute for Agriculture and Trade Policy*, January 2012.

3. High Level Panel of Experts on Food Security and Nutrition of the Committee on World Food Security, "Investing in Smallholder Agriculture for Food Security," HLPE Report 6 (Rome, Italy: Committee on World Food Security, June 2013).

4. For a more thorough discussion of these problems, see chapters 2 and 3 of Frances Moore Lappé and Joseph Collins, *World Hunger: 10 Myths* (New York: Grove Press, 2015).

5. GRAIN and Institute for Agriculture and Trade Policy, "Emissions Impossible: How Big Meat and Dairy Are Heating Up the Planet" (Minneapolis, MN, July 2018).

6. FAO researchers projected that agricultural production (not just food production) needed to grow 60 percent by 2050. For a full review, see: Timothy A. Wise, "Can We Feed the World in 2050? A Scoping Paper to Assess the Evidence," Working Paper No. 13-04 (Global Development and Environment Institute, September 2013).

7. Doug Boucher, "The World's Population Hasn't Grown Exponentially for at Least Half a Century," *Union of Concerned Scientists* (blog), April 9, 2018.

8. Lappé and Collins, *World Hunger*.

9. Timothy A. Wise, "Feeding the World: The Ultimate First-World Conceit," *Triple Crisis Blog* (blog), October 7, 2014.

10. "Who Will Feed Us? The Peasant Food Web vs. the Industrial Food Chain," 3rd Edition (ETC Group, 2017).

11. Steve Wiggins and Keats Sharada, "Rural Wages in Asia" (Overseas Development Institute, October 2014).

12. Timothy A. Wise, "Are High Agricultural Prices Good or Bad for Poverty?" *GDAE Globalization Commentaries*, from *Triple Crisis Blog* (blog), November 19, 2010.

Part I: Into Africa: The New Colonialism

1. See Stefano Liberti, *Land Grabbing: Journeys in the New Colonialism*, 2013.

2. Wise and Murphy, "Resolving the Food Crisis: Assessing Global Policy Reforms Since 2007."

3. Sigrid Schmalzer, *Red Revolution, Green Revolution: Scientific Farming in Socialist China* (Chicago; London: University of Chicago Press, 2016), 2.

4. For a sober assessment of India's green revolution, see chapter 4 of Joel K. Bourne, *The End of Plenty: The Race to Feed a Crowded World* (New York: W. W. Norton & Company, 2016); or Vandana Shiva, *Who Really Feeds the World? The Failures of Agribusiness and the Promise of Agroecology* (Berkeley, CA: North Atlantic Books, 2016).

5. "Enabling the Business of Agriculture 2017" (Washington, DC: World Bank Group, n.d.).

6. "The New Alliance for Food Security and Nutrition," Global Justice Now, accessed May 21, 2018.

7. "How Does the Gates Foundation Spend Its Money to Feed the World?," Against the Grain (Barcelona, Spain: GRAIN, November 2014).

8. AGRA Board of Directors, "2016 Financials," AGRA, April 7, 2017.

9. Kapil Subramanian, "Revisiting the Green Revolution: Irrigation and Food Production in Twentieth-Century India" (University of London, King's College, United Kingdom, 2015).

2. The Malawi Miracle and the Limits of Africa's Green Revolution

1. Thomas S. Jayne et al., "Review: Taking Stock of Africa's Second-Generation Agricultural Input Subsidy Programs," *Food Policy* 75 (February 1, 2018): 1–14, doi:10.1016/j.foodpol.2018.01.003.

2. Glenn Denning and Jeffrey Sachs, "The Rich World Can Help Africa," *Financial Times*, May 29, 2007.

3. Charity Chimungu Phiri, "Malawi's Drought Leaves Millions High and Dry," Inter Press Service, May 27, 2016.

4. Ephraim Chirwa et al., "Evaluation of the 2014/15 Farm Input Subsidy Programme, Malawi" (Wadonda Consult Limited and School of Oriental and African Studies, October 2015), 51–52, 58.

5. Christopher Chibwana et al., "Measuring the Impacts of Malawi's Farm Input Subsidy Programme," *African Journal of Agriculture and Resource Economics* 9, no. 2 (2010): 132–47.

6. Roshni Menon, "Famine in Malawi: Causes and Consequences," Human Development Report 2007/2008: Fighting Climate Change: Human Solidarity in a Divided World (United Nations Development Programme, August 2007); Malawi maize production data downloaded from "FAOSTAT," Database, Food and Agriculture Organization of the United Nations, May 16, 2018.

7. Bill Corcoran, "Five Million Face Death as Famine Grips Malawi," *The Guardian*, October 1, 2005, sec. World news.

8. "Malawi Corn Production by Year," Index Mundi, accessed May 16, 2018.

9. Jayne et al., "Review."

10. Chirwa et al., "Evaluation of the 2014/15 Farm Input Subsidy Programme, Malawi," 51.

11. Ibid., 56–57.

12. Stein Holden and Julius Mangisoni, "Input Subsidies and Improved Maize Varieties in Malawi: What Can We Learn from the Impacts in a Drought Year?," Working Paper (Centre for Land Tenure Studies, Norwegian University of Life Sciences, 2013).

13. "Running to Stand Still: Small-Scale Farmers and the Green Revolution in Malawi" (Melville, South Africa: African Centre for Biodiversity, September 2014).

14. "Soils, Food, and Healthy Communities," n.d.

15. Chirwa et al., "Evaluation of the 2014/15 Farm Input Subsidy Programme, Malawi," 57.

16. Murayama Daiki et al., "Superiority of Malawian Orange Local Maize Variety in Nutrients, Cookability, and Storability," *African Journal of Agricultural Research* 12, no. 19 (May 11, 2017): 1618–28, doi:10.5897/AJAR2017.12138.

17. Ibid.

18. Blessings Chinsinga, "Seeds and Subsidies: The Political Economy of Input Programmes in Malawi," Working Paper (Future Agricultures Consortium, August 2010), 19–20.

19. Ephraim W. Chirwa and A. Dorward, *Agricultural Input Subsidies: The Recent Malawi Experience*, first edition (Oxford: Oxford University Press, 2013).

20. Ibid., 124–42, 196–218.

21. Chirwa et al., "Evaluation of the 2014/15 Farm Input Subsidy Programme, Malawi," 53, 61–62.

22. Ephraim Chirwa and Andrew Dorward, "Private Sector Participation in the Farm Input Subsidy Programme in Malawi, 2006-07-2011/12," Policy Brief, June 2012, 2–4.

23. See the recent book by Nina Munk, *The Idealist: Jeffrey Sachs and the Quest to End Poverty*, First Anchor Books edition (New York: Anchor Books, 2014).

24. Chirwa and Dorward, *Agricultural Input Subsidies*, 90.

25. "Running to Stand Still: Small-Scale Farmers and the Green Revolution in Malawi," xiv.

26. FAO, ed., *Meeting the 2015 International Hunger Targets: Taking Stock of Uneven Progress*, The State of Food Insecurity in the World 2015 (Rome: FAO, 2015), 44.

27. Data downloaded from FAO, "Food Security Indicators," Food and Agriculture Organization of the United Nations, February 9, 2016.

28. S. Alkire and U. Kanagaratnam, "Multidimensional Poverty Index Winter 2017–18: Brief Methodological Note and Results," OPHI Methodological Notes 45 (University of Oxford: Oxford Poverty and Human Development Initiative, 2018); World Bank Global Poverty Working Group, "Rural Poverty Headcount Ratio at National Poverty Lines (percent of Rural Population) Data," World Bank Data, accessed August 6, 2016.

29. Rachel Bezner Kerr, "Seed Struggles and Food Sovereignty in Northern Malawi," *Journal of Peasant Studies* 40, no. 5 (September 2013): 887, doi: 10.1080/03066150.2013.848428.

30. Olumuyiwa Adedeji and Manuk Ghazanchyan, "IMF Survey: IMF Lends Malawi $156 Million to Help Boost Foreign Reserves," International Monetary Fund, August 9, 2012.

31. Data downloaded in July 2017 from "FAOSTAT," Database, Food and Agriculture Organization of the United Nations, n.d.; and "DataBank," Database, the World Bank.

32. "New Alliance for Food Security and Nutrition: Part 1," ONE, December 10, 2012.

33. Agnes Towera Nkhoma, "Factors Affecting Sustainability of Agricultural Cooperatives: Lessons from Malawi" (Massey University, 2011), 63.

34. "Malawi Corn Production by Year"; estimated yields from "Ministry of Agriculture, Irrigation, and Water Development," Republic of Malawi, n.d.

35. Innocent Helema, "Malawi Fertiliser Imports Double," *The Nation Online*, October 14, 2014.

36. Ephraim Chirwa, Personal Communication, "Hybrid Adoption Rates in Malawi," September 4, 2016, based on 2015–16 FISP Evaluation.

37. "The Drought Tolerant Maize for Africa Initiative," CIMMYT, n.d.; P. S. Setimela et al., "Evaluation of Regional On-Farm Variety Trials in Eastern and Southern Africa 2011" (CIMMYT, 2012).

38. Gareth Jones, "Profiting from the Climate Crisis, Undermining Resilience in Africa: Gates and Monsanto's Water Efficient Maize for Africa (WEMA) Project" (Johannesburg, South Africa: African Centre for Biodiversity, April 2015).

39. IFPRI Malawi, "Launching Key Facts Series: Key Facts Sheet on Agriculture and Food Security," IFPRI Key Facts Series (Lilongwe, Malawi: IFPRI, February 2018).

40. Taeyoung Hwang et al., "Provitamin A Potential of Landrace Orange Maize Variety (Zea Mays L.) Grown in Different Geographical Locations of Central Malawi," *Food Chemistry* 196 (April 2016): 1315–24, doi:10.1016/j.foodchem.2015.10.067.

41. Daiki et al., "Superiority of Malawian Orange Local Maize Variety in Nutrients, Cookability, and Storability," 1627.

42. Hillary Muheebwa, "ARIPO Reviews Draft Regulations on Implementation of Arusha Protocol on Plant Varieties," Intellectual Property Watch, June 24, 2016.

43. "ARIPO PVP Regulations: Ferocious Campaign Against Seed Saving Farmers in Africa and State Sovereignty," Alliance for Food Sovereignty in Africa, June 13, 2016.

44. FAO, "Farmers' Rights," International Treaty on Plant Genetic Resources for Food and Agriculture, n.d.

45. Jayne et al., "Review."

46. Vandana Shiva, *Monocultures of the Mind: Perspectives on Biodiversity and Biotechnology* (London, UK: Zed Books; Third World Network, 1993).

3. The Rise and Fall of the Largest Land Grab in Africa

1. "Formulation of Agricultural Development Master Plan in the Nacala Corridor: Concept Note" (ProSAVANA-PD, September 2013).

2. Timothy A. Wise, "Food Price Volatility: Market Fundamentals and Commodity Speculation," *Triple Crisis Blog* (blog), January 27, 2011.

3. 24/7 Wall Street, "Memo to Congress: 'Buy Land, They Ain't Making Any More of It,'" *Time*, January 28, 2009.

4. This data, and the information in the next paragraph (except where noted), come from "Land Matrix Newsletter— October 2014" (Land Matrix, October 2014).

5. Kerstin Nolte, Wytske Chamberlain, and Markus Giger, "International Land Deals for Agriculture: Fresh Insights from the Land Matrix: Analytical Report II" (Bern, Montpellier, Hamburg, Pretoria: Centre for Development and Environment, University of Bern; Centre de coopération internationale en recherche agronomique pour le développement; German Institute of Global and Area Studies; University of Pretoria; Bern Open Publishing, 2016).

6. Song Jung-A, Christian Oliver, and Tom Burgis, "Daewoo to Cultivate Madagascar Land for Free," *Financial Times*, November 19, 2008.

7. Stefano Liberti, *Land Grabbing: Journeys in the New Colonialism* (London: Verso, 2013), 81.

8. Joseph Hanlon, ed., "Land Moves up the Political Agenda," *Mozambique Political Process Bulletin*, no. 48 (February 2011): 1–18.

9. Anna Locke, "Mozambique Land Policy Development Case Study," Evidence on Demand: Climate & Environment Infrastructure Livelihoods (Overseas Development Institute, March 2014), doi:10.12774/eod_hd.march 2014.locke.

10. Filipe Di Matteo and George Christoffel Schoneveld, *Agricultural Investments in Mozambique: An Analysis of Investment Trends, Business Models, and Social and Environmental Conduct* (Center for International Forestry Research [CIFOR], 2016).

11. For more information on Tanzania, see Timothy A. Wise, "Picking Up the Pieces from a Failed Land Grab Project in Tanzania," *Public Radio International* (blog), June 27, 2014.

12. Teresa Smart and Joseph Hanlon, "Chickens and Beer: A Recipe for Agricultural Growth in Mozambique" (Maputo, Mozambique: Kapicua, 2014).

13. "The Land Grabbers of the Nacala Corridor: A New Era of Struggle Against Colonial Plantations in Northern Mozambique" (UNAC and GRAIN, February 2015).

14. "Land Matrix Newsletter—October 2014."

15. Ward Anseeuw et al., *Transnational Land Deals for Agriculture in the Global South: Analytical Report Based on the Land Matrix Database* (Bern/Montpellier/Hamburg: The Land Matrix Partnership, 2012); and Land Matrix database for Mozambique.

16. "ProSAVANA's Communication Strategy and Its Impact: An Analysis of JICA's Disclosed and Leaked Documents" (No! to Land Grab, Japan, August 22, 2016).

17. "Mozambique Offers Brazilian Farmers 6 Million Hectares to Develop Agriculture," *MercoPress, South Atlantic News Agency*, August 16, 2011.

18. Timothy A. Wise, "What Happened to the Biggest Land Grab in Africa? Searching for ProSavana in Mozambique," *Food Tank* (blog), December 20, 2014; Frederico Pavia et al., "Nacala Corridor Fund," FGV Projetos, n.d.; "ProSAVANA's Communication Strategy and Its Impact."

19. Sergio Schlesinger, "Brazilian Cooperation and Investment in Africa: The Case of ProSavana in Mozambique," TEMTI Series of Economic Perspectives on Global Sustainability (TEMTI-CEESP/IUCN, 2014).

20. "Open Letter from Mozambican Civil Society Organisations and Movements to the Presidents of Mozambique and Brazil and the Prime Minister of Japan," farmlandgrab.org, May 28, 2013.

21. "No to ProSavana! Launch of National Campaign," n.d.; Pavia et al., "Nacala Corridor Fund."

22. Locke, "Mozambique Land Policy Development Case Study."

23. Ibid.

24. Data downloaded in February 2017 from "FAOSTAT," Database, Food and Agriculture Organization of the United Nations; data downloaded in April 2018 from "DataBank: World Development Indicators," the World Bank.

25. Rogier J. E. Van den Brink, "Land Reform in Mozambique," Agriculture & Rural Development Notes: Land Policy and Administration (Washington, DC: World Bank, December 2008).

26. Pavia et al., "Nacala Corridor Fund"; for more on the Kanakwe conflict, watch "Daqui a Nada," a short video documentary by ActionAid on the land grabbing in the Nacala Corridor, *Daqui a Nada* (ActionAid Brazil, YouTube, 2015).

27. Smart and Hanlon, "Chickens and Beer."

28 "ProSAVANA's Communication Strategy and Its Impact."

29. I covered this issue in more detail at the time in Timothy A. Wise, "History Repeats as Farce: Giving Away Land Without Consultation in Mozambique," *Food Tank* (blog), May 19, 2015.

30. Ibid.

31. GRAIN & ADECRU, "Mozambique's Council of Ministers Must Say 'No' to Resettlement of 100,000 in the Nacala Corridor," May 11, 2015.

32. Ibid.

33. "Principles for Responsible Investment in Agriculture and Food Systems" (Committee on World Food Security, October 2014); "Nairobi Action

Plan to Promote Land-Based Investments That Benefit Africa," African Development Bank Group, July 10, 2011.

34. Archdiocesan Commission for Justice and Peace of Nampula and *ADECRU*, "Exigimos a Suspensão e Invalidação Imediata Da 'Auscultação Pública Do Plano Director Do ProSavana'/ We Demand the Suspension and Invalidation of Immediate 'Public Consultation Plan Director ProSavana,'" *ADECRU* (blog), May 11, 2015.

35. I wrote about this in more detail at the time in Timothy A. Wise, "Looking for Food in All the Wrong Places," *Food Tank* (blog), June 2016.

36. "Mozambique: Drought Humanitarian Situation Report," Situation Report (UNICEF, April 29, 2016).

37. "Running to Stand Still: Small-Scale Farmers and the Green Revolution in Malawi" (Melville, South Africa: African Centre for Biodiversity, September 2014).

38. New Alliance for Food Security, "Cooperation Framework to Support the New Alliance for Food Security & Nutrition in Mozambique," Partner Countries (G8 New Alliance for Food Security, n.d.).

39. AFSA, "ARIPO PVP Regulations: Ferocious Campaign Against Seed Saving Farmers in Africa and State Sovereignty," Alliance for Food Sovereignty in Africa, June 13, 2016.

40. "The GM Maize Onslaught in Mozambique: Undermining Biosafety and Smallholder Farmers" (Johannesburg, South Africa: African Centre for Biodiversity, April 2017).

41. I described this in more detail in Timothy A. Wise, "Seeds of Climate Resilience in Mozambique," *Food Tank* (blog), April 2017.

42. "El Niño in Southern Africa," United Nations Office for the Coordination of Humanitarian Affairs, accessed January 5, 2018.

43. Saleemul Huq, "Getting Climate Finance to Where It Is Needed Most," *The Daily Star*, March 9, 2017.

44. Marek Soanes et al., "Delivering Real Change: Getting International Climate Finance to the Local Level," Working Paper (London: International Institute for Environment and Development, March 2017).

45. "Mapping Farmer Seed Varieties in Manica, Mozambique: Report on Initial Investigations into Agricultural Biodiversity," Field Work Report (African Centre for Biodiversity, September 2016).

46. Sérgio Chichava, "Xai-Xai Chinese Rice Farm and Mozambican Internal Political Dynamics: A Complex Relation," Occasional Paper 2 (LSE IDEAS Africa Programme, July 2013); Sérgio Chichava, "Chinese Agricultural Investment in Mozambique: The Case of the Wanbao Rice Farm," in *The SAIS China Africa Research Initiative at Johns Hopkins University*

(Agricultural Investment in Africa: "Land Grabs" or "Friendship Farms"?, Washington, DC, 2014).

47. Chichava, "Chinese Agricultural Investment in Mozambique."

48. Kojo S. Amanor and Sérgio Chichava, "South–South Cooperation, Agribusiness, and African Agricultural Development: Brazil and China in Ghana and Mozambique," *World Development*, China and Brazil in African Agriculture, 81 (May 1, 2016): 13–23, doi:10.1016/j.worlddev.2015.11.021.

49. For more information see Zhang Chuanhong et al., "Interpreting China–Africa Agricultural Encounters: Rhetoric and Reality in a Large Scale Rice Project in Mozambique," Working Paper 126, China and Brazil in African Agriculture (CBAA) Project (Future Agricultures Consortium, August 2015).

50. For more on the myths and realities of land grabbing, see Timothy A. Wise, "Land Grab Update: Mozambique, Africa Still in the Crosshairs," *Food Tank* (blog), October 2016; Deborah Brautigam, *Will Africa Feed China?* (Oxford; New York: Oxford University Press, 2015).

51. Eléusio Filipe and Simon Norfolk, "Understanding Changing Land Issues for the Rural Poor in Mozambique" (London: IIED, 2017).

52. Smart and Hanlon, "Chickens and Beer."

53. Chichava, "Chinese Agricultural Investment in Mozambique."

54. Gizela Zunguze, "At the Lower Limpopo Irrigated Area" (Justiça Ambiental—Friends of the Earth Mozambique, 2016).

55. Wanbao also pursued a concession in the nearby Chókwè irrigation district on 15,000 acres. Sérgio Chichava, "Mozambican Elite in a Chinese Rice 'Friendship': An Ethnographic Study of the Xai-Xai Irrigation Scheme," *Future Agricultures*, Working Paper no. 111 (February 2015): 1–10.

56. Chichava, "Xai-Xai Chinese Rice Farm."

57. Chuanhong et al., "Interpreting China–Africa Agricultural Encounters."

58. Jing Gu et al., "Chinese State Capitalism? Rethinking the Role of the State and Business in Chinese Development Cooperation in Africa," *World Development* 81 (May 2016): 24–34, doi:10.1016/j.worlddev.2016.01.001.

59. Ibid.

60. Chichava, "Chinese Agricultural Investment in Mozambique."

4. Land-Poor Farmers in a Land-Rich Country: Zambia's Maize Paradox

1. Official government categories treat farmers with up to 125 acres as "smallholders," but most consider farms under 2 hectares—5 acres—to be small farms.

2. Hilal Elver, "Preliminary Observations Special Rapporteur on the Right to Food, Hilal Elver, on Her Mission to Zambia 3–12 May 2017" (Office of the High Commissioner on Human Rights, May 12, 2017).

3. Thomas S. Jayne et al., "Is the Scramble for Land in Africa Foreclosing a Smallholder Agricultural Expansion Strategy?," *Journal of International Affairs* 67, no. 2 (Spring 2014): 35–53.

4. Ha-Joon Chang, "Rethinking Public Policy in Agriculture: Lessons from Distant and Recent History," Policy Assistance Series (Rome, Italy: Food and Agriculture Organization, 2009).

5. Refiloe Joala et al., *Changing Agro-Food Systems: The Impact of Big Agro-Investors on Food Rights* (Institute for Poverty, Land, and Agrarian Studies, 2016).

6. Ibid.

7. Munguzwe Hichaambwa and T. S. Jayne, "Poverty Reduction Potential of Increasing Smallholder Access to Land," Working Paper (Lusaka, Zambia: Indaba Agricultural Policy Research Institute [IAPRI], March 2014).

8. Jordan Chamberlin, T. S. Jayne, and D. Headey, "Scarcity Amidst Abundance? Reassessing the Potential for Cropland Expansion in Africa," *Food Policy* 48 (October 2014): 51–65, doi:10.1016/j.foodpol.2014.05.002.

9. "People's Manual on the Guidelines on Governance of Land, Fisheries, and Forests: A Guide for Promotion, Implementation, Monitoring, and Evaluation" (International Planning Committee for Food Sovereignty, 2016); "Principles for Responsible Investment in Agriculture and Food Systems" (Committee on World Food Security, n.d.); "Guiding Principles on Large Scale Land Based Investments in Africa" (Addis Ababa: United Nations Economic Commission for Africa, 2014); Carlo Bolzoni, "Approaching a United Nations Declaration on Peasant Rights," *Sustainable Food Trust* (blog), August 31, 2017.

10. The following story draws on my piece published in *Food Tank*: Timothy A. Wise, "Securing Land Rights in Zambia," *Food Tank* (blog), April 3, 2017.

11. Admos Chimhowu and Phil Woodhouse, "Customary vs. Private Property Rights? Dynamics and Trajectories of Vernacular Land Markets in Sub-Saharan Africa," *Journal of Agrarian Change* 6, no. 3 (July 2006): 346–71, doi:10.1111/j.1471-0366.2006.00125.x.

12. "Responsible Land Governance: Towards an Evidence Based Approach: Annual World Bank Conference on Land and Poverty," March 2017.

13. Nicholas J. Sitko and Jordan Chamberlin, "The Geography of Zambia's Customary Land: Assessing the Prospects for Smallholder

Development," *Land Use Policy* 55 (September 2016): 50–55, doi:10.1016/j.landusepol.2016.03.026.

14. Hichaambwa and Jayne, "Poverty Reduction Potential of Increasing Smallholder Access to Land."

15. Antony Chapoto and Nicholas J. Sitko, *Agriculture in Zambia: Past, Present, and Future* (Lusaka, Zambia: Indaba Agricultural Policy Research Institute, 2015), 36.

16. Hichaambwa and Jayne, "Poverty Reduction Potential of Increasing Smallholder Access to Land."

17. "New Alliance for Food Security and Nutrition: Part 1," ONE, December 10, 2012.

18. Monsanto, "Notice of Annual Meeting of Shareowners and 2015 Proxy Statement" (Monsanto, December 10, 2015), 55.

19. Claire Provost, Liz Ford, and Mark Tran, "G8 New Alliance Condemned as New Wave of Colonialism in Africa," *The Guardian*, February 18, 2014, sec. Global development.

20. Olivier De Schutter, "Farmers Must Not Be Disempowered Labourers on Their Own Land," Special Rapporteur on the Right to Food, October 24, 2011; Olivier De Schutter, "The Right to Food" (UN General Assembly, August 2011).

21. Ward Anseeuw et al., *Transnational Land Deals for Agriculture in the Global South*.

22. Timothy A. Wise, "Picking Up the Pieces from a Failed Land Grab Project in Tanzania," *GlobalPost*, June 27, 2014, sec. Conflict & Justice.

23. "Government to Look for Partner in Nansanga Farming Block," *Lusaka Voice* (blog), August 1, 2014.

24. Human Rights Watch, "'Forced to Leave': Commercial Farming and Displacement in Zambia" (New York: Human Rights Watch, October 25, 2017).

25. Ibid.

26. Ibid.

27. Antony Chapoto and Brian Chisanga, "Zambia: Agriculture Status Report 2016" (Lusaka, Zambia: Indaba Agricultural Policy Research Institute, 2016), 15–16, 20.

28. Nicholas J. Sitko et al., "A Comparative Political Economic Analysis of Maize Sector Policies in Eastern and Southern Africa," *Food Policy* 69 (May 2017): 246, doi: 10.1016/j.foodpol.2017.04.010.

29. Nicholas J. Sitko and T. S. Jayne, "Structural Transformation or Elite Land Capture? The Growth of 'Emergent' Farmers in Zambia," *Food Policy* 48 (2014): 194–202, doi:10.1016/j.foodpol.2014.05.006.

30. Author's calculations using data downloaded in February 2017 from "FAOSTAT," Database, Food and Agriculture Organization of the United Nations.

31. Sitko et al., "A Comparative Political Economic Analysis."

32. William J. Burke et al., "Understanding Fertilizer Effectiveness and Adoption on Maize in Zambia," Working Paper, MSU International Development Working Papers (East Lansing: MSU Department of Agricultural, Food, and Resource Economics, October 2016), iv.

33. Chapoto and Chisanga, "Zambia: Agriculture Status Report 2016," 17–18.

34. Hambulo Ngoma, "E-Vouchers Bring Welcome Choice to Zambian Farmers," *AgriLinks* (blog), January 3, 2018.

35. "Push-Pull Technology for the Control of Stemborers and Striga Weed," International Centre of Insect Physiology and Ecology, n.d.

36. Elver, "Preliminary Observations"; Hilal Elver, "Report of the Special Rapporteur on the Right to Food on Her Mission to Zambia" (Human Rights Council, United Nations General Assembly, March 26, 2018).

37. Government of the Republic of Zambia, "Second National Agricultural Policy 2016" (Lusaka, Zambia: Government of the Republic of Zambia, February 2016).

Part II: The Roots of Our Problems

1. This section draws on the excellent biographical sketch in Charles C. Mann, *The Wizard and the Prophet: Two Remarkable Scientists and Their Dueling Visions to Shape Tomorrow's World* (New York: Alfred A. Knopf, 2018).

2. "World Food Prize Receives $5 Million Pledge from Monsanto to Honor Norman Borlaug," News Releases, Monsanto, February 15, 2008.

3. "Ethanol Plants," Iowa Corn, n.d.

5. Iowa and the Cornification of the United States

1. Timothy A. Wise and Kristin Sundell, "Rising to the Challenge: Changing Course to Feed the World in 2050" (Washington, DC: ActionAid USA, October 2013).

2. "Farm Drainage in the United States: History, Status, and Prospects," Miscellaneous Publication (Washington, DC: U.S. Department of Agriculture, Economic Research Service, December 1987), 18.

3. MacKenzie Elmer, "Water Works Plans $15 Million for Expanded Nitrate Facility," *Des Moines Register*, May 24, 2017.

4. Deanna Conners, "2014 Gulf of Mexico Dead Zone Has Grown to 5,052 Square Miles," *EarthSky*, August 18, 2014, sec. Earth.

5. Wallace would plant two carefully selected "inbred" varieties in alternating rows, "de-tassel" one of them to remove the pollen so that the remaining "female" plants would be pollinated by the other inbred's tassels, the male parent, and harvest the resulting "single-cross" hybrid for seed. Only a few seed varieties performed better than their parents, but those that did were selected as single-cross hybrids. Unfortunately, they did not produce much seed. When Wallace began using the "double-cross" method, crossing two single-cross hybrids, he could get larger quantities of productive seed.

6. Jean-Pierre Berlan and Richard C. Lewontin, "The Political Economy of Hybrid Corn," *Monthly Review* 38, no. 3 (July 5, 1986), doi:10.14452/MR -038-03-1986-07_5; the preceding paragraph also draws from this article.

7. For more on Henry A. Wallace see John C. Culver and John Hyde, *American Dreamer: The Life and Times of Henry A. Wallace* (New York: Norton, 2001).

8. Harold Lee, *Roswell Garst: A Biography*, first edition, the Henry A. Wallace Series on Agricultural History and Rural Studies (Ames: Iowa State University Press, 1984).

9. Richard Sutch, "The Impact of the 1936 Corn Belt Drought on American Farmers' Adoption of Hybrid Corn," in *The Economics of Climate Change: Adaptations Past and Present*, ed. Gary D. Libecap and Richard H. Steckel, National Bureau of Economic Research Conference Report (Chicago; London: University of Chicago Press, 2011), 195–223; "1941 Annual Crop Summary: Acreage, Yield, and Production of Principal Crops" (Washington, DC: U.S. Department of Agriculture, Agricultural Marketing Service, December 1941), 44.

10. Berlan and Lewontin, "The Political Economy of Hybrid Corn."

11. Frank Kutka, "Open-Pollinated vs. Hybrid Maize Cultivars," *Sustainability* 3 (2011): 1531–54, doi:10.3390/su3091531.

12. Sutch, "The Impact of the 1936 Corn Belt Drought," 204, 214–17.

13. Daniel P. Bigelow and Borchers Allison, "Major Uses of Land in the United States, 2012," Economic Information Bulletin (United States Department of Agriculture Economic Research Service, August 2017), 13.

14. Willard W. Cochrane, *The Curse of American Agricultural Abundance: A Sustainable Solution*, Our Sustainable Future, vol. 16 (Lincoln: University of Nebraska Press, 2003).

15. Historical Iowa corn yield data downloaded from "Quick Stats" (United States Department of Agriculture, National Agricultural Statistics Service), on May 15, 2018.

16. Sutch, "The Impact of the 1936 Corn Belt Drought," 199, 202, 208–9.

17. Donald N. Duvick, "The Contribution of Breeding to Yield Advances in Maize (Zea Mays L.)," in *Advances in Agronomy*, vol. 86 (San Diego, CA: Academic Press, 2005), 83–145, doi:10.1016/S0065-2113(05)86002-X; Stephen Smith et al., "Maize," in *CSSA Special Publications* (American Society of Agronomy, Inc., Crop Science Society of America, Inc., and Soil Science Society of America, Inc., 2014), doi:10.2135/cssaspecpub33.c6.

18. Lee, *Roswell Garst*, ix.

19. "Stop Factory Farms," Iowa Citizens for Community Improvement, n.d.

20. For further explanation and examples of the effects of fertilizer runoff on watersheds, see A. N. Sharpley and Seppo Rekolainen, "Phosphorus in Agriculture and Its Environmental Implications," in *Phosphorus Loss from Soil to Water* (Center for Agriculture and Bioscience International, 1997); and J. L. Hatfield, L. D. McMullen, and C. S. Jones, "Nitrate-Nitrogen Patterns in the Raccoon River Basin Related to Agricultural Practices," *Journal of Soil and Water Conservation* 64, no. 3 (May 1, 2009): 190–99, doi:10.2489/jswc.64.3.190.

21. "Corn Facts," Iowa Corn, n.d.

22. "CRP Enrollment and Rental Payments by State, 1986–2017" (Conservation Reserve Program Statistics, United States Department of Agriculture, Farm Service Agency, May 2018).

23. Charles M. Benbrook, "Trends in Glyphosate Herbicide Use in the United States and Globally," *Environmental Sciences Europe* 28, no. 1 (December 2016), doi:10.1186/s12302-016-0070-0.

24. Carey Gillam, *Whitewash: The Story of a Weed Killer, Cancer, and the Corruption of Science* (Washington, DC: Island Press, 2017).

25. Sarah P. Saunders et al., "Local and Cross-Seasonal Associations of Climate and Land Use with Abundance of Monarch Butterflies *Danaus Plexippus*," *Ecography* 41, no. 2 (February 2018): 278–90, doi:10.1111/ecog.02719.

26. Maps are available with such detail from E. Brandes et al., "Subfield Profitability Analysis Reveals an Economic Case for Cropland Diversification," *Environmental Research Letters* 11, no. 1 (January 20, 2016).

27. "Fertilizer Use and Price: All Fertilizer Use and Price Tables in a Single Workbook" (United States Department of Agriculture, Economic Research Service, February 21, 2018).

28. "2012 Census Highlights: Farm Demographics—U.S. Farmers by Gender, Age, Race, Ethnicity, and More," United States Department of Agriculture, Census of Agriculture, May 2014.

29. For more on speculative investment in U.S. farmland, including by investors like TIAA-CREF, see Lukas Ross, "Down on the Farm: Wall Street: America's New Farmer" (Oakland Institute, 2014), 19–20 for TIAA.

30. I pulled my permission for them to use me in the film, *Food Evolution*, and several notables—Michael Pollan, Marion Nestle—objected when they saw their views so misrepresented in what was a far more propagandistic film than Naylor and I suspected at the time. For more, read Stacy Malkan, "Food Evolution GMO Film Showcases Chemical Industry Agenda," *HuffPost*, June 26, 2017.

31. Iowa Department of Agriculture and Land Stewardship, "Iowa State Average Corn Prices for October 2012" (Agricultural Marketing Bureau, n.d.); Iowa Department of Agriculture and Land Stewardship, "Iowa State Average Corn Prices for October 2014" (Agricultural Marketing Bureau, n.d.).

32. This section, unless otherwise noted, draws data from "The Economic Cost of Food Monopolies" (Food and Water Watch, November 2012).

33. Timothy A. Wise, "Agribusiness and the Food Crisis: A New Thrust at Anti-Trust," *GDAE Globalization Commentaries* (blog), March 22, 2010.

34. "The DRAFT 2016 Iowa List of Clean Water Act Section 303(d) Impaired Waters" (Water Quality Monitoring & Assessment Section, Water Quality Bureau, Iowa Department of Natural Resources, April 2017), 6.

35. More detail in chapter 6.

36. Ms. Kinman now works for the Iowa Association of Water Agencies.

37. Margaret McCasland et al., "Nitrate: Health Effects in Drinking Water," Cornell University Cooperative Extension, 2012.

38. Ricardo Salvador, "Breaking News: USDA and EPA Clearly Enlist™ to Ignore Science and Protect Industry Profits," *Union of Concerned Scientists* (blog), October 17, 2014.

39. Adam S. Davis et al., "Increasing Cropping System Diversity Balances Productivity, Profitability, and Environmental Health," *PLOS ONE* 7, no. 10 (October 10, 2012): e47149, doi:10.1371/journal.pone.0047149.

40. "Rotating Crops, Turning Profits: How Diversified Farming Systems Can Help Farmers While Protecting Soil and Preventing Pollution," Union of Concerned Scientists, May 2017.

41. Donnelle Eller, "With Water Works' Lawsuit Dismissed, Water Quality Is the Legislature's Problem," *Des Moines Register*, March 17, 2017.

42. "Gulf of Mexico 'Dead Zone' Is the Largest Ever Measured," *National Oceanic and Atmospheric Administration, US Department of Commerce* (blog), August 2, 2017.

43. "Garst Seed Company, Inc." (Encyclopedia.com, 2006); "Hartung Seed Facility Slated to Open in January," *Daily Times Herald*, December 4, 2014.

6. Fueling the Food Crisis

1. High Level Panel of Experts, "Biofuels and Food Security" (Rome: Committee on World Food Security, June 2013); *Renewable Fuel Standard: Potential Economic and Environmental Effects of U.S. Biofuel Policy* (Washington, DC: National Academies Press, 2011), doi:10.17226/13105.

2. "Committee on World Food Security: Fortieth Session Report" (Rome, Italy, October 7, 2013).

3. Author's calculations from data downloaded on April 10, 2018, from "FAOSTAT," Database, Food and Agriculture Organization of the United Nations, n.d.

4. High Level Panel of Experts, "Biofuels and Food Security," 50.

5. Kirsten Appendini, "Reconstructing the Maize Market in Rural Mexico," *Journal of Agrarian Change* 14, no. 1 (March 25, 2013): 1–25, doi:10.1111/joac.12013.

6. "Mexico's Poor Seek Relief from Tortilla Shortage," *National Geographic News*, June 4, 2008,

7. Marco Lagi, Karla Z. Bertrand, and Yaneer Bar-Yam, "The Food Crises and Political Instability in North Africa and the Middle East" (Cambridge, MA: New England Complex Systems Institute, September 28, 2011), 4; David J. Lynch, "Tensions in Egypt Shows Potency of Food Crisis," *USA Today*, April 29, 2008.

8. "Biofueling Hunger: How US Corn Ethanol Policy Drives Up Food Prices in Mexico" (ActionAid International USA, May 2012); "Energy Independence and Security Act of 2007," H.R.6 § Sec. 202(a)(1), Sec. 202(b)(4), and Sec. 210(a) (2007).

9. Daryll E. Ray, Daniel G. De La Torre Ugarte, and Kelly J. Tiller, "Rethinking US Agricultural Policy: Changing Course to Secure Farmer Livelihoods Worldwide" (Agricultural Policy Analysis Center, 2003).

10. For a more detailed analysis of the rise in corn ethanol and its impacts, see Timothy A. Wise and Marie Brill, "Fueling the Food Crisis: The Cost to Developing Countries of US Corn Ethanol Expansion" (ActionAid International USA, October 2012).

11. "Methyl Tertiary Butyl Ether (MTBE): Overview," EPA Web Archive, February 20, 2016; "Methyl Tert-Butyl Ether" (US Environmental Protection Agency, January 2000).

12. Mary Farrell-Stieve, "Power Formula: Gas Price Hikes Fuel Drive for Ethanol Production; Farmers Look to Co-ops to Gain Market Share," *USDA Rural Cooperatives*, June 2000, 8–9.

13. Ibid., 10–12.

14. Ibid., 10–11.

15. "The 5 Largest Ethanol Producers," Farm Industry News, March 12, 2012.

16. Bruce A. Babcock, "The Impact of US Biofuel Policies on Agricultural Price Levels and Volatility" (Geneva, Switzerland: International Centre for Trade and Sustainable Development, 2011).

17. High Level Panel of Experts, "Biofuels and Food Security" (appendix A1 has a useful compilation of recent estimates); Renewable Fuel Standard (refers to 20 to 40 percent of the increase in a period when prices approximately doubled).

18. "Directive 2003/30/EC of the European Parliament and of the Council of 8 May 2003 on the Promotion of the Use of Biofuels or Other Renewable Fuels for Transport," Pub. L. No. 32003L0030, OJL 123 42 (2003); "Directive 2009/28/EC of the European Parliament and of the Council of 23 April 2009 on the Promotion of the Use of Energy from Renewable Sources and Amending and Subsequently Repealing Directives 2001/77/EC and 2003/30/EC," Pub. L. No. 32009L0028, OJL 140 16 (2009).

19. "EU Parliament Ends Support to Highest-Emitting Palm Oil Biofuel While Freezing All Food-Based Biofuels at Current Levels," Transport and Environment, January 17, 2018; "Prospects for Agricultural Markets in the EU 2017–2030" (European Union, 2017), 9.

20. F. F. Kesaulija et al., "Oil Palm Estate Development and Its Impact on Forests and Local Communities in West Papua: A Case Study on the Prafi Plain" (Center for International Forestry Research, 2014), doi:10.17528 /cifor/005068; "Vegetable Oil Markets and the EU Biofuel Mandate" (International Council on Clean Transportation, February 2013); "Demand for Palm Oil Fuels Land-Grabbing," IRIN (blog), July 6, 2010.

21. Sarantis Michalopoulos, "EU Parliament Ends Palm Oil and Caps Crop-Based Biofuels at 2017 Levels," Euractiv.Com (blog), January 17, 2018.

22. Jarrett Renshaw, "EPA Abandons Changes to U.S. Biofuel Program After Lawmaker Pressure," Reuters, October 20, 2017.

23. "Petroleum & Other Liquids, Data: U.S. Imports by Country of Origin," Database, U.S. Energy Information Administration, downloaded March 19, 2018; I explain this in more detail in a blog post, Timothy A. Wise, "Running on Empty: US Ethanol Policies Set to Reach Their Illogical Conclusion" (Global Development And Environment Institute, Tufts University, July 23, 2012).

24. High Level Panel of Experts, "Biofuels and Food Security"; Marco Lagi et al., "The Food Crises: A Quantitative Model of Food Prices Including Speculators and Ethanol Conversion," 2011, 8, 16.

25. "Price Volatility and Food Security" (Committee on World Food Security, High Level Panel of Experts on Food Security and Nutrition, July 2011), 32.

26. Data downloaded on April 11, 2018 from "FAOSTAT."

27. High Level Panel of Experts, "Biofuels and Food Security," 71.

28. Wise and Brill, "Fueling the Food Crisis," 3, 16, 22.

29. Timothy A. Wise, "Two Roads Diverged in the Food Crisis: Global Policy Takes the One More Travelled," *Canadian Food Studies* 2, no. 2 (September 2015): 9–16, doi:10.15353/cfs-rcea.v2i2.98.

30. Ibid.

31. Wise and Brill, "Fueling the Food Crisis," 17–18.

32. Elisabeth Rosenthal, "As Biofuel Demand Grows, So Do Guatemala's Hunger Pangs," *New York Times*, January 5, 2013, sec. Environment.

33. Ibid.

34. According to reports by the Iniciativa de Copenhague para Centroamérica y México, the Comité de Unidad Campesina, and the Guatemala Human Rights Campaign, via ActionAid: Wise and Brill, "Fueling the Food Crisis," 21.

35. Rosenthal, "As Biofuel Demand Grows, So Do Guatemala's Hunger Pangs."

36. Timothy A. Wise, "Food Price Volatility: Market Fundamentals and Commodity Speculation," *Triple Crisis Blog* (blog), January 27, 2011; Timothy A. Wise, "Spotlight G20: New Evidence of Speculation in Financialized Commodities Markets," *Triple Crisis Blog* (blog), July 14, 2011; Kaufman offers an extensive guided tour of the financialization of food in Frederick Kaufman, *Bet the Farm: How Food Stopped Being Food* (Hoboken, NJ: John Wiley & Sons, 2012).

37. Robert Pollin and James Heintz, "How Wall Street Speculation Is Driving Up Gasoline Prices Today" (Political Economy Research Institute, University of Massachusetts Amherst, June 2011), 1; Jayati Ghosh, "Global Oil Prices," International Development Economics Associates, July 13, 2011.

38. Wise, "Food Price Volatility."

39. Ibid.

40. I summarized these dynamics in more detail at the time in Wise, "Spotlight G20"; and Wise, "Food Price Volatility."

41. Michael W. Masters and Adam K. White, "The Accidental Hunt Brothers: How Institutional Investors Are Driving Up Food and Energy Prices," Special Report, July 31, 2008.

42. One of the effects of this "financialization" of commodity markets was to eliminate the rationale for their value as an investment vehicle in the first

place. The following short policy brief from UNCTAD showed that commodities stopped being a safe haven when other markets were falling. Instead of moving "countercyclically"—up when the stock market went down—they began to move in parallel. "Don't Blame the Physical Markets: Financialization Is the Root Cause of Oil and Commodity Price Volatility" (United Nations Conference on Trade and Development, September 2012).

43. Lagi et al., "The Food Crises: A Quantitative Model," 4.

44. Lagi et al., 8–10. The following UNCTAD report confirmed that such speculation can have significant impacts in the short run on prices, consistent with the kinds of spikes NECSI studies. "Price Formation in Financialized Commodity Markets: The Role of Information" (United Nations Conference on Trade and Development, June 2011); See also Jayati Ghosh, James Heintz, and Robert Pollin, "Speculation on Commodities Futures Markets and Destabilization of Global Food Prices: Exploring the Connections," *International Journal of Health Services* 42, no. 3 (July 2012): 465–83, doi:10.2190 /HS.42.3.f. For more on NECSI's modeling and its findings, see the NECSI website and its additional studies of food price movements.

45. Lagi et al., "The Food Crises: A Quantitative Model," 1.

46. "Financial Crisis 2: Rise of the Machines" (Robin Hood Tax, n.d.), 2–4.

47. "Don't Blame the Physical Markets: Financialization Is the Root Cause of Oil and Commodity Price Volatility," 4.

48. Patrick Barta, "Jatropha Plant Gains Steam in Global Race for Biofuels," *Wall Street Journal*, August 24, 2007.

49. For more on the Sun Biofuels story, see Timothy A. Wise, "Picking Up the Pieces from a Failed Land Grab Project in Tanzania," *GlobalPost*, June 27, 2014, sec. Conflict & Justice; Josie Cohen, "How a Biofuels Landgrab Has Destroyed the Life of an African Village," *ActionAid* (blog), October 31, 2011; Liberti, *Land Grabbing*, chapter 6.

50. W. Gerbens-Leenes, A. Y. Hoekstra, and T. H. van der Meer, "The Water Footprint of Bioenergy," *Proceedings of the National Academy of Sciences* 106, no. 25 (June 23, 2009): 10222, doi:10.1073/pnas.0812619106.

51. Donald L. Kgathi et al., "A Review of the Sustainability of Jatropha Cultivation Projects for Biodiesel Production in Southern Africa: Implications for Energy Policy in Botswana," *Agriculture, Ecosystems & Environment* 246 (August 2017): 314–24, doi:10.1016/j.agee.2017.06.014.

52. Valerie Fernandes, "RE: Request to an Interview/Meeting," June 3, 2014; her email stated: "With all due respect, surely the villagers do not expect to be consulted on the plans for a farm that belongs to Sun Biofuels? I agree the villages surround the land but do they contribute to the upkeep of the land that they expect to be consulted?"

53. "Diligent Tanzania Ltd," Trickle Out Africa, n.d.; Finnigan Wa Simbeye, "Tanzania: Dutch Firm Goes Bust Leaving Thousands of Farmers in Limbo," *Tanzania Daily News* (Dar Es Salaam), January 6, 2015.

54. Rod Nickel, "Special Report: Drowning in Grain—How Big Ag Sowed Seeds of a Profit-Slashing Glut," Reuters, September 27, 2017, sec. Business News.

55. Ben Wolfgang, "E15 Ethanol Debate Reaches Tipping Point in Congress," *Washington Times*, June 14, 2017; Daniel De La Torre Ugarte, "10-Year Review of Renewable Fuel Standard Impacts to the Environment, the Economy, and Advanced Biofuels Development: An Update," *American Council for Capital Formation Blog*, June 2016

56. Timothy A. Wise and Emily Cole, "Mandating Food Insecurity: The Global Impacts of Rising Biofuel Mandates and Targets," Working Paper (Global Development and Environment Institute, February 2015), 1–4.

7. Monsanto Invades Corn's Garden of Eden in Mexico

1. "Mexican Judge Throws Out Monsanto Appeal to Confirm GM Maize Ban," *Sustainable Pulse*, December 30, 2013.

2. *Maiz* is the Spanish word for corn, and *maize* is the English word used internationally to refer to corn. In Mexico, the word *corn* is seen to refer to U.S. yellow dent corn used for feed, ethanol, and processed foods, distinct from their maize, much of which is consumed directly. Out of deference, for the rest of this chapter I use the terms interchangeably but mainly use the term *maize*.

3. José Antonio Serratos Hernández, "The Origin and Diversity of Maize in the American Continent" (Greenpeace, January 2009).

4. Daniel Zizumbo-Villarreal and Patricia Colunga-GarcíaMarín, "Origin of Agriculture and Plant Domestication in West Mesoamerica," *Genetic Resources and Crop Evolution* 57, no. 6 (August 2010): 813–25, doi:10.1007/s10722-009-9521-4.

5. José Antonio Serratos Hernández, "Bioseguridad y Dispersión de Maíz Transgénico en México" (Ciencias, October 2008).

6. The information in this section, except where noted, is drawn from *Maize & Biodiversity: The Effects of Transgenic Maize in Mexico: Key Findings and Recommendations* (Montréal: Commission for Environmental Cooperation, 2004).

7. Hector R. Bourges, "El Maiz: Su Importancia En La Alimentacion de La Poblacion Mexicana," in *El Maíz En Peligro Ante Los Transgénicos?: Un Análisis Integral Sobre El Caso de México.*, ed. Elena R. Alvarez-Buylla and Alma Pinero Nelson (Mexico City: Universidad Nacional Autónoma de

México, Centro de Investigaciones Interdisciplinarias en Ciencias y Humanidades, 2013), 231–48.

8. Comments on the report *Maize & Biodiversity*.

9. Donna Tingley, "Joint Public Advisory Committee (JPAC) RE: Maize and Biodiversity Symposium of the Commission for Environmental Cooperation," April 13, 2004, 2.

10. "Public Comments on Article 13 Report, Comision de Biotecnologia Agroalimentaria" (Consejo Nacional Agropecuario, 2004), 2.

11. "About the IAASTD Report," Global Agriculture, n.d.

12. "Independent Reports: Maize and Biodiversity: The Effects of Transgenic Maize in Mexico," Commission for Environmental Cooperation, n.d.

13. Efrén Flores, "México Se Inundó en 30 Años con Transgénicos de Monopolios, y Hoy Sólo 4 Estados Están 'Libres,'" *SinEmbargo*, March 5, 2018, sec. Investigaciones.

14. David Sandoval Vázquez, "'Treinta Años de Transgénicos en México" (Centro de Estudios para el Cambio en el Campo Mexicano, August 2017), 20; J. A. Serratos, "La Ley de Bioseguridad y los Centros de Origen y Diversificación," in *Origen y Diversificaión del Maíz: Una Revisión Analítica* (México, D.F.: Universidad Nacional Autónoma de México, Instituto de Biología, 2009).

15. T. A. Kato et al., *Origen y Diversificaión del Maíz: Una Revisión Analítica* (México, D.F.: Universidad Nacional Autónoma de México, Instituto de Biología, 2009).

16. Serratos, "La Ley de Bioseguridad y los Centros de Origen y Diversificación."

17. José Antonio Serratos Hernández, "La Sobrevivencia del Maíz Nativo en la Megalópolis de la Ciudad de México," *La Jornada*, June 20, 2012, sec. Sociedad.

18. Michelle Chauvet and Elena Lazos, "El Maíz Transgénico en Sinaloa: ¿Tecnología Inapropiada, Obsoleta o de Vanguardia? Implicaciones Socioeconómicas de la Posible Siembra Comercial," *Sociológica* 29, no. 82 (August 2014): 7–44.

19. Lisa Abend, "Mexico's Chefs Are Fighting a Future of Genetically Modified Corn," *Munchies*, October 13, 2015.

20. "Percy Schmeiser's Battle," *CBS News Online*, May 21, 2004, sec. In Depth.

21. Committee on Genetically Engineered Crops: Past Experience and Future Prospects et al., *Genetically Engineered Crops: Experiences and Prospects* (Washington, DC: National Academies Press, 2016), 154, doi:10.17226/23395.

22. Andrew Jacobs and Matt Richtel, "A Nasty, Nafta-Related Surprise: Mexico's Soaring Obesity," *New York Times*, December 11, 2017, sec. Health.

23. Vandana Shiva, *Monocultures of the Mind: Perspectives on Biodiversity and Biotechnology* (London: Zed Books; Third World Network, 1993).

24. A. I. Monterroso Rivas et al., "Assessing Current and Potential Rainfed Maize Suitability Under Climate Change Scenarios in México," *Atmósfera* 24, no. 1 (2011): 53–67.

25. Zoe VanGelder, "Agroecological Transition in Mexico: ANEC's Journey to a Better Farm and Food System" (Asociación Nacional de Empresas Comercializadoras de Productores del Campo and the Institute for Agriculture and Trade Policy, September 2007), 3.

26. E. Schnepf et al., "Bacillus Thuringiensis and Its Pesticidal Crystal Proteins," *Microbiology and Molecular Biology Reviews* 62, no. 3 (September 1998): 775–806; Clayton C. Beegle and Takashi Yamamoto, "Invitation Paper: History of Bacillus Thuringiensis," *The Canadian Entomologist* 124, no. 04 (August 1992): 587–616, doi:10.4039/Ent124587-4.

27. VanGelder, "Agroecological Transition in Mexico," 4.

28. Antonio Turrent Fernández, Timothy A. Wise, and Elise Garvey, "Achieving Mexico's Maize Potential," Working Paper No. 12-03 (Medford, MA: Global Development and Environment Institute, October 2012).

29. Ibid.

30. Ibid.

31. High Level Panel of Experts on Food Security and Nutrition of the Committee on World Food Security, "Investing in Smallholder Agriculture for Food Security," HLPE Report 6 (Rome, Italy: Committee on World Food Security, June 2013).

32. A documentary film, ViralMx, *Sierra Norte por la Vida*, tells the story.

33. "Unión de Cooperativas Tosepan," Producción Social del Hábitat, n.d.

34. Reuters Staff, "Monsanto Says Mexico Revokes Permit to Market GMO Soy in Seven States," Reuters, n.d., sec. Business News.

35. E. González-Ortega et al., "Pervasive Presence of Transgenes and Glyphosate in Maize-Derived Food in Mexico," *Agroecology and Sustainable Food Systems* 41, no. 9–10 (November 26, 2017): 1146–61, doi:10.1080/21683565.2017.1372841.

Part III: Trading Away the Right to Food

1. Richie Santosdiaz, "The Future of the 14 Free Trade Agreements America Has Under Trump," *Forbes*, December 7, 2016, sec. Opinion.

2. "International Investment Agreements Navigator: United States of America," Investment Policy Hub, UNCTAD, United Nations, n.d.

3. Paolo D'Odorico et al., "Feeding Humanity Through Global Food Trade: D'ODORICO et al.," *Earth's Future* 2, no. 9 (September 2014): 458–69, doi:10.1002/2014EF000250.

8. NAFTA's Assault on Mexico's Family Farmers

1. Timothy A. Wise, "Making Rural Mexico Great Again: Leading Candidate Endorses Farmers' Reform Program," *Food Tank* (blog), April 2018.

2. James McBride and Mohammed Aly Sergie, "NAFTA's Economic Impact," *Council on Foreign Relations* (blog), October 4, 2017.

3. Luis Téllez Kuenzler, *La Modernización del Sector Agropecuario y Forestal* (Fondo de Cultura Económica, 1994).

4. Ginger Thompson, "Ex-President in Mexico Casts New Light on Rigged 1988 Election," *New York Times*, March 9, 2004, sec. World.

5. Victor Suárez Carrera, *Rescate del Campo Mexicano: Organización Campesina y Políticas Públicas Posneoliberales* (Mexico City: ANEC and ITACA, 2018).

6. Alejandro Nadal, "The Environmental & Social Impacts of Economic Liberalization on Corn Production in Mexico" (Oxfam GB and WWF International, September 2000), 5, 21.

7. Harry Cleaver and Canning House Library (Hispanic & Luso Brazilian Councils), *Zapatistas!: Documents of the New Mexican Revolution* (New York: Autonomedia, 1994), 72.

8. Eduardo Zepeda, Timothy A. Wise, and Kevin P. Gallagher, "Rethinking Trade Policy for Development: Lessons From Mexico Under NAFTA," *Policy Outlook* (Carnegie Endowment for International Peace, 2009), 4.

9. Ibid., 13.

10. Ibid.

11. Nadal, "The Environmental & Social Impacts of Economic Liberalization on Corn Production in Mexico," 26.

12. This and other figures in this section, except where noted, come from: Timothy A. Wise, "Agricultural Dumping Under NAFTA: Estimating the Costs of U.S. Agricultural Policies to Mexican Producers," Working Paper (Global Development and Environment Institute, December 2009). For a full assessment of NAFTA at twenty years, see: Steven Zahniser et al., "NAFTA at 20: North America's Free-Trade Area and Its Impact on Agriculture" (U.S. Department of Agriculture, Economic Research Service, February 2015).

13. Kirsten Appendini, "Reconstructing the Maize Market in Rural Mexico," *Journal of Agrarian Change* 14, no. 1 (March 25, 2013): 1–25, doi:10.1111/joac.12013.

14. Alejandro Nadal and Timothy A. Wise, "The Environmental Costs of Agricultural Trade Liberalization: Mexico-U.S. Maize Trade Under NAFTA," Discussion Paper (Working Group on Development and Environment in the Americas, June 2004), 26.

15. Zepeda, Wise, and Gallagher, "Rethinking Trade Policy for Development," 15.

16. John Scott, "Agricultural Subsidies in Mexico: Who Gets What?" (Centro de Investigación y Docencia Económicas, n.d.), 76.

17. "Mexico: US-Mexico Trade Facts," Office of the United States Trade Representative, n.d.

18. Zepeda, Wise, and Gallagher, "Rethinking Trade Policy for Development," 10.

19. Suárez Carrera, Rescate del Campo Mexicano, 413.

20. Timothy A. Wise, "The Cost to Mexico of U.S. Corn Ethanol Expansion," Working Paper (Global Development and Environment Institute, May 2012), 7.

21. Jacobs and Richtel, "A Nasty, Nafta-Related Surprise."

22. September 2010 conference Transparencia y Rendición de Cuentas de los Subsidios Agrícolas: Políticas Públicas y Modelos de Desarrollo Rural; for media coverage of the conference, see: Victor Suárez Carrera, "En Defensa de un Procampo Reformado," La Jornada del Campo, September 18, 2010.

23. Catherine Rampell, "Why Are Mexican Smugglers' Fees Still Rising?," New York Times, May 18, 2009, sec. Economix. As of early 2018, the price had reportedly risen to as high as $8,000 due to U.S. president Donald Trump's anti-immigration policies, "Smugglers Up Prices for Crossing Mexican Border into US," Mexico News Daily, February 18, 2017.

24. Antonio Turrent Fernández, Timothy A. Wise, and Elise Garvey, "Achieving Mexico's Maize Potential," Working Paper No. 12-03 (Medford, MA: Global Development and Environment Institute, October 2012).

25. Timothy A. Wise, "The True Cost of Cheap Food," Resurgence & Ecologist, April 2010.

26. J. K. Boyce, "The Globalization of Market Failure? International Trade and Sustainable Agriculture" (Political Economy Research Institute, 1999), 18.

27. Conny Almekinders, "Management of Crop Genetic Diversity at Community Level" (Eschborn, Germany: Deutsche Gesellschaft für Technische Zusammenarbeit, January 2001).

28. See T. M. Swanson, D. W. Pearce, and R. Cervigni, "The Appropriation of the Benefits of Plant Genetic Resources for Agriculture: An Economic Analysis of the Alternative Mechanisms for Biodiversity Conservation," First

Extraordinary Session (Rome, FAO: Commission on Plant Genetic Resources, 1994).

29. "Technologies to Maintain Biological Diversity" (Washington, DC: Government Printing Office: Office of Technology Assessment of the U.S. Congress, March 1987), 4, 50.

30. Based on extensive fieldwork, much more is known today about the biological nature of on-farm diversity, the location of key centers of diversity for important food crops, the causes of genetic erosion, and the farm-management practices that can promote in situ conservation. Robert Tripp and Wieneke van der Heide, "The Erosion of Crop Genetic Diversity: Challenges, Strategies, and Uncertainties" (Overseas Development Institute, March 1996); Stephen B. Brush, ed., *Genes in the Field: On-Farm Conservation of Crop Diversity* (Boca Raton, FL: Lewis [u.a.], 2000); Esbern Friis-Hansen and Bhuwon Ratna Sthapit, eds., *Participatory Approaches to the Conservation and Use of Plant Genetic Resources* (Rome, Italy: International Plant Genetic Resources Institute, 2000); Melinda Smale et al., "Economic Concepts for Designing Policies to Conserve Crop Genetic Resources on Farms," *Genetic Resources and Crop Evolution* 51, no. 2 (March 2004): 121–35.

31. Miguel A. Altieri, M. Kat Anderson, and Laura C. Merrick, "Peasant Agriculture and the Conservation of Crop and Wild Plant Resources," *Conservation Biology* 1, no. 1 (May 1987): 49–58, doi:10.1111/j.1523-1739.1987 .tb00008.x.

32. The data in this section comes from Alejandro Nadal and Hugo García Rañó, "Trade, Poverty, and the Environment: A Case Study in the Sierra De Santa Marta Biosphere Reserve" (World Wildlife Fund, May 2009).

33. Much of the local detail in this section comes from David Bacon, "How US Policies Fueled Mexico's Great Migration," *The Nation*, January 4, 2012.

34. Wise, "Agricultural Dumping Under NAFTA," 25.

35. Bacon, "How US Policies Fueled Mexico's Great Migration."

36. Timothy A. Wise and Betsy Rakocy, "Hogging the Gains from Trade: The Real Winners from U.S. Trade and Agricultural Policies," Policy Brief (Global Development and Environment Institute, January 2010), 2.

37. Bacon, "How US Policies Fueled Mexico's Great Migration."

38. Ibid.

39. Ibid.

40. Bacon, "How US Policies Fueled Mexico's Great Migration." Those raids were captured on video by union organizers powerless to stop the actions, the footage featured in the popular documentary *Food Inc.*

41. Steven Greenhouse, "After 15 Years, North Carolina Plant Unionizes," *New York Times*, December 12, 2008, sec. U.S.

42. Bacon, "How US Policies Fueled Mexico's Great Migration"; Rufino Domínguez, "Cultural Roots as a Source of Strength: Educating and Organizing a Fragmented Immigrant Community" (Oaxacan Indigenous Binational Front, September 2003); David Bacon, *The Right to Stay Home: How US Policy Drives Mexican Migration* (Boston, MA: Beacon, 2014).

43. This section draws on my prior reporting, including an article for Mexico's *La Jornada del Campo*: Timothy A. Wise, "El Arte de Entregar Los Valores," *La Jornada del Campo*, November 16, 2013.

44. Fernández, Wise, and Garvey, "Achieving Mexico's Maize Potential," 12, 27.

45. Zahniser et al., "NAFTA at 20," 88; "Mexico: US-Mexico Trade Facts."

46. Wise, "Agricultural Dumping Under NAFTA," table 1; Veronica Nigh, "NAFTA: No U.S. Barley, No (Mexican) Beer," *Farm Bureau* (blog), June 30, 2017.

47. David Agren, "Mexico Protesters Fear US-Owned Brewery Will Drain Their Land Dry," *The Guardian*, February 4, 2018.

48. Aliza Kellerman, "The Mexican Cerveza You Know Is Actually European," *Vinepair* (blog), April 29, 2015; "Cracking Down on Corporate Monopolies and the Abuse of Economic and Political Power" (A Better Deal, n.d.).

49. Redacción, "López Obrador Firma el 'Plan de Ayala 2.0,'" *El Financiero*, April 10, 2018.

50. "Technical Progress During Seventh NAFTA Round," *Feed & Grain* (blog), March 9, 2018; Steve Suppan, "NAFTA 2.0: Doing Harm with Ag Biotech Approval Shortcuts," *Institute for Agriculture & Trade Policy* (blog), September 29, 2017.

51. Azam Ahmed, Matt Richtel, and Andrew Jacobs, "In Nafta Talks, U.S. Tries to Limit Junk Food Warning Labels," *New York Times*, March 20, 2018, sec. Americas.

9. Trading in Hypocrisy: India vs. World Trade Organization

1. Agriculture Census Division, "Agriculture Census 2010–11: All India Report on Number and Area of Operational Holdings" (New Delhi, India: Department of Agriculture & Co-operation, 2014), 6; World Bank, "Employment in Agriculture (Percent of Total Employment)," World Bank Data, accessed April 8, 2016.

2. Amartya Sen, *Poverty and Famines: An Essay on Entitlement and Deprivation* (Oxford; New York: Clarendon Press; Oxford University Press, 1981).

3. Right to Food Campaign, "The 'Right to Food' Case," n.d.

4. Right to Food Campaign, "The 'Right to Food' Case"; Shareen Hertel, "Hungry for Justice: Social Mobilization on the Right to Food in India: Social Mobilization on the Right to Food in India," *Development and Change* 46, no. 1 (January 2015): 74, doi:10.1111/dech.12144; Biraj Patnaik, "The Right to Food," Law Resource India, November 6, 2006.

5. Sakshi Balani, "Functioning of the Public Distribution System: An Analytical Report" (PRS Legislative Research, December 2013), 1–2, 7, 14.

6. "Integrated Child Development Services (ICDS) Scheme," Ministry of Women and Child Development, Government of India, n.d.

7. Yamini Jaishankar and Jean Drèze, "Supreme Court Orders on the Right to Food: A Tool for Action" (Right to Food Campaign, October 2005), 18.

8. Ibid., 52.

9. Abhijit Sen Himanshu, "In-Kind Food Transfers—I: Impact on Poverty," *Economic & Political Weekly* 48, no. 45–46 (November 16, 2013): 46–54; Abhijit Sen Himanshu, "In-Kind Food Transfers—II: Impact on Nutrition and Implications for Food Security and Its Costs," *Economic and Political Weekly* 48, no. 45–46 (November 16, 2013): 61.

10. Jean Dreze, "Democracy and Right to Food," *Economic and Political Weekly* 39, no. 17 (April 24, 2004): 1723–31; Jaishankar and Drèze, "Supreme Court Orders on the Right to Food," 26.

11. Jaishankar and Drèze, "Supreme Court Orders on the Right to Food," 28.

12. "MGNREGA Public Data Portal," Ministry of Rural Development, Government of India, accessed April 11, 2016. The number who actually received paid work is lower, peaking at 54 million in 2009–2010 according to Jayati Ghosh, "India's Rural Employment Programme Is Dying a Death of Funding Cuts," *The Guardian*, February 5, 2015, sec. Global Development.

13. Mihir Shah, "Report of the Joint Commission of Enquiry: Incidence of Repeated Deaths Due to Malnutrition, Sheopur District, Madhya Pradesh" (Joint Commission of Enquiry, November 2006), 3, 15–19.

14. IIPS and MOHFW, "National Family Health Survey-4 State Fact Sheet: Madhya Pradesh," State Fact Sheet, NFHS-4 (Mumbai and New Delhi, India: International Institute for Population Sciences and Ministry of Health and Family Welfare, 2016), 2, 4.

15. "CAB Madhya Pradesh Fact Sheet," Clinical, Anthropometric and Biochemical (CAB), Annual Health Survey (New Delhi: Ministry of Home Affairs, Government of India, 2014), 1.

16. IIPS and MOHFW, "National Family Health Survey-4 State Fact Sheet: Madhya Pradesh," 2.

17. "About Madhya Pradesh," UNICEF India, accessed January 17, 2016; Government of India, ed., *Madhya Pradesh Development Report* (New Delhi: Academic Foundation, 2011), 259.

18. "About Madhya Pradesh"; Anumeha Yadav, "In Rajasthan, Sahariyas Throw Off Generations of Slavery," *The Hindu*, February 25, 2013.

19. ACF International, "Acute Malnutrition: Situational Analysis in the States of Rajasthan and Madhya Pradesh, India" (Action contre la Faim, December 2010), 20.

20. Ghosh, "India's Rural Employment Programme Is Dying a Death of Funding Cuts."

21. Author's calculations, data for India 2005 and 2015 from "Mortality Rate, Under-5 (per 1,000 Live Births)" (World Bank, Data), accessed March 30, 2018.

22. The next two sections draw on the author's reporting in a two-part series for *Food Tank*: Timothy A. Wise, "WTO and Food Security: Biting the Hand That Feeds the Poor," *Food Tank* (blog), December 2017; Timothy A. Wise, "India's Public Stockholding: 'Much More Than a Welfare Program,'" *Food Tank* (blog), December 2017.

23. Himanshu, "In-Kind Food Transfers—II," 64; Jean Drèze and Reetika Khera, "Rural Poverty and the Public Distribution System," Working Paper No. 235 (Centre for Development Economics, September 2013).

24. Harsh Mander, "State Food Provisioning as Social Protection: Debating India's National Food Security Law" (Rome: Food and Agriculture Organization of the United Nations, 2015), 21; Sachin Kumar Jain, "Children's Right to Food in the NFS Bill 2011: A Raw Deal for Our Children," Policy Brief for Parliamentarians (New Delhi: Centre for Legislative Research and Advocacy (CLRA), December 2012), 3; Avinash Kishore, P. K. Joshi, and John Hoddinott, "India's Right to Food Act: A Novel Approach to Food Security," in *2013 Global Food Policy Report*, ed. Andrew Marble and Heidi Fritschel (Washington, DC: International Food Policy Research Institute, 2014), 41.

25. For a detailed review of the debate on NFSA leakage estimates, see Jean Drèze and Reetika Khera, "Understanding Leakages in the Public Distribution System," *Economic & Political Weekly* 50, no. 7 (February 14, 2015): 39–42; and Jean Drèze et al., "Clarification on PDS Leakages," *Economic & Political Weekly* 50, no. 39 (September 26, 2015).

26. Shweta Saini and Ashok Gulati, "The National Food Security Act (NFSA) 2013—Challenges, Buffer Stocking, and the Way Forward," Working Paper 297 (Indian Council for Research on International Economic Relations [ICRIER], March 2015), 3–4.

27. Himanshu, "In-Kind Food Transfers—II," 68–69; Marta Kozicka et al., "Modelling Indian Wheat and Rice Sector Policies," Discussion Papers on Development Policy (Bonn, Germany: Center for Development Research [ZEF], March 2015), 76.

28. Abhijit Das, "India's Public Stockholding of Agricultural Products: Will Exports of Procured Food Grains Cause Trade Distortion?," *India Law News* (blog), April 13, 2015.

29. Press Information Bureau, "Initiatives to Ensure Targeted Disbursement of Government Subsidies and Financial Assistance to Actual Beneficiaries," Government of India Press Information Bureau, February 29, 2016.

30. See Sachin Kumar Sharma, *The WTO and Food Security: Implications for Developing Countries* (New Delhi: Springer, 2016).

31. "Federal Surplus Commodities Corporation (FSCC) (1933)," The Living New Deal, n.d.

32. Timothy A. Wise, "Agricultural Dumping Under NAFTA: Estimating the Costs of U.S. Agricultural Policies to Mexican Producers," Mexican Rural Development Research Report No. 7 (Washington DC: Woodrow Wilson International Center for Scholars, 2010).

33. At the time, I wrote about this hypocrisy in a widely circulated article for the Indian press, Timothy A. Wise, "Ten Signs of US Hypocrisy on India's Food Security Programme," *FirstPost* (blog), December 7, 2013.

34. Timothy A. Wise and Biraj Patnaik, "WTO Takes a Wrong Turn for Development," *Down to Earth*, February 23, 2016.

10. Conclusion: The Battle for the Future of Food

1. "Voluntary Guidelines to Support the Progressive Realization of the Right to Adequate Food in the Context of National Food Security," adopted by the 127th Session of the FAO Council, November 2004 (Rome: Food and Agriculture Organization of the United Nations, 2005).

2. International Assessment of Agricultural Knowledge, Science, and Technology for Development (Project) et al., eds., *Agriculture at a Crossroads Synthesis Report: A Synthesis of the Global and Sub-Global IAASTD Reports*, Agriculture at a Crossroads (Washington, DC: Island Press, 2009).

3. Ha-Joon Chang, "Rethinking Public Policy in Agriculture: Lessons from Distant and Recent History," Policy Assistance Series (Rome, Italy: Food and Agriculture Organization, 2009).

4. C. Peter Timmer, *Food Security and Scarcity: Why Ending Hunger Is So Hard*, first edition (Philadelphia: University of Pennsylvania Press, 2015).

5. Author's calculations from data downloaded in February 2017 from "FAOSTAT," Database, Food and Agriculture Organization of the United Nations.

6. AfDB, "Abuja Declaration on Fertilizer for the African Green Revolution," African Development Bank, accessed May 18, 2017.

7. "The Inequalities of Hunger: 2017 Global Hunger Index by Severity," Global Hunger Index, 2017; Rural poverty headcount data downloaded in May 2018 from "DataBank," Database, World Bank.

8. Thomas S. Jayne et al., "Review: Taking Stock of Africa's Second-Generation Agricultural Input Subsidy Programs," *Food Policy* 75 (February 1, 2018): 1–14, doi:10.1016/j.foodpol.2018.01.003.

9. Roger Thurow, *The Last Hunger Season: A Year in an African Farm Community on the Brink of Change*, 2013.

10. Rod Nickel, "Special Report: Drowning in Grain—How Big Ag Sowed Seeds of a Profit-Slashing Glut," Reuters, September 27, 2017, sec. Business News.

11. "The State of Food Security and Nutrition in the World: Building Resilience for Peace and Food Security" (Rome: Food and Agriculture Organization of the United Nations, 2017).

12. Roger Thurow, *The First 1,000 Days: A Crucial Time for Mothers and Children—and the World*, first edition (New York: PublicAffairs, 2016).

13. IPES-Food, "From Uniformity to Diversity: A Paradigm Shift from Industrial Agriculture to Diversified Agroecological Systems" (International Panel of Experts on Sustainable Food Systems, 2016).

14. "Family Farmers Must Remain Central to Agroecology Scale-Up," Food and Agriculture Organization of the United Nations, April 5, 2018.

15. Jules Pretty, Camilla Toulmin, and Stella Williams, "Sustainable Intensification in African Agriculture," *International Journal of Agricultural Sustainability* 9, no. 1 (2011).

16. IPES-Food, "From Uniformity to Diversity," 57.

17. GRAIN and Institute for Agriculture and Trade Policy, "Emissions Impossible: How Big Meat and Dairy Are Heating Up the Planet" (Minneapolis, MN, July 2018).

18. "Lobbying: Ranked Sectors," Database, OpenSecrets.org, Center for Responsive Politics, May 2018.

Index

Page numbers in *italic* refer to illustrations.

About the Author

Timothy A. Wise is a senior researcher at the Small Planet Institute, collaborating with director Frances Moore Lappé to start its new Land and Food Rights Program. He is also a senior research fellow at Tufts University's Global Development and Environment Institute. He lives in Cambridge, Massachusetts.